PSYCHOLOGY
for WJEC AS Level

Julia Russell
Matt Jarvis

Hodder Arnold

A MEMBER OF THE HODDER HEADLINE GROUP

The authors and publishers would like to thank the following for the use of photographs in this volume:

p.24 Ria Novosti/Science Photo Library; p.25 From John B. Watson & Rosalie Rayner Watson (1928) Psychological Care Of Infant and Child, W.W.Norton, New York; p.27 © Professor Albert Bandura; p.33 Isopress/Rex Features; p.41 Getty Images; p.113 From Wright, Loftus & Hall (2001), picture drawn by Soni Wright; p.118 Getty Images; p.130 TopFoto/ImageWorks

This material has been endorsed by WJEC and offers high quality support for the delivery of WJEC qualifications. While this material has been through a WJEC quality assurance process, all responsibility for the content remains with the publisher.

Orders: please contact Bookpoint Ltd, 130 Milton Park, Abingdon, Oxon OX14 4SB. Telephone: +44 (0)1235 827720. Fax: +44 (0)1235 400454. Lines are open from 9.00–5.00, Monday to Saturday, with a 24-hour message-answering service. You can also order through our website www.hoddereducation.co.uk.

British Library Cataloguing in Publication Data
A catalogue record for this title is available from the British Library

ISBN 978 0 340 94312 0

First edition 2007
Impression number   10 9 8 7 6 5 4 3 2 1
Year   2012 2011 2010 2009 2008 2007

Cover photo © Paul Edmondson/Corbis

Typeset by Fakenham Photosetting Limited, Norfolk.
Printed in Great Britain for Hodder Arnold, an imprint of Hodder Education and a member of the Hodder Headline Group, an Hachette Livre UK Company, 338 Euston Road, London NW1 3BH by CPI Bath.

Contents

This book has been written for students following the WJEC AS Psychology specification, but might be of use to students taking any AS course. The following explanation of the examination structure applies only to those readers following the WJEC specification.

WJEC AS exams

At AS there are two exams:

PSY 1 Approaches in Psychology is 1 hour long and worth 40 per cent of the AS marks.

PSY 2 Psychology: Core Studies and Applied Research Methods is 1½ hours long and is worth 60 per cent of the AS marks.

Exam questions are designed to test your skills, specifically, three different ones, identified as different assessment objectives:

- Assessment Objective 1 (AO1): a measure of your knowledge and understanding. This tests how well you understand and can describe information such as psychological theories, studies, concepts and research methods. Your communication should be clear and effective; you should aim for logical, well-structured answers and remember that spelling and use of psychological terms will be assessed.
- Assessment Objective 2 (AO2): a measure of your ability to analyse and evaluate. This tests how well you can interpret information and assess its strengths and weaknesses. This can include analysing and evaluating psychological theories, studies, concepts and research methods. As for AO1, your communication should be effective.
- Assessment Objective 3 (AO3): a measure of your understanding of the process of psychological investigation. This tests your knowledge of the issues involved in designing, conducting and reporting studies in psychology. It covers a range of research methods, problems of reliability, validity and ethics and how to solve them and how to deal with data collection and draw conclusions from findings.

The examination papers for PSY 1 and PSY 2 differ in structure.

PSY 1 has five compulsory questions, testing AO1 and AO2 (and, from 2009, AO3 also). These questions are about:

- the approaches
- their related therapies
- research methods.

They use 'command' words, such as:

- outline
- describe
- evaluate
- strengths
- weaknesses
- limitations
- compare
- contrast
- similarities
- differences.

PSY 2 has three sections:

- Sections A and B are about the Core Studies and test AO1 and AO2
- Section C is about research methods and tests AO3.

WJEC A Level

The AS qualification you are taking is the first half of the WJEC A Level in Psychology. If you continue with Psychology and take the A2 exams, you will sit PSY 3 and PSY 4 exams. *Psychology for WJEC A2 Level* will help you to complete the whole A Level.

Acknowledgements

With thanks to Emma, Nina and Alison.

Dedication

To Joe Cocker, with thanks for his much-valued contribution to psychology.

1

Approaches
and
applications

The biological approach

What should I know?

- The main assumptions of the biological approach.
- Selye's General Adaptation Syndrome as an explanation of stress.
- How the biological approach has been put to use in drug therapy.

In addition I should be able to:

- describe and evaluate the contributions the biological approach has made to psychology
- evaluate the biological approach in terms of its strengths and weaknesses
- compare and contrast the biological approach with other perspectives.

The biological approach to psychology has its roots in the much older science of biology, so has a very long history. 'Modern' research into the structure of the nervous system began as early as the eighteenth century with the microscopic study of brain cells and investigations of the brain through autopsy. Techniques have moved on enormously with much more detailed and informative research methods, such as brain scans of people performing different actions. Nevertheless, many of the early findings about the biological structures and their functions were accurate and informative and those discoveries are still relevant today. This is not, however, the case for all aspects of the biological approach – as you will see.

Assumptions of the biological approach

The biological approach looks at psychology from a physiological perspective, that is, it considers physical changes in the body. It investigates how chemical and electrical events that occur within us affect our thinking, emotions and behaviour. The main assumptions of the approach are based on biology and include the following ideas:

- the structure and function of **neurones** (nerve cells)
- the structure and function of the brain
- the structure and function of the **endocrine system** (the system of

hormones that helps to control bodily events).

Understanding these ideas is important because it enables us to see how our thinking, emotions and behaviour are controlled. Furthermore, psychologists can use this understanding to develop therapies to help people to overcome mental health problems, for example, through:

- **psychosurgery** – operating on the brain to control mental disorders
- **chemotherapy** – the use of drugs to control mental disorders.

Glossary

neurone: a nerve cell.
central nervous system: the brain and spinal cord (CNS).
synapse: the junction between two neurones.
neurotransmitter: chemical that passes a message between one neurone and another.
receptor: location on the post-synaptic membrane of a neurone to which specific neurotransmitters (or drugs) can attach and stimulate or inhibit the action of that neurone.

The structure and function of neurones

The nervous system is made up of cells called neurones that form connections through structures called synapses. Neurones themselves conduct minute electrical messages (called action potentials) around the brain and body. There are different types that serve to carry information in different ways:

- **Sensory neurones** convey information about stimuli (such as light, sound or pain) to the brain.
- **Motor neurones** convey instructions out from the brain (e.g. to make muscles contract or to stimulate the release of hormones from glands).
- **Interneurones** are found only in the central nervous system (CNS) and so are important in thinking and decision making.

Neurones consist of a long, thin **axon**, the part that transmits the electrical message, and branched ends. The electrical message can be sent in one direction only, from the **dendrites** (the branching tree at the 'front') to the **axon terminals** (the branches at the 'end'). Many interconnections are formed between axon terminals and dendrites of adjacent neurones. Each interconnection is called a '**synapse**'. At this junction, the neurones do not physically touch and the electrical message from one neurone is transferred to the next by chemicals called '**neurotransmitters**' (see Figure 1.1). There are many different neurotransmitters, including serotonin, dopamine and noradrenalin.

Receptors on the post-synaptic membrane are specific to particular neurotransmitters. One consequence of this is that, in addition to neurotransmitters, similarly shaped drug molecules can attach to specific receptor sites. This is important in understanding the action of drugs used to treat mental disorders (see pages 15–18).

1 An electrical impulse passes down the axon of the first neurone.
2 Vesicles containing neurotransmitters move towards the pre-synaptic membrane.
3 Vesicles fuse with the pre-synaptic membrane and release neurotransmitters into the synaptic cleft.

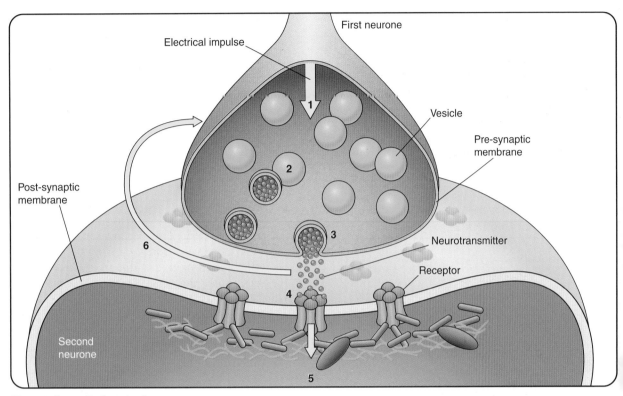

Fig. 1.1 Synaptic functioning

4 Neurotransmitters diffuse across the synapse and attach to receptors on the post-synaptic membrane.
5 Activity in the receptors causes a change in the second neurone which increases (or in some cases decreases) the likelihood of an action potential in the second neurone.
6 Neurotransmitter molecules are recycled into the pre-synaptic neurone.

The structure and function of the brain

The central nervous system consists of the brain and spinal cord. The brain is a highly organised structure. The central brain stem, which connects to the spinal cord, is surrounded by the cerebral hemispheres. These are roughly similar structures on the left and right sides, thus many (but not all) structures are found on both sides of the brain.

A surface view (without the covering of the skull) shows the brain has four 'lobes'. These lobes are areas of the outer layer called the 'cortex'. Beneath this, there are many other structures, each with different, although complex and interacting, functions.

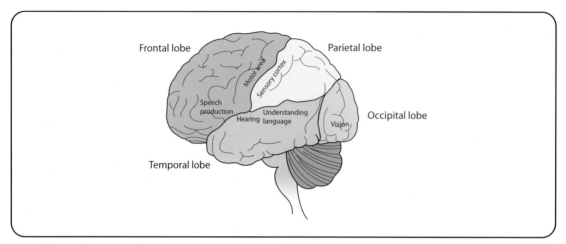

Fig. 1.2 A surface view of the brain

The cortex is only the outer few millimetres of the brain and is deeply folded. The resulting 'hills' and 'valleys' give the cortex an enormous surface area. Different areas of the cortex have different functions, being devoted to vision, movement and language for example (see Figure 1.2). The link between particular areas and functions in the brain is called '**localisation**'. One consequence of this is that if damage is caused to a small area of brain tissue, specific functions may be lost.

The endocrine system

Within the body there are two communication systems, the nervous system (a fast, electrical process) and the **endocrine system** (a slower, chemical one). The endocrine system is composed of many glands which secrete **hormones** into the blood stream. Hormones are chemicals that travel around the body in the blood and affect the action of target organs. As a result, hormones can influence our thinking, behaviour and emotions. For example, the hormone melatonin affects whether we feel sleepy or awake. One important role for hormones is in the co-ordination of our response to stress; we will look at this next.

Glossary

endocrine system: a set of glands that releases hormones into the bloodstream.
hormone: a chemical released from a gland into the bloodstream that affects a target organ. This can influence our thinking, emotions or behaviour.
stress: the physical and psychological reaction to a threat that appears to be too difficult for us to be able to deal with.
stressor: a source of threat that may be internal or external that could initiate a stress response in the individual.

Selye's General Adaptation Syndrome (GAS)

One biological event that involves both the nervous system and the endocrine system is the body's response to stress. **Stress** is a physical and psychological response experienced when we encounter a threat that we feel we do not have the resources to overcome. Such threats, called '**stressors**', may be internal or external and can come from sources such as loud noise, crowds or a lot of work. These situations may be acceptable when we feel able to cope with them, but become stressors when we cannot. For example, a large animal running towards us might be perfectly okay if it's a friendly horse coming in from the field, but is unlikely to be judged positively if it is a bull with horns (and you are not a matador). The difference is simply that, in the first situation, we assess the situation and decide we have the means to cope (a calm voice and a handful of food). In the second example, however, we are likely to decide that we might be flattened or stabbed and there wouldn't be much we could do about it – so we experience stress.

The changes that occur in the face of a stressor are adaptive – they have evolved to help us to survive. Clearly, being able to respond to a threat in a way that will increase the chances of survival is beneficial – hence it has evolved. So, how is our response to stress beneficial?

Selye (1947) began investigating how rats responded to different unpleasant situations and stimuli that he judged to be stressful (e.g. heat and fatigue). They produced the same kinds of response regardless of the stressor used (hence 'general'). These responses reflected an attempt by the body to cope with the situation (i.e. resulted in 'adaptation'). The responses included a range of physiological and behavioural changes rather than a single effect so were described as a 'syndrome'. The initial changes included increased pulse rate, blood pressure and breathing rate, dilated pupils and a diversion of blood away from organs such as the digestive system to the muscles. These all help to prepare the individual for an emergency, such as fleeing danger or engaging in a fight. This first response is called the 'alarm reaction'. Selye identified a further two phases in the body's response that arise if the stressor persists. The sequence of the General Adaptation Syndrome (GAS) is therefore:

- **alarm reaction**: the immediate activation of the body's mechanisms for dealing with a threat
- **resistance stage**: the attempt by the body to return to a steady physiological state despite the persistence of the stressor

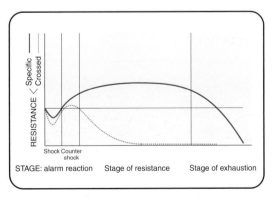

Fig. 1.3 Loss of cross resistance

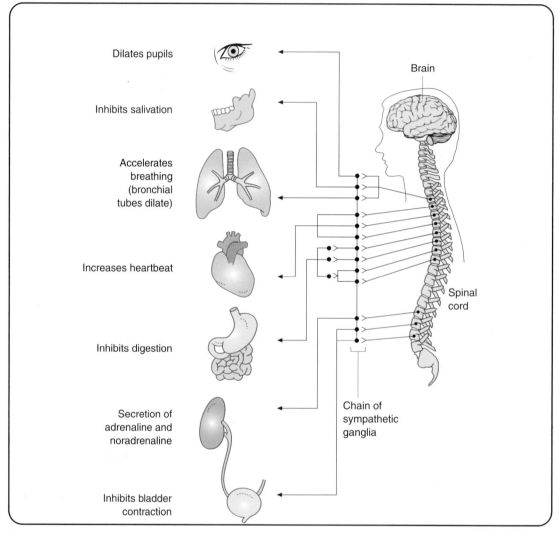

Dilates pupils

Inhibits salivation

Accelerates breathing (bronchial tubes dilate)

Increases heartbeat

Inhibits digestion

Secretion of adrenaline and noradrenaline

Inhibits bladder contraction

Brain

Spinal cord

Chain of sympathetic ganglia

Fig. 1.4 Sympathetic nervous system

● **exhaustion stage**: the failure of the body to return to a normal physiological state in the on-going presence of a stressor that causes depletion of bodily resources and eventual collapse.

Selye saw this syndrome as an increase in the capacity of the individual to cope with (or resist) the impact of a *specific* stressor and the failure of this coping in the final stage. He also recognised that this response was effective only against that particular threat and, in many other ways, the body became less effective at coping. He described this as 'the loss of **cross resistance**'. (See Figure 1.3.)

The alarm reaction

The immediate changes that occur in the alarm reaction are caused by the nervous system. Specifically, messages from the sensory organ that detects the threat (such as eyes seeing a ghost or ears hearing an explosion) are rapidly transmitted to the brain and the sympathetic part of the **autonomic nervous system** (ANS) is activated (see Figure 1.4). The ANS consists of two approximately antagonistic halves:

● the **sympathetic** part – this is responsible for activating the body when arousal is high
● the **parasympathetic** part – which is active during relaxation (e.g. when we have eaten a big meal or are asleep).

The neurones of the ANS are part of the peripheral nervous system, i.e. they lie outside the CNS and are distributed around the body, reaching all the vital organs. The bodily changes caused by sympathetic activation help to prepare us for action. For example, faster heart and breathing rate supply more oxygen and redirecting blood to the muscles assists this, so we are more likely to have the energy to fight or run away. The messages to the sympathetic system are located alongside the spinal cord. They are all together in a 'line' (called the 'sympathetic chain') and tend to be activated together. Activation of the different roles of the parasympathetic system tends to occur independently.

In addition to the response of the nervous system, the endocrine system is activated. This occurs because the sympathetic nervous system (SNS) stimulates the adrenal glands (specifically the **adrenal medulla**) to release a hormone called **adrenaline**. The effects of adrenaline are similar to those of the SNS itself. The effects of the hormone, however, are slower but longer lasting than those of the SNS. This allows the defensive reactions to be maintained in the face of the danger. If the threat

subsides, the parasympathetic part of the ANS can return the body to normal. The link between the sympathetic nervous system and the adrenal medulla is referred to as the **sympathetic adrenal medullary system** (SAM). The SAM is therefore responsible for the body's reaction to acute (short term) stressors.

Glossary

adrenal glands: a pair of glands that lie on top of the kidneys that are part of the endocrine system. Each really consists of two glands, the **adrenal medulla** (which produces adrenaline) and the **adrenal cortex** (which produces cortisol).
hypothalamus: a small but complex part of the brain which interacts with both the nervous and endocrine systems.

The resistance stage

If the danger persists, the bodily state of alert cannot be maintained by adrenaline. Other hormones are released to sustain the body's defence reactions. Levels of these hormones may remain high for months or even years if a stressor persists. They include:

● **cortisol** (from the adrenal cortex), which makes more energy available through the breakdown of fats and release of glucose from the liver
● **aldosterone** (from the adrenal cortex), which maintains elevated blood pressure
● **thyroxine** (from the thyroid gland), which increases basal metabolic rate so maintains elevated heart and breathing rate and allows energy from food to be used quickly and efficiently.

The key hormones in this stage are the glucocorticoids, such as cortisol, released from the **adrenal cortex**. Cortisol is released in

Glossary

carcinogens: chemicals that cause cancer.
immune system: the structures and mechanisms that the body uses to fight disease, including several kinds of lymphocytes released from lymph glands.
lymphocyte: a type of white blood cell produced to combat disease. Some produce antibodies, othes release anti-viral chemicals such as interleukins that fight infection. Further types engulf and destroy infected cells or target cancerous cells.

response to the presence of adrenocorticotropic hormone (ACTH) in the blood. ACTH itself is released from the **pituitary gland** under the influence of corticotropin releasing factor (CRF), a small protein released by the hypothalamus. This link between the hypothalamus, the pituitary gland and the adrenal cortex is called the **hypothalamic pituitary–adrenocortical axis** (HPA). The HPA is responsible for the body's response to chronic (long term) stressors. However, the effects of persistently elevated hormone levels are themselves damaging and ultimately lead to illness and the exhaustion stage.

The exhaustion stage

Selye observed that, whatever the cause of stress, if the threat persisted his animals became sick and died. The exhaustion stage reflects the body's inability to sustain attempts to cope under chronic stress. One significant impact is on the immune system, the structures and mechanisms that the body employs to fight disease. Under prolonged stress, this system becomes less effective. A high level of hormones such as cortisol appears to impair immune functioning. This is associated with an increase in allergic reactions, such as asthma and eczema,

a change in the activity of lymphocytes and an increased risk of heart disease and cancer.

Evaluation of the GAS

Selye identified many of the key aspects of a biological response to stress:

- the increase and then decrease in availability of energy (through the metabolism of glucose and fat)
- the physiological changes associated with the stress response, such as changes in blood pressure and heart rate
- the involvement of both the nervous system and the endocrine system in the stress response
- the initial rise and then fall in the ability of lymphocytes to produce antibodies
- the damaging effect of prolonged stress on the cardiovascular system (e.g. higher risk of heart disease under stress) and on the digestive system (e.g. the increased incidence of stomach ulcers).

Selye also recognised the importance of specific hormones in these functions. For example, he identified the roles of adrenaline and corticosteroids (such as cortisol) from the adrenal glands and that of ACTH from the pituitary gland. Although Selye recognised that there was a link between the nervous system and the adrenal medulla that could initiate the release of adrenaline, he did not specifically identify the link between the SAM and HPA, i.e. the unifying role played by the hypothalamus.

There is evidence to support many of the effects proposed by Selye. The reduction in lymphocyte production during prolonged exposure to a stressor has been demonstrated experimentally. De Groot *et al.* (2002) injected rats with a virus and exposed some of them to a social stressor. The stressed individuals produced fewer antibodies and virus-specific interleukins to fight the infection. There is also a strong link between stress and cancer but it is difficult to demonstrate that this relationship is causal. Studies such as that of Herbert and Cohen (1993) have shown that the activity of special lymphocytes (natural killer cells) that attack cancerous cells is impaired by prolonged stress. However, stressed people may also experience other effects that increase their risk of cancer, for example exposure to carcinogens if they smoke more cigarettes.

There are also ways in which Selye's explanation of stress is incomplete. If biological processes alone could explain the response to stress, all individuals would respond to a particular stressor in the same way. This is not, however, the case; for example, some students suffer far more from exam nerves than others. These individual differences cannot be accounted for by a purely biological model. Factors such as personality have been shown to influence the extent to which a stressor is problematic for different individuals. Friedman and Rosenman (1974) described people with a 'Type A' personality. These individuals seem to get more stressed and suffer more stress-related illnesses such as heart disease. Perry and Baldwin (2000) found that people exhibiting

Where are we now?

Selye undoubtedly developed a highly comprehensive explanation of stress for his time. Since then, both physiological and psychological investigations of stress have shown that the overall picture is even more complex than he envisaged. Progress is still being made, with explanations encompassing ever wider examples of the stress response. Modern research indicates that post traumatic stress disorder (PTSD) is the result of physiological responses to stress, not a sign of a weak personality or malingering, as was believed in cases of 'shell shock' during the first and second world wars. Soldiers exposed to the horrors of the battlefield sometimes developed severe and lasting reactions that included symptoms such as panic, confusion and paralysis.

As modern research discovers more about the physiology and psychology underlying PTSD, potential new ways to treat PTSD are being identified. One chemical thought to be involved is corticotropin-releasing factor. While its release under stress is normal, in PTSD its release seems to be indiscriminate, provoking intense feelings of fear and anxiety. Experiments with animals have informed this understanding. Plotsky and

Meaney (1993) demonstrated that infant rats that are stressed by separation from their mothers have abnormally high CRF levels as adults. Investigating the action of CRF in mice, Risbrough et al. (2004) showed that it controls hyper-responsiveness to stressful stimuli. They identified two types of receptors for CRF. Both of these increase defensive reactions but they work in different ways and an imbalance between them may be central to the disruption in PTSD.

In an experiment comparing controls to Vietnam veterans suffering from combat-related PTSD, Liberzon et al. (1999) found that the war veterans with PTSD were more sensitive to combat-related sounds than either non-veterans or war veterans without PTSD. They showed greater sensitivity to stress in terms of reactions such as heart rate and adrenaline and cortisol levels. Sautter et al. (2003) compared PTSD sufferers with and without psychotic symptoms. Those most severely affected, i.e. with psychotic symptoms, had higher levels of CRF. Together, the findings suggest that a drug that selectively affected only one of the CRF receptors could, in the future, provide an effective therapy for PTSD (Zorrilla and Koob, 2004).

'Type A' behaviours are frequently involved in road rage. Of course, it is possible that having a 'Type A' personality leads people to engage in stressful situations (such as driving too fast or having a demanding job) rather than lowering their ability to cope with stress.

Another criticism is that the GAS does not include the active steps that people take to cope with a stressor. For example, some people tackle problems objectively (e.g. by using social support from others) so can reduce the impact stressors have on them. This is important, as different kinds of coping strategies affect health differently. Epping-Jordan *et al.* (1994) studied the progress of people with cancer. In those who used avoidance strategies to deal with their stress (e.g. ignoring the problem), the disease developed faster than in those who confronted the issues.

Applying the biological approach to therapy: psychosurgery

Localisation and the aims of psychosurgery

As we discovered earlier in the chapter, brain functions are localised (see page 6). As a result, damage to particular brain areas can have specific effects on psychological functions. This idea is the basis of psychosurgery – the use of surgery on the brain to treat psychological disorders. In the case of the procedures discussed below, the objective was to relieve distress and anxiety, particularly in patients who did not respond to any other treatment. Although the function of the targeted brain areas had not

Thinking psychologically

1 Carwyn is a student in his AS year and is under a lot of pressure to complete his homework. As he experiences this stress and begins to tolerate it during the year, his cortisol levels rise.
  a What stage of the GAS would he be in?
  b Carwyn is trying to learn to drive but is finding it really difficult. He can't cope with this source of stress at all and wants to scream at the instructor and abandon his lessons. How would Selye explain Carwyn's ability to cope with one source of stress but not another?
2 The release of which hormone would be associated with each of the following situations?
  a Nearly being hit by a car.
  b A long spell of unemployment.
  c Waiting in the wings before a performance.
3 a Recently bereaved people often find they get ill. Why might this be?
  b Suggest two other events that might happen in a person's life that might trigger stress and ill-health.

web watch

There are many internet sites offering advice about how to deal with stress. Look at a selection that explains what effects sufferers of stress are likely to experience. Use your understanding of the physiology of the response to stress to explain some of these effects.

been identified, the effect of the surgery was deemed, at least at first, to have a specific effect.

Techniques in psychosurgery

One of the first widespread uses of psychosurgery was a procedure called a **lobotomy**. Early lobotomies were called 'leucotomies' (from *leuco*, referring to the white matter of the brain, and *tome*, to cut). The technique was pioneered by Egas Moniz and developed by Walter Freeman. It was based on a report that Moniz heard in 1935. A laboratory chimpanzee that became very distressed when she made errors on tests was subdued by a bilateral lesion to the prefrontal areas of her left and right frontal lobes. The safety of this treatment for highly emotionally distressed people was supported by a case in which a person had their frontal lobes removed to destroy a tumour. This patient appeared not to suffer any intellectual impairment, despite the physical damage to the brain. These two observations, of a different species and a single human, were the basis for the development of several techniques which in principle aimed to destroy, or cut connections from, the frontal lobes. These included:

- **leucotomy** – an operation in which a narrow device called a leucotome was inserted (via holes made in the skull) into the frontal lobe. The 'blade' of the leucotome, a wire loop, was then extended and the device was rotated to lesion a core of tissue. This procedure could be repeated several times to destroy pieces of prefrontal cortex
- **transorbital lobotomy**, which used a special knife, called an 'ice pick', inserted under the eye lid and into the back of the eye socket. This was used to break through the skull into the brain and was moved around to destroy connections between

the prefrontal area and other brain areas. This was repeated on both hemispheres.

This treatment was used on patients who were emotionally unstable and violent and did not respond to other forms of therapy. It did generally have the effect of relieving emotional distress and anxiety, thus calming the patient down. As a consequence, the surgery became common. Tooth and Newton (1961) reported that more than 10,000 such operations were performed in the UK alone. The transorbital procedure, which did not even require hospitalisation, was especially popular. Now, however, such procedures are rare because of their severe side effects. Problems included changes in the patients' personality: for example they became lethargic, apathetic, irresponsible or socially withdrawn. Although the patients' intellectual ability did not seem to be affected, they lacked the ability to plan their own behaviour or judge its appropriateness.

Evaluation of psychosurgery

The evidence on which lobotomies were based was very limited. Findings from the chimpanzee would not necessarily have been relevant to humans. The species differ in both brain structure and function (e.g. cognition and behaviour). The findings from the human case may not have been generalisable, as the medical reason for the lobotomy was a physical not a psychological one and a single instance is not sufficient to indicate the success of a procedure on others. The rapid growth of the technique was based not only on its efficacy for reducing distress in patients but also on making difficult individuals more manageable for staff in institutions. Such manipulation is now seen as unethical. At the time, however, the treatment was perceived to be an improvement in the care of patients who were suffering severe and incurable distress, or whose behaviour could not be controlled other than by confinement or restraint.

Both Moniz and Freeman claimed high success rates for their operations. Initial evidence supported this, for example Pippard (1955 a, b) reported worthwhile or good results for 62 per cent of leucotomised depressive patients and good results with 50 per cent of those with affective (mood) disorders. In 95 per cent of these cases, Pippard reported no more than slight personality changes. However, many other sources reported severe side effects, and the original procedures were abandoned in favour of alternative treatments which became available in the 1950s, including drugs for mental illnesses.

Glossary

bilateral: both sides of the brain.
limbic system: an area deep within the brain that plays a role in emotional responses.

Current procedures

Despite the problems with psychosurgery, less dramatic procedures, such as the **bilateral cingulotomy**, are still occasionally performed. This has been used to help very depressed patients and sufferers of obsessive-compulsive disorder (OCD) who do not respond to other treatments. It is also used to reduce pain in cancer patients. In this operation the cingulate gyri, which link the limbic system to the frontal lobe, are destroyed. There is one cingulate gyrus on each side of the brain (hence 'bilateral'). This modern operation uses very accurate stereotactic magnetic resonance imaging to assist surgeons to identify the exact location of the area to be lesioned. The lesion can be performed

with a fine electrode, which destroys the tissue directly. Alternatively, a gamma knife can be used. In this procedure, beams of radiation are focused on the location to be destroyed. So, unlike early lobotomies, a cingulotomy can be restricted to a minute area and the skull does not have to be breached.

web watch

Use key terms from the text above to search for information about the benefits and risks of modern psychosurgery. Descriptions of the side effects of the cingulotomy are a good place to start.

There are also many sites that describe the history of lobotomies. Find one with images of the two techniques. Remember that many sites sensationalise issues such as psychosurgery. Some of the most accurate ones are likely to have academic or university addresses that end in .ac or .edu.

Click on the links in this lobotomy timeline (or search for 'lobotomy timeline') and hear Walter Freeman discussing his lobotomy patients: http://www.soundportraits.org/on-air/my_lobotomy/timeline.php3

Evaluation of current procedures

There is mixed evidence for the effectiveness of the cingulotomy as a treatment of psychological disorders such as depression and OCD and although it does seem to reduce the subjective response to pain, it does not appear to affect the pain threshold. Despite the reduced nature of the lesion, and its greater accuracy, there are also similar side effects. Cohen *et al.* (1999) compared the pre-operative performance of 12 cingulotomy patients being treated for chronic pain with 20 control patients (also with chronic pain). Over 60 per cent of the cingulotomy patients reported less pain post-operatively and most required less medication to control their pain. However, Cohen *et al.* also found some consistent post-operative problems. On average, the cingulotomy patients lacked the ability to spontaneously initiate responses (such as verbal responses) and showed deficits in attention compared with the controls.

Investigating the use of cingulotomy for OCD, Baer *et al.* (1995) followed 44 patients. They found the treatment to be effective in 32 per cent of cases and partially so in a further 14 per cent. Here, too, some patients reported side effects, including seizures.

Mashour *et al.* (2005) suggest that one legacy of psychosurgery is the usefulness of modern electrical brain-stimulation techniques. Some of these, using stimulation that ultimately has the effect of inhibiting brain activity, can be used to generate a temporary simulation of the effects of a lesion. This enables clinicians to decide on the efficacy of possible procedures on specific individuals. Thus, the effect of possible psychosurgery in combination with other treatments can also be evaluated. This is clearly a much safer and more ethically sound approach.

Applying the biological approach to therapy: chemotherapy

Neurotransmitters and the aims and techniques of psychosurgery

As we saw at the beginning of the chapter, communication between neurones is chemical in nature and uses neurotransmitters (see page 4). As a result of this, it is possible for other chemicals to affect brain function. Drug molecules – which resemble neurotransmitters – can affect synapses, thus artificially influencing emotions, cognition or behaviour. These effects can be useful in the treatment of mental illness, i.e. in **chemotherapy**, the therapeutic use of drugs. Two ways that drugs can interfere with synaptic transmission are to:

- **mimic neurotransmitters** – and imitate their action at the receptor sites, for example causing stimulation and an increase in action potentials
- **block receptors** – so preventing neurotransmitters from attaching to receptors, thus reducing the likelihood of action potentials occurring.

One of the earliest drugs to be understood was morphine. This works by imitating the action of neurotransmitters called '**endorphins**'. These 'natural opiates' are molecules that are structurally like the drug morphine and are even more powerful pain killers (think: *endo* – internal, *orphins* – morphine like). Morphine molecules attach to the receptors that naturally respond to endorphins and control our experience of pain. As morphine also causes activation at these receptors, it too has an analgesic effect. The nature of this effect was understood after the discovery of endorphin receptors in the brain by Pert and Snyder (1973). Morphine and many related drugs (other opiates) are extensively used in medical practice for the relief of pain. One disadvantage of morphine use is that, in the long term, it causes dependence, i.e. patients find it difficult to cope without the drug after prolonged use. As a result it is used for the control of pain only in acute cases, such as after surgery, and for severe chronic pain, such as in terminal cancer patients.

The mental disorder schizophrenia is linked to a high level of the neurotransmitter dopamine. Some drug treatments for schizophrenia, such as chlorpromazine, are effective because they block dopamine receptor sites. This action reduces the access of dopamine molecules to the receptor sites and so counters the effect of high dopamine levels and reduces symptoms.

In depressed individuals, levels of another neurotransmitter, serotonin, are low compared with those of non-depressed people. A drug group called 'selective serotonin reuptake inhibitors' (SSRIs) block the return of serotonin to the pre-synaptic membrane. This means that there is relatively more of the neurotransmitter remaining in the synaptic cleft. This increases the likelihood of serotonin molecules attaching to the receptors, countering the low neurotransmitter levels.

Glossary

agonist: a drug that attaches to a receptor site and mimics or increases the effect of the normal neurotransmitter.
antagonist: a drug that attaches to a receptor site and blocks or decreases the effect of the normal neurotransmitter.
opiate: drugs extracted from the opium poppy (morphine and codeine). They work by attaching to opioid receptors.
opioids: synthetic drugs (e.g. pethidine) and ones manufactured from morphine (e.g. heroin).
natural (endogenous) opioids: compounds that normally exist in the body and attach to opioid receptors (e.g. endorphin).
opioid receptor: a post-synaptic site to which opiates and opioids bind and have agonistic or antagonistic effects.
SSRI (selective serotonin reuptake inhibitor): an anti-depressant drug which works by preventing the reabsorption of the neurotransmitter serotonin into the pre-synaptic membrane. This causes more serotonin to be available in the synapse to stimulate the post-synaptic receptor sites.

Evaluation of chemotherapy

In depression and schizophrenia, the nature of the condition is more complex than has been considered here, so drug treatments alone are rarely fully effective. For example, several other neurotransmitters are important in depression, so for some individuals other treatments that target neurotransmitters such as noradrenalin are more effective. Furthermore, differences between individuals, such as the causes and symptoms of schizophrenia, mean that a

Box 1.1
Examples of mental disorders: schizophrenia and depression

Schizophrenia is characterised by the disruption of both emotions and cognition, so affects perception, thinking, language, behaviour and emotional responses. It can be identified by:
- positive symptoms – diagnosed by their presence (such as hallucinations and the belief that the individual's thoughts are being controlled or have been 'inserted')
- negative symptoms – diagnosed by the absence of responses (such as immobility or lack of speech).

Depression is a mood disorder characterised by a persistent and overwhelming sadness. This can be diagnosed by symptoms such as loss of pleasure or interest in most activities, significant loss or gain in weight, sleeping very much more or less than normal, feeling fatigued and having low self-esteem.

treatment which is effective for one patient may not be so for all.

The complexity of the disorders and multiple roles of neurotransmitters in the brain mean that even highly targeted drugs can have side effects. One common and serious side effect of the drug chlorpromazine used to treat schizophrenia is tardive dyskinesia. This condition results in involuntary movements of parts of the body including the mouth, face and limbs. For SSRIs, there is a small risk of suicide, especially in the early weeks on the drug; more common side effects include changes in sleep patterns, such as insomnia.

Adams *et al.* (2005) conducted a meta-analysis of 50 randomised controlled trials of the use of chlorpromazine for schizophrenia. In total, they included 5,276 individuals (in treatment or placebo groups). Overall, they found that chlorpromazine failed to produce global improvement in 76 per cent of patients and commonly produced adverse side effects such as sedation, a risk of movement disorders and dizziness. Despite this, it is a low-cost treatment that is effective for one in seven people with schizophrenia. Adams *et al.* report that it is still one of the most common treatments used and is a standard against which other drugs can be evaluated.

Trivedi *et al.* (2006) evaluated the efficacy of the SSRI Citalopram in treating depression. They followed up 2,876 out-patients from a variety of environments (e.g. psychiatric and primary care settings). Their depressive characteristics were measured on a number of scales, both prior to and after treatment of up to 14 weeks. One scale, a 16-item self report, found that 33 per cent of the participants had experienced remission while taking Citalopram and 47 per cent had shown a response to the drug that had halved their depression score. For many patients, this effect had been achieved by eight weeks. The effectiveness of Citalopram varied between different groups of people. It was most effective for well-educated, employed, white Caucasian women who were not suffering from other psychological or physical disorders. Insel (2006) observed that while these results show that Citalopram can treat depression effectively, around 70 per cent of the patients did not recover, so alternative courses of action would need to be considered. Furthermore, it is possible that some of those who recovered would have gone into remission spontaneously and, in the absence of a placebo group, this effect cannot be identified.

Glossary

meta-analysis: a review study that combines the findings of many similar previous investigations.
placebo: an apparent treatment in which no active element is present (e.g. a pill containing no drug or an operation that opens the skull but does not affect the brain at all).
randomised controlled trial: a design for a clinical investigation which compares the outcome for patients randomly assigned to different conditions usually including treatment and placebo groups.

Where are we now?

Psychosurgery, at least in its original form, is no longer performed and even more modern techniques are used relatively infrequently. In terms of having a specific effect on emotional state, cognition or behaviour, chemical rather than physical routes are proving more effective. The relationship between structure and function in the brain is highly complex and appears to be more than simply a matter of physical location. Networks of interconnected neurones or 'circuits' are often responsible for co-ordinating particular functions. These networks are more readily and effectively modified using drugs.

One of the most recent advances has been the development of new drugs for schizophrenia that are antagonistic to both dopamine and serotonin. This targeting of brain receptors helps to make the action of chemotherapy more specific and reduce the risk of side effects. Research such as Masui *et al.* (2005) and Borison (1995) suggests that these drugs, such as Respiridone, are especially effective in controlling negative symptoms.

As we have seen, drug treatments can be effective in reducing distressing symptoms and more modern drugs have fewer side effects and can be taken for longer periods of time. Conversely, all drug treatments can be criticised because they treat the symptoms of the disorder rather than identifying and eradicating the cause of the problem. It is often the case, however, that it is not possible to change the individual's past or their biology and chemotherapy may offer a way to manage symptoms that would otherwise be distressing.

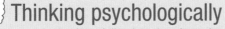

Thinking psychologically

1 In which of the following situations do you think it would be appropriate to treat a patient suffering from depression with drugs rather than considering alternative therapies such as counselling? Why?

a   An adult who is recently divorced, has had to move house and is feeling that they have no friends because everyone seems to be supporting their ex-partner.

b   A young man who has discussed his feelings of hopelessness with his GP and college counsellor but is not making progress.

c   A bereaved husband who, for many months, has attended group sessions with other people who have lost loved ones but who is still unable to function effectively as a result of the death.

2 Naloxone is a drug that blocks endorphin receptors.

a   Would you expect it to increase or decrease the experience of pain? Why?

b   It is used medically to reverse the effects of drug overdoses, for example from the use of heroin.

   i   To which drug group must heroin therefore belong?

   ii   How does Naloxone protect against the effect of an overdose?

Summing it up

● **Neurones** are nerve cells that send electrical messages. They communicate across synapses using chemicals called neurotransmitters that attach to special receptor sites.

● The **brain** is part of the central nervous system. It is highly organised and different structures have different functions – this is called localisation. The nervous system is vital to our emotions, cognition and behaviour. It co-ordinates our responses and triggers rapid reactions.

● The **endocrine system** is composed of hormones released from glands into the blood. It is another important communication system in the body and is slower but longer acting than the nervous system. It is important in controlling our response to stress.

● **Stress** is a response to a threat that we perceive ourselves to be unable to cope with. Such threats may be internal or external and include noise, crowding and fear.

● The General Adaptation Syndrome (GAS) was proposed by Selye and consists of three stages:

1   Alarm reaction – an initial, rapid response to a threat that mobilises bodily resources. This is effected by the sympathetic nervous system and adrenaline.

2   Resistance stage – a later and more prolonged response that allows the body to remain ready for defensive action in ways that can be sustained. It is achieved through hormones such as cortisol.

3   Exhaustion stage – the effect of prolonged attempts to deal with a stressor that diminish bodily resources and cause an elevated risk of illness (and death).

- **Psychosurgery** – treating mental illnesses by operating on the brain. Lobotomies and cingulotomies were examples used when no other treatment had worked. The lobotomy was widely used but had a poor success rate. It was popular in part because it made it possible to control difficult patients. Cingulotomies have a higher success rate and fewer side effects but still carry considerable risks.

- **Chemotherapy** – treatments using drugs. Many drugs are used to help people to cope with mental illnesses (e.g. anti-depressants). They often act by mimicking or blocking the effects of a neurotransmitter (e.g. by stimulating or occupying post-synaptic receptor sites). Although often very successful at reducing symptoms, they have side effects and cannot solve the cause of the condition.

What have I learned?

1   Describe (without using a diagram) how messages are transmitted between neurones.

2   a What is meant by localisation?

    b Why is localisation important to psychosurgery?

3   a Outline the three stages of the General Adaptation Syndrome.

    b In which stage is stress-related illness unlikely?

    c When is the individual best able to cope with a stressor and why?

4   a Describe one therapy based on the biological approach.

    b Evaluate the therapy you have described in part a.

Reading around

- Carlson, N. R. (1998) *Physiology of Behavior*. London: Allyn & Bacon.

- Stroebe, W. (2000) *Social Psychology and Health*. Buckingham: Open University Press.

What should I know?

- The main assumptions of the behaviourist approach.
- How the social learning theory can explain aggression.
- How behaviourist ideas have been put to use in psychological therapy.

In addition I should be able to:

- describe and evaluate the contributions the behaviourist approach has made to psychology
- use psychological research to support social learning theory
- suggest criticisms of the approach in general and of social learning theory in particular.

The behaviourist approach arose from the research of several individuals working largely in isolation from one another who developed ideas about ways to study the behaviour that simply allowed them to focus on the observable reactions of organisms to their environments. Specifically, these researchers – now known as behaviourists – attempted to explain psychological processes in terms of acquired responses to stimuli. Behaviourism is thus sometimes referred to as 'stimulus-response' psychology (see page 55 for a comparison to cognitive psychology). This approach allowed the behaviourists to concentrate exclusively on those aspects of psychological events that could be seen, i.e. the environmental trigger and the individual's behavioural response. Behaviourism thus represented a departure from both the early psychologists who had tried to study thinking through introspection and the psychodynamic psychologists (see Chapter 3) who focused on explaining events in terms of the unconscious. This distinction is important because the phenomena the behaviourists were recording, unlike thoughts or unconscious motives, were entirely observable and measurable. In this respect, behaviourism paved the way for a more scientific approach to psychology. Explanations from the behaviourist approach predominantly account for learning that is the range of ways in which we, and non-human animals, can acquire new behaviours. They also offer reasons for some of the effects that are common to many learning situations, such as generalisation and discrimination.

Glossary

introspection: studying mental processes by looking inwardly at one's own thinking.
learning: a relatively permanent change in behavioural potential that arises as a result of experience.

Assumptions of the behaviourist approach

These are:

● the role of the environment
● the importance of observable events in research
● the common principles in learning.

The role of the environment

The environment is a significant influence on our behaviour. It can provide stimuli that act as triggers for behaviours, such as the presence of food producing salivation. Through learning, new different stimuli can acquire the ability to trigger responses. The environment is also a source of consequences that affect the likelihood that we will repeat a behaviour. Good things, such as praise, make us more likely to do something again. Receiving punishment, on the other hand, means we are less likely to do the same thing again.

The environment also provides models allowing individuals to learn by copying. A child growing up in a home where adults have a regional accent will acquire that accent by imitation. Manipulating an individual's environment is therefore a way to alter their

learning experience. Other approaches also suggest that aspects of the external environment may affect behaviour, such as the psychodynamic approach, which says that childhood experiences are important. The behaviourist approach is different, because it focuses directly on the role of the environment. Other approaches, in contrast, include internal aspects too, such as the role of the unconscious in psychodynamic psychology.

The importance of observable events in research

The behaviourist approach focuses on external rather than internal factors, so its methodology is distinctive. Whereas other approaches must rely, to an extent, on assumptions about thinking, feeling, attitudes or the unconscious, the behaviourist approach relies exclusively on observable data. While behaviourists do not deny the existence of an unconscious, the emphasis of their investigations is on the visible, measurable changes that occur in behaviour in response to known manipulations of the environment.

The common principles in learning

Behaviour learned in response to one stimulus may appear in response to another, similar stimulus; this is called '**generalisation**'. For example, a child might learn that aggression at home makes a sibling surrender their sweets. They may then be aggressive to peers at school too.

Discrimination is the process of distinguishing between two similar but different stimuli and responding to only one of them.

For example, a child may be aggressive at home to a younger sibling but not to an older one.

These ideas are central to the behaviourist approach because they apply to behaviours acquired by any mechanism, e.g. classical or operant conditioning, or social learning (see below). They are also important because they have survival value for the learner. An animal that can generalise a response can apply the behaviour to new situations which might be beneficial (for example, a bird that learns to open milk bottle tops to reach the cream can generalise this to foil-top yoghurt or cream pots and gain new sources of food). Discrimination can help the individual to avoid dangerous or unpleasant situations (for example, a bird might learn to eat only nice-tasting berries or insects on the basis of their colour).

When behaviours have been learned, they are not necessarily permanent. Following the learning period, a newly acquired behaviour may be lost from the repertoire. This is called 'extinction' of the response. After a period of time during which this response is not produced, it may suddenly reappear, triggered by the original stimulus. This is called 'spontaneous recovery'.

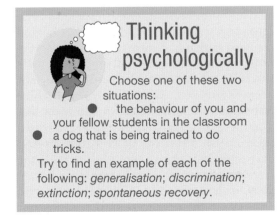

Thinking psychologically

Choose one of these two situations:
● the behaviour of you and your fellow students in the classroom
● a dog that is being trained to do tricks.
Try to find an example of each of the following: *generalisation*; *discrimination*; *extinction*; *spontaneous recovery*.

Early behaviourist theories

Classical conditioning

Classical conditioning occurs when an individual acquires the response of reproducing an action that they can already perform, but in response to a new situation. For example, a puppy will learn that going in the car leads to exciting places to walk. Soon it gets excited every time the car door is opened. The learned response becomes an automatic and unavoidable consequence of exposure to this new stimulus.

In order to describe this process you need to understand the correct terms:

● **unconditioned stimulus** (UCS) – the existing cause of a behaviour (which may be a reflex) prior to conditioning
● **neutral stimulus** (NS) – a new stimulus which, prior to conditioning, did not produce this response
● **unconditioned response** (UCR) – the pre-existing response to the unconditioned stimulus
● **conditioned response** (CR) – a response, similar to the unconditioned response, which is produced in response to the conditioned stimulus
● **conditioned stimulus** (CS) – the name given to the neutral stimulus after conditioning when it has acquired the capacity to produce the conditioned response.

The CR may differ from the UCR in terms of latency (the time it takes to start) and strength (how vigorous the response is). The conditioned response is likely to occur more slowly and less vigorously than to the UCR.

Fig. 2.1 Ivan Pavlov with one of his dogs during an experiment

- **Before conditioning:**
  UCS (meat powder) –> UCR (salivation).
- **During conditioning:**
  UCS + NS (beat of metronome) –> UCR.
- **After conditioning:**
  CS (beat of metronome) –>UCR.

Many behaviours can be classically conditioned. For example, you may find yourself looking up expectantly and considering crossing the road because you have heard the sound of the 'clear to cross' beeping – that's the product of classical conditioning. We are even conditioned to salivate. Ask someone to rattle a biscuit tin or unwrap a chocolate bar near you. Even if you can't smell the food, you may salivate because the visual and auditory triggers act as conditioned stimuli. Humans can also learn a fear response through classical conditioning.

John Watson, another famous behaviourist, studied the phenomenon of conditioned emotional responses. Watson and Rayner (1920) requested the co-operation of the mother of a 9-month-old boy (called Albert). The infant was unafraid of a range of objects such as a white rat and wooden blocks but was startled by a loud noise (see Figures 2.2a and b). He was classically conditioned by being repeatedly shown a rat and simultaneously hearing a loud noise caused by the striking of a metal bar behind his head with a hammer. His response to the noise alone was observed, and to objects (such as the wooden blocks) that had not been associated with the noise. These responses were observed over a long period. Watson and Rayner observed that the infant appeared afraid of the noise (from a metal bar) and, after the second pairing with the rat, also seemed afraid of the rat as he leaned away. After five days the child cried in response to the rat and to similar white, soft

Ivan Pavlov was the first researcher to identify and explore classical conditioning (see Figure 2.1). He was a physiologist studying digestion and knew that animals produced saliva in response to food, but the dogs in his experiments also seemed to salivate in response to the sound of footsteps. Pavlov (1927) aimed to investigate whether they had learned that the sound was associated with food.

During the experiment, salivation was measured with:

- meat powder alone
- meat powder and a ticking metronome (the conditioning phase)
- a ticking metronome alone.

Pavlov found that the dogs initially salivated to the meat powder (UCS) but not the metronome (NS). After the conditioning phase, during which the noise and the food were presented together repeatedly, the dogs also salivated to the metronome. The dogs acquired an association between the existing response of salivation and the new stimulus – the sound of the metronome (then a CS).

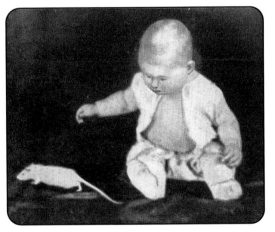

Fig. 2.2a *Before conditioning, Albert shows no fear of the rat*

Fig. 2.2c *After conditioning, Albert's fear generalises to other fluffy, white objects*

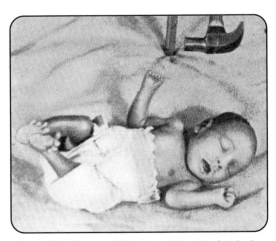

Fig. 2.2b *Before conditioning, Albert is afraid of the loud noise*

objects (such as a fur coat and Father Christmas beard – see Figure 2.2c). After seven weeks, these responses were still present but at no point did he show distress to the wooden blocks. These observations suggest that Albert had acquired an association between the sight of the rat and the new stimulus – the loud noise – through classical conditioning. This response generalised to other, similar, white fluffy objects but not to different objects such as the wooden blocks.

Operant conditioning

When an animal is placed in a new situation, it responds with a range of behaviours triggered by stimuli in the environment. Some of the responses have no effect, some produce pleasant, and others unpleasant, consequences. These consequences determine the future frequency of the behaviours that elicited them. If a behaviour results in an overall pleasant effect this is called '**reinforcement**' and the behaviour will be repeated more often. When this pleasant effect is the result of something good happening, this is called '**positive reinforcement**'. If the pleasant effect is the result of something nasty stopping, it is called '**negative reinforcement**'. In either case, remember, the behaviour increases in frequency. However, if the behaviour has unpleasant effects, this consequence is called '**punishment**' and the behaviour is repeated less often. Punishers can be either the end of

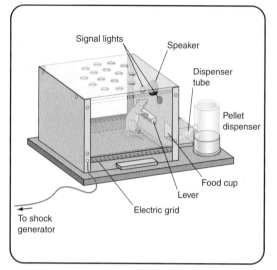

Fig. 2.3 Skinner box

Figure 2.3) also recorded the frequency of the animal's responses. Skinner conducted many different experiments, for example showing that rats which received food for pressing the bar in a box (i.e. were reinforced) pressed the bar more often than those which received no food. Interestingly, rats which received food on only some bar presses (a partial reinforcement schedule) responded faster and were more resistant to extinction than those reinforced for every bar press.

The social learning theory of aggression

In addition to the processes of conditioning, humans and animals can acquire new behaviours by observation. This is explained by the 'social learning theory'. This theory says that social learning happens when one individual acquires the ability to perform a new behaviour by watching that behaviour in another (the **model**). The observed behaviour is then imitated. Behaviours acquired in this way can therefore be learned without necessarily being performed.

Social learning may account for the acquisition of aggressive responses. Some children may observe violent acts by their parents but many more will be exposed to aggressive behaviours in media such as TV, computer games and films. It has been estimated by Eron (1995) that a child entering secondary school will have seen 8,000 murders and 100,000 other violent acts on TV. So, if social learning does occur, these opportunities for observation are likely to have an influence. That children are affected

something nice (**negative punishment**) or the start of something nasty (**positive punishment**).

These consequences may occur every time the action is performed or only sometimes (**partial reinforcement**). This pattern is called the schedule of reinforcement and affects both the rate of responses and extinction.

Much of our understanding of operant conditioning comes from the extensive work of B. F. Skinner. He devised a way to test learning in animals, minimising the need for human interference. He created a mechanised box in which an animal such as a rat or pigeon could perform a range of responses and (for some but not others) gain automatic reinforcement. This apparatus, now called the 'Skinner box', allowed him to vary the nature and frequency of reinforcement (e.g. food, which was delivered in tiny pellets). A Skinner box (see

Box 2.1

Bandura (1977) identifies four processes in social learning. These are:

- **attention** – the model must actually be observed, rather than just present
- **retention** – the observer must remember what they have seen
- **reproduction** – the observer must be capable of doing the behaviour they have seen
- **motivation** – the observer must have a reason to perform the new action.

The first three criteria will result in the acquisition of the new response, the fourth is also required if the behaviour is to be demonstrated.

by what they see on-screen was illustrated by Troseth (2003) who showed that even two-year-olds can be affected by what they see on TV. The children were filmed hiding a toy and were more likely to be able to find the toy later if they had watched their own actions on TV.

Several factors increase the likelihood that an observer will perform a behaviour that they have observed. Some affect whether the behaviour will be acquired, for example if the model is:

- the same gender
- the same age
- powerful or high status
- friendly or likeable.

Observers are more likely to identify with models to whom they aspire. So individuals with these characteristics, such as adults (high status), peers (same age) and characters on TV (powerful and likeable), are all potentially effective models.

In addition, the probability of the behaviour actually being performed is influenced

by external events, for example it is more likely if:

- the observer has seen the model being rewarded for the behaviour (this is called '**vicarious reinforcement**')
- the observer is reinforced (this, of course, is an effect of operant conditioning, i.e. positive reinforcement).

Fig. 2.4a, b

Fig. 2.4c, d Children imitate the aggressive actions of an adult model

In films and even in cartoons, violent characters tend to have attributes such as those listed above and, furthermore, are rewarded for their actions. For example, a cartoon 'baddy' gets a laugh and many film heroes, both good and bad, achieve material gain or hero status through acts of violence. As a result, viewers also are exposed to vicarious reinforcement for aggression.

Evaluation of social learning theory

There is much evidence to support social learning theory. Using a laboratory experiment, Bandura *et al.* (1961) showed that children will imitate aggression from a live model. They tested 36 boys and 36 girls aged between three and six years. Initially, they observed the children and rated them individually for aggressive behaviour. This allowed the researchers to match the groups of children for aggressiveness. Each child was then allowed to watch an adult model playing. Children either saw:

- aggressive or non-aggressive behaviour by the model, or no model, or
- a same or different sex model.

The non-aggressive model played for ten minutes with Tinker toys (building sets). The aggressive model played with the Tinker toys for one minute, then spent nine minutes displaying both verbal and physical aggression to a Bobo doll. The children were subsequently shown attractive toys which they could play with, but were then told they were for other children. This served to frustrate them and increase the likelihood of them demonstrating aggression if it had been acquired. Finally, the children were moved to another room with toys including a Bobo doll. They were observed there for 20 minutes through a one-way mirror.

The children, especially the boys, who saw aggressive models showed more violent behaviour towards the Bobo doll than those who had observed non-aggressive behaviour. Girls reproduced slightly more verbal aggression and boys more physical aggression. Boys were more likely to imitate same-sex models, while although the same pattern existed for girls, it was less evident. Children who saw the non-aggressive model were even less aggressive than those who saw no model. These findings suggest that observation and imitation can account for the learning of specific aggressive behaviours and that children are more likely to imitate same-gender models.

In a similar experiment, Bandura *et al.* (1963) compared the behaviour of children exposed to different kinds of aggressive modelling situations. Participants saw either:

- a real-life aggressive model with a Bobo doll, or
- the same model performing the same behaviours but recorded on film and projected onto a screen, or
- a film of an aggressive cartoon character 'Herman the Cat' presented on a TV (the film looked like a cartoon but was acted by one of the models dressed as a cat who performed the same sequence of behaviours as in the other conditions), or
- no film or live model (control group).

As in Bandura *et al.* (1961), the children were then frustrated and subsequently observed for aggression. In all of the model groups significantly more aggression was displayed (average score of 91) than the control group (average score of 54). The differences between the effects of different models were small, although, where differences existed (e.g. for total aggression, imitative aggression and gun play), the filmed model was most effective. This suggests that violent humans on film are potent models for aggression.

It could be argued that the evidence from studies such as Bandura's is weak support for the idea that violent TV affects children's aggression in the real world since they used an artificial set-up. It is possible, for example, that the children responded aggressively because they believed that they were being 'invited' to hit the Bobo doll and were merely copying the adults because that is what adults expect children to do. However, evidence from studies based on the effects of exposure to actual TV violence also supports the effect of social learning. Eron *et al.* (1972) observed aggressiveness in eight-year-old children and recorded the amount of violent TV they watched. They found a positive correlation, that is, there was a link between the children's aggressive behaviour and their TV viewing. Of course, precisely because this was not a controlled study, we cannot be sure that the TV viewing was responsible for the high levels of aggression. It is possible that both were influenced by some other factor, such as violence in the home or a personality that tends the individual towards both actual violence and a preference for viewing violent programmes. The children were followed up 11 and 22 years later. At 19 years of age, the association that had been observed in childhood was even stronger in the boys (though not girls) as teenagers and they were likely to be aggressive if they had watched more television even if they had not been particularly aggressive at the age of eight.

Eron and Huesmann (1986) reported on the effects of childhood TV viewing on adult violence. Again, the boys from Eron *et al.* (1972) were followed up to find out whether each individual had been convicted of any violent crimes by 30 years of age. They found

that the more violent TV the boys watched as children, the more likely they were to be violent criminals as adults. These results also suggest that childhood viewing of violent TV is linked to adult aggressive behaviour. The longitudinal design of this study means that it is testing a more realistic, long-term effect than laboratory experiments such as Bandura's can – these can study only the immediate effects of viewing violence. Furthermore, the findings were robust – the pattern persisted even when other variables, such as baseline aggressiveness, socio-economic status and intelligence, had been controlled for.

One study that had the advantage of an experimental design over a correlational one, i.e. that could exclude other possible influences on aggression, but which still looked at real-world evidence was Joy *et al.* (1986). In this study, an opportunity was taken to observe Canadian children who lived in a remote rural area which had been unable to receive transmitted TV because of poor signal reception (they called this group 'Notel'). The children's physical aggression was recorded before and after the introduction of TV and in two control towns which already had TV reception (called 'Unitel' – with one TV station – and 'Multitel' – with several). The findings showed an increase in the incidence of aggression of 160 per cent in the Notel children following exposure to TV, compared with children in areas which already had access to TV during the same two years. This change occurred in both boys and girls and included children who had not been aggressive prior to the introduction of TV, as well as those who were.

Not all real-world evidence suggests that TV violence leads to aggression. Charlton *et al.* (2000) investigated the effect of the introduction of satellite TV on the aggressive behaviour of children. They observed children aged between three and eight at school on St

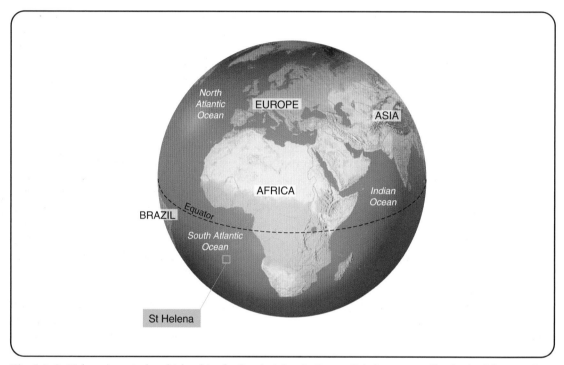

Fig. 2.5 St Helena is an isolated island in the South Atlantic Ocean. It is just 10.5 miles (17 km) long and 6.5 miles (10 km) wide

Helena Island (see Figure 2.5). Children in this isolated community had not seen transmitted TV prior to 1995 and were filmed in the playground before and after satellite TV became available. The aggression they displayed, including hitting and kicking, was recorded.

The violent content of the programmes was slightly higher than on British TV and there was no watershed. However, following exposure to satellite TV, no radical changes in behaviour were observed in the children. This suggests that the opportunity to observe televised violence does not necessarily result in an increase in aggressive behaviour. It was also noted, however, that the children were exceptionally well-behaved compared with those in other geographical areas and that

those children who were, prior to 1995, the most badly behaved also exhibited the greatest interest in violent TV.

Nevertheless, the findings may well be a more valid reflection of the effects of genuine exposure to media violence than laboratory studies. In experiments such as Bandura's, the participants would have been aware that they were being studied, whereas this is unlikely in the St Helena study, so they were less likely to be responding to demand characteristics, making the behaviour more true to life. While this is an advantage, there are also disadvantages to natural experiments. It would have been difficult for the researchers to control other factors that could influence aggression, such as the fact that the children were unusually well-behaved, or any other influences on their behaviour other than TV, such as the social values of the community, so the findings may not be representative of its effect on others.

It is not only television that can provide inappropriate models for social learning, but the home environment too. A longitudinal study conducted by Ehrensaft *et al.* (2003) looked at many consequences for children living in a violent household. One of the factors they isolated was the influence of exposure to violence between parents. They report that witnessing parents expressing their anger through physical aggression can teach young people that this is a way to resolve conflicts. Through social learning, the children learn from the models of their parents that physical violence is a means by which to overcome problems within a relationship.

As we have seen, there is a wealth of evidence to support the social learning theory explanation for aggression. Studies employing a range of designs, in different contexts, have shown that models are important to the acquisition of aggressive behaviours. Even more striking are the direct examples of 'copy-cat' violence, such as the wave of school killings that spread across the USA in the wake of the Columbine High School tragedy (e.g. Kostinsky *et al.*, 2001). Not all the available evidence supports social learning theory, however. The findings of Charlton *et al.* (2000), described earlier, clearly contradict those of Joy *et al.* (1986). Similarly, not all correlational studies find a link between TV viewing and aggressiveness. For example, Hagell and Newbury (1994) found that young people in an institution for juvenile offenders had watched no more violent TV than a control group, suggesting that their delinquent behaviour was not the result of imitating models on television.

There are also weaknesses within the social learning approach. Evidence for the theory is obtained by observing changes in behaviour. However, behaviours acquired through imitation may not be demonstrated immediately. As a consequence, it is difficult to measure learning accurately (as behaviours may be acquired but not performed), so conclusions based on studies of social learning may be flawed. The studies themselves, such as laboratory experiments of aggression, are often artificial. This reduces the validity of the findings. For example, the children in Bandura's studies may not have hit the Bobo doll because they were imitating the adult's aggression but because they believed that they had been invited to do so. Also, in unfamiliar settings (such as in experiments) children – who are not accustomed to being deliberately shown aggressive acts – may reason that they are meant to copy. Furthermore, such studies raise ethical issues about exposing participants to aggression, which may have detrimentally affected their behaviour. This is of especial concern if they are children. Ethical guidelines say that participants should not be negatively affected by research.

Thinking psychologically

Find an article on the internet reporting Ehrensaft's research that suggests that children learn violence from watching parents (some examples are listed below). Use the principles of social learning theory to explain how this pattern of behaviour might be perpetuated.
http://news.bbc.co.uk/1/hi/health/3092847.stm
http://www.psychologytoday.com/articles/pto-20030725-000003.html

Finally, social learning theory is not the only possible explanation which can account for the consequences of exposure to aggressive models. Alternative explanations include the effects of:

- arousal
- desensitisation.

The arousal explanation suggests that watching a model, such as on a violent TV programme, makes the observer excited. This effect occurs with all emotionally arousing content, for example with sexual or funny programmes too. This idea suggests that what is different about violence is that it causes the viewer to interpret their raised arousal as anger and that this source of motivation then triggers aggressive behaviours. However, this explanation would account only for short-term changes, as the physiological effect would subside quickly, and it is contradicted by experimental evidence. For example, Anderson and Dill (2000) compared aggressive responses following exposure to two very exciting computer games that differed only in the extent of their violent content. The games were chosen for the matched physiological arousal they generated. Aggressiveness was measured by the duration of a blast of noise that participants believed they were inflicting on an opponent. They found that participants using the aggressive game responded more aggressively after playing. This suggests that some factor other than arousal, such as the promotion of aggressive thoughts, must be at work.

The desensitisation idea suggests that repeated exposure to violent models would result in a decreased level of emotional reaction to observed aggression (e.g. on-screen)

web watch

You can find Anderson and Dill's original article (2000) at: http://www.apa.org /journals/features/ psp784772.pdf

Look at the factors involved in the General Affective Aggression Model (GAAM). Identify those which have been discussed above.

Read about the method and findings of study 2 (the experiment). What differences were found between men and women?

and a corresponding rise in acceptability of real-life aggression. For example, when Vidal-Vazquez and Clemente-Diaz (2000) showed violent films to adolescents they found that this increased their acceptance of, and attraction to, violent behaviour. One way in which individuals may become less sensitive to violence is through a change in their self-perceptions. Ulmann and Swanson (2004) recorded participants' self-concept after playing the violent video game 'Doom'. Video-game players generally believe that this activity does not make them more violent. However, the self-concept of participants after ten minutes of playing 'Doom' was significantly more likely to be associated with aggressive traits and behaviours than after playing a non-violent video game. The GAAM suggests that this may arise because automatic associations are made between arousal and aggressive emotions, thoughts and behaviours.

Fig. 2.6 Violent video games increase violent emotions and behaviours

Note also the possible role of catharsis – the discharging of built-up emotions. (You will learn more about catharsis when you read Chapter 3.) It has been suggested that by watching media violence an individual might reduce the likelihood of committing actual acts of violence. If their behaviour is caused by pent-up aggression, this could be diverted and released harmlessly by becoming absorbed in on-screen violence.

Together, these findings suggest that social learning is one factor in the acquisition of aggressive behaviours during exposure to aggressive models. However, it is also clear that imitation is not the only important consequence of observing a model and that other hypotheses can refine this explanation.

Where are we now?

As a theory, social learning encompasses both environmental factors (such as models and the effect of reinforcement) and internal factors (such as cognitive aspects, e.g. retaining the information and the relative importance of different kinds of models; and motivation). It is therefore more flexible and complete as an explanation of learning than other theories, such as classical or operant conditioning. As a consequence, social learning is better able to explain some aspects of human learning, which is complex, than are conditioning theories. For example, humans can appear to have acquired new behaviours without any learning. Social learning can explain this through observation in the absence of repetition, whereas in both operant and classical conditioning, the acquisition phase requires that the individual performs the behaviour that they are learning. Finally, social learning theory has many useful applications. For example, it can help

psychologists to understand how we can become aggressive through exposure to violent television. This can be used to guide broadcasting restrictions and film classifications.

Although social learning theory is valuable in understanding the acquisition of aggression, there is also the potential to broaden its application to understand more about the way the social context affects violent behaviour. For example, social learning may be responsible for the acquisition of beliefs about acceptable behaviour, such as social norms and an understanding of sanctions. The social environment can also potentially provide reinforcement for violent behaviour (e.g. through peer acceptance or material gain). Together, these factors may in the future provide a more complete picture of the role played by social learning in acquisition of aggressive behaviour, such as is offered by the GAAM.

Applying the behaviourist approach to therapy

According to the behaviourist approach, mental disorders develop in the same way as other aspects of our behavioural repertoire, through the processes of classical and operant conditioning and social learning. This suggests that disorders have arisen because of the effect of the environment rather than faulty emotions, physiology or cognitions. Behavioural techniques can thus attempt to alter associations between stimuli using the principles of classical conditioning. The manipulation of the environment should allow maladaptive responses to extinguish and enable individuals to learn new, more adaptive behaviours to replace them.

Aversion therapy

Some disorders, such as alcoholism, can be controlled using aversion therapy (AT). This uses classical conditioning (see page 23), pairing an unpleasant CS with a maladaptive behaviour that is to be eliminated. This therapy has also been used to help people to stop smoking and is the principle behind the use of nasty-tasting nail varnish to stop nail-biting. The basic action is shown in Figure 2.7.

The pairings are repeated and, as a result, an association is built up. The stimulus associated with the disorder (such as the tempting sight of a nail to bite) becomes linked to an unpleasant conditioned response (e.g. the nasty taste of the nail treatment).

Evaluating aversion therapy

Aversion therapy has been used effectively with a range of problems. Weinrott *et al.* (1997) successfully treated juvenile sex

---

UCS (naturally aversive stimulus) → UCR (unpleasant consequence)

UCS + NS (stimulus relating to the disorder) → UCR (unpleasant consequence)

CS (stimulus relating to the disorder) → CR (unpleasant consequence)

Fig. 2.7 Basic action of aversion therapy

Box 2.2
Treating alcohol dependence with aversion therapy

Patients with alcohol addiction can be treated with the drug Antabuse, which causes vomiting if it is combined with alcohol. It works like this:

UCS (Antabuse) → UCR (unpleasant sensation of vomiting)
UCS + NS (alcohol) → UCR (expectation of unpleasant sensation of vomiting)
CS (alcohol) → CR (unpleasant expectation)

As the CR is unpleasant (aversive), the drinking of alcohol is deterred.

offenders by pairing the aversive stimulus of videotaped negative consequences of sex offences with the arousal they experienced on listening to an audio-taped scenario of a sexually deviant crime. The intention was to create an association between their sexual arousal and the negative effects. Following treatment, they demonstrated significantly less physiological and self-reported arousal.

Duker and Seys (2000) used aversion therapy to reduce self-injury in 12 children with severe learning difficulties. The children needed to be physically restrained to prevent them from harming themselves repeatedly. They were conditioned by pairing the undesirable behaviour with electric shocks administered by remote control. This unpleasant UCS of shocks became associated with the undesirable behaviour, hence the self-harming behaviour was eliminated in seven of the individuals and reduced in a further three. The effectiveness of aversion therapy can be increased by supplementing it with the reinforcement of alternative behaviours. So, for example, alcoholics could be reinforced for going out and *not* drinking alcohol.

One major problem with aversion therapy is that it does not resolve the underlying cause of the problem. Therefore, it only provides a means to limit symptoms and may even mask the symptoms without dealing with the cause, thus prolonging the effects of disorder in the long term. Another issue is that aversion therapy is necessarily unpleasant. It therefore has the potential to be unethical in its use; patients may feel unable to refuse treatment they have been told is 'good' for them but which is also painful or upsetting. Finally, since the effects of learning may not be permanent, there is a risk of 'spontaneous recovery', that is, of the reappearance of the old (maladaptive) response or extinction (loss) of the new (adaptive) one.

Systematic desensitisation

Systematic desensitisation was developed by Wolpe (1958) and is used in the treatment of phobias. Like aversion therapy, it is based on the principle of classical conditioning. The therapist initially agrees an anxiety hierarchy with the client. This is a graduated sequence of feared stimuli that rise in subjective units of discomfort. For example, for a client who has a phobia of lifts, this may range from watching other people getting into a lift to being stuck in one themselves. The sequence is a list of increasingly challenging conditioned stimuli. These can be real, imagined or achieved using a virtual reality simulator. The aim is to decondition, or desensitise, the client to each of the items on the hierarchy systematically. To achieve this, the therapist must relax the client and preserve this state throughout each level of the hierarchy. A state

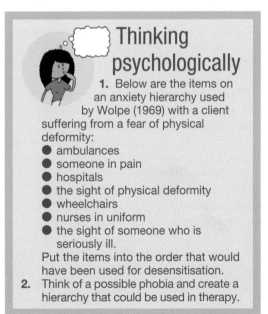

Thinking psychologically

1. Below are the items on an anxiety hierarchy used by Wolpe (1969) with a client suffering from a fear of physical deformity:
   - ambulances
   - someone in pain
   - hospitals
   - the sight of physical deformity
   - wheelchairs
   - nurses in uniform
   - the sight of someone who is seriously ill.

   Put the items into the order that would have been used for desensitisation.

2. Think of a possible phobia and create a hierarchy that could be used in therapy.

of relaxation (the unconditioned response) may be induced using a range of techniques, for example progressive muscle relaxation or hypnosis. The technique used to induce and maintain relaxation is the unconditioned stimulus. We cannot feel two opposite emotions simultaneously (due to reciprocal inhibition) so fear is prevented by the maintenance of relaxation. The therapist works gradually up through the hierarchy, returning to the previous stimulus if the client becomes distressed. The aim is for the client to stay relaxed when confronted with the top of the hierarchy, i.e. the feared stimulus itself.

Evaluating systematic desensitisation

Lang and Lazovik (1963) used systematic desensitisation to help a group of college students who were all suffering from a snake phobia. They underwent 11 sessions to work through a hierarchy which included such items as 'writing the word "snake"' and 'accidentally treading on a dead snake'. Hypnosis was used to assist in the maintenance of relaxation. The participants' fear rating fell between the beginning and end of the sessions. It was found to be effective for most (although not all) of the treatment group and the improvement was still evident six months later.

Similar success has been found in the treatment of a fear of flying. Rothbaum et al. (2000) used either standard or virtual reality presentation of the anxiety hierarchy to participants who were afraid of flying. Following treatment, 93 per cent of both groups agreed to take a trial flight. Their anxiety levels were lower than those of a control group who had not received systematic desensitisation and this improvement was maintained when they were followed up six months later.

Where are we now?

In the use of behavioural techniques in therapy, many are being combined successfully with cognitive strategies (such as in cognitive behavioural therapies). In systematic desensitisation, the recent use of virtual reality has provided an effective means to treat phobias that would be unsafe or impractical to treat within a therapist's office (for example fear of fire or of flying). The use of aversion therapy, in contrast, has declined over several decades. For example, Toneatto and Kosky (2006) surveyed journal articles reporting the use of different techniques in the treatment of addictive gambling from 1966–2005. While from 1966–1972 reports of aversion therapy were common, there were no reports in the last 30 years of Toneatto and Kosky's study. Instead, treatments have used more complex behavioural programmes or drugs. However, the use of aversion therapy has not ceased altogether. Marshall (2006) reports on the successful use of aversion (using smelling salts) to reduce inappropriate behaviour in a habitual exhibitionist.

There are some problems with systematic desensitisation. Simply engaging with overcoming the fear may be distressing for clients, which raises ethical concerns. Furthermore, if the client is so traumatised that they abandon the treatment, this will reinforce their escape behaviour from the fear-inducing stimulus, potentially making the phobia worse.

Like aversion therapy, systematic desensitisation does not necessarily remove the cause. If a phobia has been acquired through learning, it can be successfully unlearned in this manner, but if it is caused by some underlying, perhaps unconscious problem, this will remain unsolved. In such cases, systematic desensitisation would only be limiting the symptoms without dealing with the cause, so the effects of the treatment may not last and the phobic behaviour may spontaneously reappear.

Finally, standard systematic desensitisation (although not the virtual reality assisted type) can work only with people who can maintain the imagery necessary for relaxation and who can transfer their learning from the safe environment with the therapist to their life outside.

Summing it up

- Behaviourists focus on observable events, studying the relationship between **stimuli** and **responses**. Their experimental approach to learning helped to make psychology more scientific.

- The major assumptions of the approach are the importance of the environment, the emphasis of research on observable events and the general principles that underlie all learned behaviours.

- Four general principles underlie all learning: **generalisation** – a behaviour can be elicited by similar stimuli; **discrimination** – an individual can learn to distinguish between similar stimuli; **extinction** – learned behaviours fade; **spontaneous recovery** – even after extinction a behaviour may reappear.

- Early behaviourists identified two mechanisms of learning, classical and operant conditioning.

- **Classical conditioning** is the acquisition of an association between a new stimulus and an existing response. As a result, the behaviour appears in response to a 'conditioned stimulus'. Pavlov demonstrated classical conditioning with dogs which learned to salivate to a specific noise after it was paired repeatedly with food. Conditioned emotional responses, such as fear, can also be learned through classical conditioning.

- In **operant conditioning**, new behaviours are acquired through a trial-and-error process. When the consequences of an action are pleasant, the behaviour is repeated more often. This is the result of reinforcement. If the consequences are unpleasant, i.e. punished, the frequency of the behaviour decreases.

- **Social learning** occurs when a model is imitated. The learned behaviour does not have to be reproduced immediately.

- Factors such as gender, age and status make some models more effective, so characters on TV may be important models for children.

- Evidence suggests that aggressive behaviour may result from observing violent models, e.g. in the home and on TV. However, not all instances support this and many other factors influence aggressive behaviour.

- Therapies based on the behaviourist approach manipulate the client's environment to change behaviour. Maladaptive responses may extinguish or be removed by conditioning and appropriate responses are learned in their place.

- **Aversion therapy** is used to remove inappropriate responses. Classical conditioning pairs an unpleasant experience with the behaviour that is to be 'removed'.

- **Systematic desensitisation**, used to treat phobias, also uses classical conditioning. A calm state is associated with a feared situation, allowing the client to overcome their fear.

- Aversion therapy and systematic desensitisation have been used successfully for a range of conditions, although both raise some practical and ethical concerns.

What have I learned?

1 Outline two assumptions of the behaviourist approach.

2 a Outline the process of classical conditioning.

b Explain how classical conditioning has been used in one therapy.

3 a How has social learning theory been used to account for aggressive behaviour?

b Evaluate the strengths and weaknesses of the social learning explanation of aggression.

4 Compare and contrast the behavioural approach with any one other approach to psychology.

Reading around

● Bergin, A. E. and Garfield, S. L. (1994) *Handbook of Psychotherapy and Behaviour Change.* New York: Wiley.

● Gunter, B. and McAleer, J. (1997) *Children and Television*. London: Routledge.

● Pearce, J. M. (1997) *Animal Learning and Cognition: An Introduction*. Hove: Psychology Press.

What should I know?

- The main assumptions of the psychodynamic approach to psychology.
- Freud's ideas about the unconscious mind and personality.
- Freud's ideas about psychosexual development.
- How psychodynamic ideas have been put to use in psychological therapy.

In addition I should be able to:

- evaluate the contributions the psychodynamic approach has made to psychology
- use psychological research to support and/or challenge aspects of Freud's theory
- suggest criticisms of the approach in general and of Freudian theory in particular
- compare and contrast the psychodynamic approach with other psychological approaches.

The psychodynamic approach is one of the older approaches to psychology, originating at the end of the nineteenth century. The most famous and historically important person in this approach was Sigmund Freud. Freud was a medical doctor who had a particular interest in using psychology to treat patients, including those whose symptoms were apparently medical rather than psychological. Freud's ideas came largely from his work with patients. From listening to and observing his patients Freud concluded the following principles about psychology. These continue to underlie the psychodynamic approach.

Assumptions of the psychodynamic approach

These are:

- the importance of the unconscious mind (i.e. mental processes we are not aware of)
- the importance of early experience in affecting later psychological functioning

- the importance of relationships to psychological functioning.

Glossary

psychodynamic: refers to a set of theories, concepts and therapies that depends on importance of the unconscious mind, early experience and relationships.
unconscious: mental processes of which the thinker is unaware.
lust: pleasure.
unlust: displeasure.
transference: transferring emotions from one relationship on to another.

The influence of the unconscious mind

There are a number of psychodynamic theories, each of which has a different view of the nature of the unconscious mind. In this chapter we are concerned with Freudian theory. Freud (1915) suggested that the unconscious mind functions quite differently from the conscious. The unconscious mind is not logical and makes no distinction between real external events and internal ones such as dreams. The unconscious seeks pleasure (what Freud called '**lust**') and avoids displeasure (or as Freud called it, '**unlust**'). The unconscious mind constantly influences our behaviour, urging us towards pleasure and away from displeasure. So we might dream of something that would give us pleasure, commit a slip of the tongue that might reveal something we really want, or forget something unpleasant.

The importance of early experience

In psychodynamic theory there is a close connection between childhood experiences and adult functioning. Many aspects of adult thinking, emotion and behaviour can be linked to particular childhood experiences. Different psychodynamic theories place their emphasis on different childhood events. Freud saw childhood development as a series of stages, each of which was linked to particular aspects of adult behaviour and particular personality characteristics. During each stage, 'lust' (pleasure) is linked to a particular part of the body, hence their names, the oral, anal and phallic stages.

The importance of relationships

In psychodynamic theory, relationships are of particular importance, especially those with family members. Freud placed great emphasis on the relationship between a developing child and its parents. He believed that the quality of the relationship with parents is reflected in how well the child progresses through each stage of development, and that as adults we are unconsciously influenced to respond to people according to the nature of the early relationship they remind us of. This is called '**transference**', because emotions directed at one relationship become transferred on to new relationships. This idea is used in psychodynamic therapy where patients build a transference relationship with their therapist.

Freud's theory

Freud's collection of ideas is vast (the Collected Works include 26 books). The focus in the early part of this chapter is on Freud's ideas about the personality and how it develops in childhood. Personality can be defined as the aspects of human behaviour that vary from one person to another but which remain fairly consistent within the individual. Later in this chapter, when we apply psychodynamic ideas to therapy, we can explore other key aspects of Freudian theory.

The structural model of personality

Freud (1923) suggested that we can think of the personality as having three aspects: an instinctive part, a logical part and a moral part. So we are influenced by instinct and morality but also have the ability to make logical decisions that satisfy our instincts to seek pleasure and avoid displeasure while not falling foul of our conscience. These three parts to the personality have become known as the '**id**', '**ego**' and '**superego**' (Figure 3.1).

- The id (originally called simply 'it' as in the phrase 'it just came over me') is the instinctive aspect of the personality. It seeks purely to receive pleasure and avoid displeasure. Thus it is said to operate on the pleasure principle. We are born without logic or morality – Freud described babies as 'bundles of id'.
- The ego (originally called simply 'I') is the logical part of the personality that can make conscious and logical decisions that reflect the demands of instinct, morality and external reality. Thus the ego is said to operate on the reality

Fig. 3.1 The id–ego–superego image has often been used in film

principle. Freud believed the ego was part of the personality by around one year of age.
- The superego (originally known as 'above-I') is the moral aspect of the personality. It is formed when an image of the same-sex parent is internalised and it functions as a mental representation of that parent, internally punishing and rewarding us according to the morality of our actions.

We constantly have to make decisions. How we go about this and how we then respond to the decisions we make can form an important part of our personality. We might, for example, find ourselves in the position of finding a wallet in the street. Our id will push us towards taking it and keeping any money it contains. Our superego, on the other hand, will influence us in a more moral direction, perhaps leading us to hand it in at a police station. If we give in to our id and take the

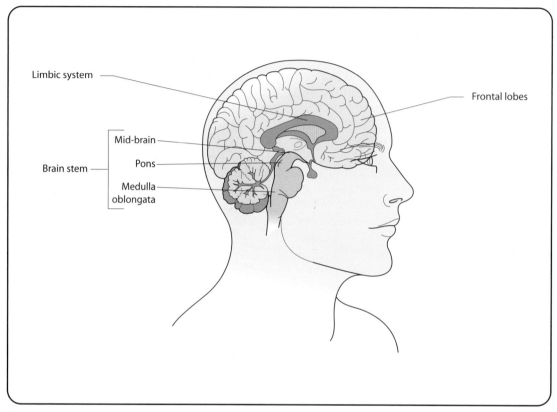

Fig. 3.2 Some psychologists have attempted to locate the Freudian personality in the brain

money, our superego will probably punish us with guilt and shame later. It is the ego that has the final say in a situation like this, and successful resolution will involve a course of action that satisfies our pleasure-seeking id and our moral superego *and* makes sense in the light of circumstances. We might, for example, hand it in but hope to receive a reward for doing so. This should satisfy the superego because it is the 'right' course of action and also satisfy the id because there is a selfish motive.

Evaluation of the structural model

By looking at the roles of instinct, logic and social morality, Freud has provided a very broad model of the human personality and in this sense he was well ahead of his time (Jarvis, 2004). Modern psychologists would widely agree that we are influenced by instinct, logic and morality. However, many would disagree that this is the best way of thinking about personality. Most modern psychologists who are concerned with personality believe it is more useful to think in terms of **traits** – stable characteristics such as how lively, sociable, agreeable and emotionally stable we are. This approach is difficult to reconcile with the Freudian structure of personality.

Some psychologists have approached the structural model differently and attempted to see whether id, ego and superego can be located in the brain. For example, Ito (1998) has proposed that the id is based in the hypothalamus and limbic system (see Figure 3.2), whilst the associative cortex (particularly the frontal lobes) is the location of the ego and superego.

Freud himself (Freud, 1933) was more concerned with the way his structural model explained the experience of being pulled in different directions by different aspects of the personality. So it may be that even if we could locate id, ego and superego in the brain, this is fairly far removed from what Freud was thinking about.

web watch

One of the applications of the structural model is in film and literature where characters can represent id, ego and superego.

1 Go to the following site and see how we can interpret Start Trek characters using Freud's model: http://ryong001.homestead.com/Freud.html

2 Think of a current TV programme and look at which characters might represent id, ego and superego.

Psychosexual development

Freud (1905) suggested that our personality develops through our childhood and that particular aspects of our personality are rooted in the experiences we have at particular stages of development. He identified five stages of development, but proposed that the adult personality is largely formed by the end of the third stage. The stages are shown in Table 3.1.

Stage	Age
Oral	0–1
Anal	1–3
Phallic	3–6
Latency	7–puberty
Genital	Puberty & adolescence

Table 3.1 Freud's stages of development

At each of the first three stages of development a region of the body has particular significance because psychic energy or **libido** is concentrated there. In the oral stage, for example, libido is concentrated on the mouth because the focus of the infant's attention is largely on the mouth.

Glossary

structural model: a model in which the mind is 'dissected' into three parts: id, ego and superego.
libido: sexual energy or sexual instinct.

The oral stage (0–1 year)

In the oral stage the child's development largely revolves around the mouth, as the child is breast-feeding and being weaned. As well as nourishment, children in the oral stage are taking comfort and information via the mouth (hence babies suck objects to calm themselves and put objects they are investigating in the mouth). From the first year of life we take away to adulthood a number of 'oral' characteristics. These can include an enjoyment of food and drink, and other mouth-related pleasure-seeking behaviour such as smoking and oral sex. We also take away aspects of the infant's relationship with the world, including the capacity for dependence on another person and acceptance of nurture.

If our oral stage goes smoothly, we take away from it the capacity for an adult enjoyment in food and drink and to be dependent on the people with whom we have relationships. However, if an individual experiences a trauma in their first year, such as being separated from their primary carer or having a feeding difficulty, they can go on to experience psychological problems centred around eating or drinking, and may be excessively dependent on others or highly gullible. These attitudes of dependence and gullibility represent the infant's attitudes of dependence on their primary carer and unconditional acceptance of nurture.

The anal stage (1–3 years)

To Freud, the next stage of development is centred on the development of bowel control and potty training, hence the term 'anal'. In this stage the focus of libido thus shifts from the mouth to the anus. The child is now fully aware that they are an independent person (they now have a fully formed ego) and that their wishes can bring them into conflict with others. This type of conflict typically comes to a head in potty training, when adults impose restrictions on when and where the child can defecate.

If the anal stage goes smoothly, we take away from it the ability to deal with authority, to assert our wishes appropriately and to maintain a balance between being ordered and being able to tolerate mess. However, excessively early or harsh potty training can lead to an adult personality dominated by the anal triad of personality characteristics:

- stubbornness – this represents the failure to resolve appropriate relationships with authority
- orderliness – this represents the intolerance of mess
- stinginess – this represents the refusal to give parents the bowel movement they want.

The phallic stage (3–6 years)

In this stage the child's focus is on gender and gendered relationships, in particular the triangular relationship between themselves and each parent and the parents with each other. The focus of libido now shifts from anus to genitals (the word 'phallic' actually refers to the penis). Initially, this may manifest itself as scopophilia, a type of infantile voyeurism in which children are fascinated by adult genitals and may attempt to see them, for example by following adults into the toilet.

This awareness of gender and concentration of libido on the genitals coincides with the child's growing awareness of their being left out of some aspects of their parents' lives. For example, parents at this stage may become less happy with a child climbing into bed with them. The resulting three-way relationship is known as the '**Oedipus complex**', named after Oedipus, a character in a play based on a Greek legend. Through a series of unhappy coincidences, Oedipus came to kill his father and marry his mother, not realising who they were. In the Oedipus complex, a rivalry relationship develops between the child and the same-sex parent for the affection of the opposite-sex parent. On an unconscious level, the child is expressing instinctive wishes to have sex with his mother and kill his father.

To Freud, the resolution of the Oedipus complex is an essential part of a child's personality development. The superego, the moral aspect of the personality, is formed at this point as the child's same-sex parent is internalised or **introjected** into the personality. To Freud, our conscience is literally the mental representation of our same-sex parent telling us what is right and wrong and rewarding and punishing us for our actions. How the Oedipus complex is handled has implications then for our moral development; parents who brutally suppress children's desire for their opposite-sex parent

risk leaving the child with a harsh, punitive superego, thus they may experience excessive guilt and shame. Failure to sensitively parent children through their Oedipus complex can also affect their sexual development, leaving them sexually over- or under-confident.

Evaluation of psychosexual development

The whole idea of psychosexual development is very tricky to study scientifically because the unconscious is inaccessible by any usual techniques – a major issue with Freud's work. His methods, such as dream interpretation, have thus been criticised for being subjective. Another criticism relates to the samples that Freud used. Much of his work was based on findings from case studies which used narrow samples, i.e. his patients. Since these were studies of single individuals, the findings may not generalise to others. However, it is not the case that there is no evidence to support Freud's ideas. We can assess orality and anality using questionnaires or projective tests such as the Rorschach inkblots, although

Box 3.1
Freud's influence on language

One way to see just how great an influence Freud's ideas about personality development have had on our culture is in the popular use of terms, particularly insults, to describe people's personality characteristics. For example, people with an excess of orality as a result of a trauma during their oral stage may be very gullible or dependent on others. Influenced by Freud, we call gullible people 'suckers' and highly dependent people 'leeches'. Similarly, we sometimes call stingy people 'tight' and sexually over-confident people 'cocky'.

web watch

One tool used to measure orality and anality is the Rorschach inkblot test. You can see examples of inkblots similar to the real Rorschach images at: http://www.deltabravo.net/custody/rorschach.php

Try looking at some images and saying what you can see. How credible do you think this type of personality test is?

the validity of the latter is a subject of fierce debate. This allows us to attempt to investigate orality and anality further. In a study by Jacobs *et al.* (1966), for example, smokers and non-smokers were compared for orality using the Rorschach inkblots. In support of Freud, smokers did emerge as significantly more oral.

A number of studies have found correlations between the three anal characteristics, i.e. stubborn people tend to also be stingy and orderly. Of course, just because this personality type exists this does not necessarily mean that it is appropriate to label it 'anal'! However, in one study, O'Neill *et al.* (1992) assessed 40 women for the three anal characteristics (using a standard questionnaire) and for their responses to toilet humour. A positive correlation emerged between stubbornness, stinginess and orderliness and the enjoyment of toilet humour, supporting the notion of anality. This is a good example of how imaginative we have to be if we are to provide scientific support for Freud's ideas. However, some psychologists would see this as a contrived way of investigating the issue and question whether it really provides strong support for anality.

One area where there is little evidence to support Freud concerns the importance of the Oedipus complex in children's development. One way of assessing the importance of the Oedipus complex is to look at the development of same-sex children from gay and single-parent families, who presumably have had no opportunity for Oedipal conflict. If the Oedipus complex is as important as Freud would have us believe, we would expect some difference in children who have and have not had the experience. In a recent review however, Golombok (2000) concluded that, once poverty is controlled for, there is no relationship between family type and psychological development.

Thinking psychologically

Baron-Cohen (2006) has suggested that Freud's ideas about psychosexual development actually lead to a number of hypotheses that have never been tested by psychologists. For example, if the Oedipus complex does exist and is important, it would predict that children who idealise their opposite-sex parent and resent their same-sex parent would be more likely to have affairs with married people as an adult. In Freudian terms, this is because they never resolved their Oedipus complex and so would be unconsciously motivated to break up existing partnerships. Design a study to test this hypothesis.

Applying the psychodynamic approach to therapy

The most important application of psychodynamic ideas is in understanding and treating people suffering from psychological distress and/or mental health problems. Thinking back to our three assumptions of the approach we can apply each of these to understanding mental health.

The unconscious mind

A basic assumption of the psychodynamic approach is that we are constantly influenced by unconscious mental processes (i.e. mental processes of which we are not aware). These unconscious processes can lead to the symptoms of mental disorder. For example, Pines (2002) found that teachers who were bullied as children were particularly likely to experience severe anxiety when disciplining children in their adult professional role. This is presumably because confronting difficult children has two distinct meanings to the teacher. To the conscious mind it is simply part of one's job, but to the unconscious mind it raises the spectre of suffering at the hands of bullies.

Early experience

Our second basic assumption of the approach is that our adult functioning can be linked to childhood experience. Sometimes this is true of symptoms. For example, Freud (1917) suggested that some instances of depression in adulthood are the direct result of childhood experiences of losses. There is some contemporary evidence to support this idea. In an investigation of the origins of depression and anxiety, Eley and Stevenson (2000) found that early losses predicted adult depression and that early frightening experiences predicted later anxiety disorders. However, they also found evidence to suggest that mental disorder has a genetic component. This fits well with Freud's ideas: he believed that only some cases of depression could be linked to loss experiences. It does also show, however, that we cannot explain mental health problems using psychodynamic ideas alone.

Relationships

Our final assumption of the psychodynamic approach concerns the importance of relationships to psychological functioning. Relationships can be linked to symptoms in a number of ways. First, poor early relationships can predispose us to mental health problems. The poet Philip Larkin expressed this when he wrote:

'They fuck you up, your mum and dad.

They may not mean to, but they do

They fill you with all the faults they had

And add some extra, just for you.'

First verse of 'This Be the Verse' (1971)

There is evidence to support this view. In one study Massie and Szeinberg (2002) followed up 76 babies from birth, assessing the quality of their relationship with their mother and noting any traumatic experiences they had during childhood. At age 30 years they were assessed for symptoms. Both childhood trauma and quality of maternal relationship were associated with adult symptoms, although childhood trauma had the stronger relationship.

In the Massie and Szeinberg study there was also a strong relationship between quality of maternal relationship and the quality of adult relationships. People do not come to therapy only because of clinical symptoms. One common problem is in establishing relationships with other people. In Freudian theory, relationship problems can result from negative **transference**, in which we transfer the emotions from one relationship on to another. Thus a patient who has had a poor early relationship with his mother might transfer the negative emotions from that relationship on to adult romantic relationships. This might lead to him behaving irrationally and failing to hold down a relationship. This is an example of the influence of early relationships on adult functioning.

The aim of psychodynamic therapies

We can understand the psychodynamic approach to therapy in terms of our three assumptions. Psychodynamic therapies aim to make unconscious material conscious, so that it can be dealt with better. Often, this unconscious material has links to early trauma or relationships. To take our example of the anxious teacher, once they understand that the reason that they become so anxious when disciplining children is linked to their early experiences of bullying (i.e. when this unconscious material becomes conscious), they can begin to tackle the problem. This would involve dealing with the left-over emotions about being bullied. With this dealt with, it would be straightforward to get better at managing discipline.

Take our other example of the man with a poor maternal relationship who struggles to maintain an adult romantic relationship. Once he is aware that he behaves irrationally towards women because they remind him of his mother, he can begin to do two things.

Box 3.2
Varieties of psychodynamic therapy

- **Classical psychoanalysis:** a very intensive and long-term therapy. Takes place 4–5 times per week and can last for several years. Sessions normally last exactly 50 minutes. The patient often lies on a couch.
- **Psychoanalytic psychotherapy:** a less intensive but still usually long-term therapy. Sessions take place 1–3 times per week. The patient may lie on a couch or face the therapist.
- **Brief dynamic therapy:** this is a generally less intensive and short-term therapy. It may focus on a single problem rather than take the very broad approach to the patient's mental functioning in psychoanalysis.

First, he can use this insight to begin to regulate his behaviour towards his girlfriends more successfully. Second, he can start to deal with his emotions towards his mother. We can say, then, that the techniques of psychodynamic therapy each aim to achieve one of two things. First, they aim to make unconscious material conscious, giving the patient insight into where their problems come from. Second, they aim to get rid of pent-up emotion related to this unconscious material. This process is called '**catharsis**'.

Techniques of psychodynamic therapies

Free association

In free association the patient makes no conscious effort to recall or focus on anything specific, but simply allows their thoughts to drift and voices whatever crosses their mind. The idea behind this is that it creates the optimum conditions for important unconscious material to come to mind. So, even if we had only a vague idea of what our problem really was and no idea where it came from, if we were to lie on the couch and free associate we would expect to start talking about both the problem and its origins. A therapist could then feed back to us the possible links between problem and origin. Some free associations just allow a patient to communicate something to the therapist that they would not have thought consciously to say. An example of this is shown in Box 3.3.

Box 3.3
An example of free association (after Malan, 1995)

A male patient in his 40s was admitted to hospital to investigate a series of severe headaches. No biological cause was discovered, but a student doctor encouraged the man to talk about his current life problems. The headaches then disappeared. Just before leaving hospital the patient said spontaneously: 'A few months ago my wife and I went out to a meal in a restaurant. We had a most enjoyable evening, and as we were about to go I called the waitress over and asked her how I could thank her for the wonderful service. She said that if I wanted to thank her perhaps I should speak about it to the manager.' The student doctor interpreted this free association as meaning that the patient was grateful to him, saying 'I think you're trying to thank me for giving you good service'.

Glossary

catharsis: discharging of built-up emotion.
free association: saying whatever comes into the mind.

Although this is tricky to test scientifically, there is some evidence to suggest that free association is associated with therapeutic benefit. Pole and Jones (1998) computer-analysed a set of 208 sessions of psychoanalytic psychotherapy with a single patient, looking at free association and symptoms. It emerged that the patient's ability to free associate increased over time, and that phases of therapy when there were particularly rich free associations were also the periods of decline in symptoms.

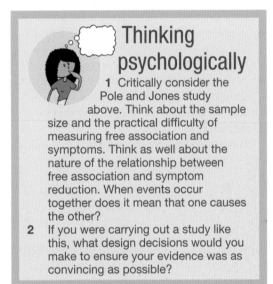

Thinking psychologically

1 Critically consider the Pole and Jones study above. Think about the sample size and the practical difficulty of measuring free association and symptoms. Think as well about the nature of the relationship between free association and symptom reduction. When events occur together does it mean that one causes the other?
2 If you were carrying out a study like this, what design decisions would you make to ensure your evidence was as convincing as possible?

Dream interpretation

Freud (1900) famously called dreams 'the royal road to a knowledge of the activities of the unconscious mind' (p. 769). He believed that dreams perform psychological functions, the most important being the satisfaction of wishes. Freud suggested that behind the scene and story of a dream (this is called the '**manifest content**') there is likely to be a hidden wish, or **latent content**. The processes in which the underlying wish is transformed into the manifest content are called '**dreamwork**'. Dreamwork is important because it allows us to continue to sleep while dreaming about the sort of latent content that would be extremely exciting and so probably wake us up! Freud identified four processes in dreamwork:

- Displacement takes place when we change one person or object into another.
- Condensation takes place when we combine the features of two or more people or objects into one.
- Symbolisation takes place when an object or action serves as a symbol for another. Thus if we dream about phallic objects like pens, swords etc., Freud might suggest these are penis symbols.
- Secondary elaboration is the final part of dreamwork and takes place as the unconscious mind strings together images into a logical storyline. This further disguises the latent content.

Dream interpretation can be an important technique in psychodynamic therapy. Of course, not all patients remember their dreams or choose to bring them to therapy. However, on occasion dreams can reveal things about the mental state of the patient, for example what they want and what is worrying them. Take the example of the dream in Box 3.4.

Note that a good therapist does not impose a particular interpretation on a patient. Rather, such interpretations are offered and may be accepted if they 'ring true' with the patient.

The link between dreaming and wish fulfilment remains a subject of some debate over a century after Freud proposed his ideas. We must remember that in Freud's time we knew pretty much nothing about the physiology of sleep and dreaming. When this was researched in the 1970s, some findings emerged that at first suggested that Freud could not be correct. Hobson and McCarley (1977) discovered that REM sleep, the period when the most vivid and best-remembered dreams take place, is associated with random firing of cells in the brain stem, these activating other centres of the brain and

Box 3.4
An example of dream interpretation

Background
The patient, Buffy, is a woman in her 30s. She always believed that she was neglected by her parents who lavished their attention on her two brothers, one of whom was extremely tall and the other of whom was bald. She also recalls being bullied by the two brothers. As an adult she has minimal contact with them or her parents. However, she has agreed to spend Christmas with them. The dream takes place a week before Christmas. She has been out to a pub with friends that evening.

The dream
Buffy is due to meet two friends – a married couple – for a drink. She takes the bus to the pub and gets there on time and buys herself a drink. The others are late and when they get there they talk to each other and ignore her. When it is the man's turn to buy a round he forgets her drink. Buffy leaves the pub early in disgust and walks to the bus stop where she waits for the bus. There is a tall, bald man at the bus stop who starts to shout at her. She grabs a brick from the ground and hits him with it. The man falls to the ground and begs not to be hit again.

Interpretation
The two neglectful friends may represent Buffy's parents. This is an example of displacement. The aggressive, tall, bald man might be interpreted as a condensation of Buffy's two brothers. Some aspects of the dream, such as the pub setting and peripheral details like travelling to meet her friends, can be seen as secondary elaboration, based on Buffy's own evening. In Freudian terms this dream would be seen as triggered by the coming difficult Christmas and expressing Buffy's wishes to walk out on her parents and take revenge on her brothers.

appearing to create the experience of dreams. If dreams are random it seems unlikely that they can perform a psychological function like wish fulfilment.

More recent research, however, suggests that there may indeed be a link between dreaming and wishing. Solms (2000) has identified an area of the brain where the limbic system (which is associated with emotion and memory processes) links to the cortex, an area associated with higher mental functions such as thinking. Damage to this region of the brain tends to inhibit two mental functions, dreaming and goal-seeing behaviour, i.e. the satisfaction of wishes. Thus on a neurological level there may indeed be a close link between dreaming and wishing.

Freud's ideas about dreamwork are harder to test. In one study Roussy *et al.* (1996) collected pre-sleep thoughts and accounts of what issues were on the minds of eight participants over a period of eight nights. The content of their dreams was also recorded. No significant association was found between the issues the dreamers were thinking about and their dream content. This is a good example of the difficulty in testing Freudian ideas. On one hand, if Freud were wrong and dreams have no meaning, this is exactly what we would expect to find. On the other hand, if Freud were right and our unconscious mind distorts dream content to disguise what is really on our mind ... this is also exactly what we would expect to find!

Evaluation of psychodynamic therapies

Unlike therapists from the other theoretical approaches discussed in this book, psychodynamic therapists are most commonly not psychologists. This is important because it means that they are often not trained researchers. Because of this, rather less research has been carried out on the effectiveness of psychodynamic therapies than is true of other brands of therapy. However, the research that does exist paints a positive picture. In one large-scale Scandinavian study, Sandell (1999) studied the symptoms of 756 patients before, immediately after and three years after receiving state-funded psychoanalysis or psychoanalytic psychotherapy. Therapy lasted up to three years. At the end of treatment there were significantly fewer symptoms in both the psychotherapy and psychoanalysis conditions, but no difference between the two groups. At three-year follow-up, the psychoanalysis group reported significantly fewer symptoms than the psychotherapy group. This suggests that both psychotherapy and psychoanalysis are effective and that patients who have psychoanalysis continue to improve after their analysis ends. The effectiveness of brief dynamic therapy has also been researched. In one recent study, Leichsenring (2001) meta-analysed results of six studies in order to compare the usefulness of brief dynamic therapy, cognitive-behavioural therapy (see Chapter 4) and behavioural therapy (see Chapter 2) for treating depression. No differences emerged between the three treatments.

Although nowadays there is little doubt that psychodynamic therapies can be very effective, there are ethical questions to be addressed. One ethical issue concerns the possibility of making a minority of patients worse. In one study Hauff *et al.* (2002) followed up 25 patients suffering from schizophrenia who had received psychodynamic therapy as in-patients. A control group of 71 patients had received standard medication and in-patient support. Seven years after they left hospital those patients with less severe symptoms prior to treatment were generally better off if they had had therapy. However, low-functioning patients had worse outcomes if they had received in-patient psychodynamic psychotherapy. Another ethical issue concerns the time and expense of the long-term psychodynamic therapies. A patient paying for daily analysis and fitting it into their daily schedule can face considerable expense and disruption to their life. This may be justifiable but it seems likely that in some cases patients might benefit from much quicker, cheaper and less disruptive interventions.

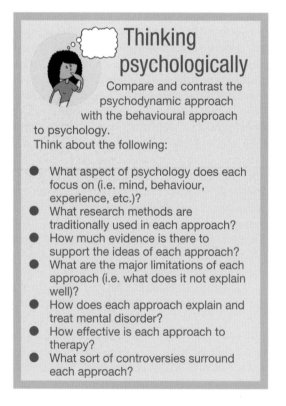

Thinking psychologically

Compare and contrast the psychodynamic approach with the behavioural approach to psychology.
Think about the following:

- What aspect of psychology does each focus on (i.e. mind, behaviour, experience, etc.)?
- What research methods are traditionally used in each approach?
- How much evidence is there to support the ideas of each approach?
- What are the major limitations of each approach (i.e. what does it not explain well)?
- How does each approach explain and treat mental disorder?
- How effective is each approach to therapy?
- What sort of controversies surround each approach?

Where are we now?

The psychodynamic approach in general and Freud's work in particular is perhaps the most controversial area in psychology. A number of criticisms have been made about the scientific status of Freud's work. He relied a lot on self-analysis and case studies of patients for his evidence. This would not generally be considered acceptable in modern psychology, which prides itself on systematic and scientific research. Freud's patients, being by and large neurotic members of the Austrian middle class, were an unrepresentative group of people on whom to base a theory intended to apply to everyone. Furthermore, Freud tended to ignore aspects of these cases that didn't fit with his ideas and often made quite contrived links between theory and case study. Another problem with the scientific status of Freud's ideas concerns the difficulty that exists in testing his ideas. For example, we have seen that it is pretty much impossible to investigate the idea of dreamwork scientifically.

Although these issues are quite genuine, we should not exaggerate their significance. There is plenty of solid evidence to support the general psychodynamic principles emphasising the importance of relationships and early trauma in child development. There is also evidence to support some aspects of Freudian theory, including the dream–wish link and the existence of oral and anal personalities. Perhaps most importantly, the psychodynamic approach has important real-world applications, ranging from the design and analysis of film to psychological therapy. Although some older studies cast doubt on the usefulness of psychodynamic therapies, it is clear from contemporary studies that their effectiveness is on a par with other therapies.

Summing it up

- The major assumptions underlying the psychodynamic approach are the importance of **the unconscious mind**, the importance of **early experience** and the importance of **relationships** in psychological development.

- Freud saw the personality in terms of an instinctive aspect (the **id**), a logical aspect (the **ego**) and a moral aspect (the **superego**).

- This way of looking at the personality differs from the approach of most current personality theorists, who look at personality as a set of stable characteristics of the individual.

- Freud saw the personality developing in childhood through a series of **stages**. Events in the **oral**, **anal** and **phallic** stages are associated with particular personality characteristics.

- There is supporting evidence for some aspects of Freud's view of child development. However, evidence is lacking for the importance of the **Oedipus complex**, which Freud considered to be particularly important.

- Psychodynamic therapies work on the basis that psychological distress and other symptoms of mental health difficulties result at least in part from unconscious influences, early experience and relationships.

- Two important techniques of psychodynamic therapies are **free association** and **dream interpretation**.

- There is now solid evidence for the effectiveness of psychodynamic therapies. However, there are other issues to consider in their use, including the time and cost required for long-term therapy.

What have I learned?

1   Outline the main assumptions of the psychodynamic approach.

2   Describe how the psychodynamic approach has been applied to one theory in psychology. Suitable examples would be Freud's structure of personality, psychosexual development or a combination of these.

3   Describe how the psychodynamic approach has been applied in one form of therapy in psychology. Suitable examples would include free association, dream analysis or a combination of these.

4   Evaluate the strengths and weaknesses of the psychodynamic approach.

5   Compare and contrast the psychodynamic and biological approaches to psychology.

Reading around

■ Gay, P. (1995) *The Freud Reader*. London: Vintage.

■ Jacobs, M. (2003) *Sigmund Freud*. London: Sage.

■ Jarvis, M. (2004) *Psychodynamic Psychology: classical theory and contemporary research*. London: Thomson.

■ Wollheim, R. (1991) *Freud*. Hammersmith: Fontana.

The cognitive approach

What should I know?

- The main assumptions of the cognitive approach to psychology.
- The distinction between pure and applied cognitive psychology.
- Attribution theory.
- How cognitive ideas have been put to use in psychological therapy.

In addition I should be able to:

- evaluate the contributions the cognitive approach has made to psychology
- use psychological research to support and/or challenge aspects of cognitive theory
- suggest criticisms of the cognitive approach in general and of attribution theory in particular
- compare and contrast the cognitive approach with other psychological approaches.

The cognitive approach originated in the 1950s and has for the last half century been the single most popular and influential approach to psychology. Recall the behaviourist approach, discussed in Chapter 2. Behaviourism was based on the principle that the mind was simply too difficult to study and explain scientifically. Thus the emphasis of behavioural psychology was on studying and explaining observable behaviour. This is sometimes called 'black box' psychology because the mind was seen as impenetrable. By the 1950s, however, the computer had been invented and this gave psychologists a new way of thinking about the mind. By comparing the way the mind processes information to that of a computer, cognitive psychologists have been able to study the mind as the behaviourists could not. The difference between behavioural and cognitive psychology is shown in Figure 4.1.

As Figure 4.1 shows, the behaviourists focused on how people respond to a stimulus (a stimulus is anything in the environment that we perceive). By contrast, the cognitive approach is concerned with how the mind makes sense of the environment and takes appropriate action. Its assumptions are explored further below.

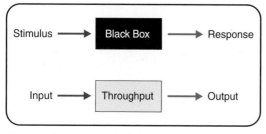

Fig. 4.1 Comparing the behaviourist (top) and cognitive (bottom) approaches

Assumptions of the cognitive approach

These are:

- an emphasis on the internal processes of the mind
- the importance of the ways information is processed in order to make sense of the environment and respond appropriately to it
- that the human mind can be understood by comparing it to a computer.

Emphasis on the internal processes of the mind

It might seem obvious that psychology is concerned with the human mind. However, consider the three approaches we have already looked at. Behaviourists essentially ignore the mind, focusing as far as possible on the effects of the environment on behaviour. Biological psychologists are interested primarily in the nervous system and the links between physical mechanisms, particularly in the brain, and psychological functioning. Here, there is an overlap with cognitive psychology, as we can use the study of brain functioning to understand better the mental processes that are happening in the brain. Psychodynamic psychology is concerned specifically with a very particular type of *unconscious* mental processes (see page 40). Cognitive psychologists are concerned with understanding the full range of mental processes, including the following:

- **Perception**: the processes by which we take in and make sense of information from the environment.
- **Attention**: the processes by which we focus on particular sources of information rather than others and maintain this focus over time.
- **Memory**: the processes by which we retain and recall information.
- **Language**: the use of mental symbols to represent information in the mind, helping thinking and communication between people.
- **Thinking**: the processes by which we manipulate information in the mind in order to reason, solve problems, make decisions and otherwise make judgements.

The importance of information processing

Most cognitive psychologists have adopted an information-processing approach to understand the mind. This means that the cognitive processes of perception, attention, memory, etc. can be seen as a series of processing systems. Working together, these processing systems allow us to make sense of and respond to the world. For example, when we look at an orange (attention) we perceive a distinctive shape, texture and colour (perception), we recognise it (memory) and name it an orange (language). Once we have identified it as an orange we can think about it. We might, for example, analyse whether it looks like a tasty orange, consider whether we are hungry, etc. We can also make the decision to eat it!

The computer analogy

Many cognitive psychologists find it useful to think of the ways in which the mind processes information as similar to the processing taking place in a computer. Like a computer, the mind has an input of information from the senses, throughput in the form of memory, thinking and language, and output in the form of decision making, speech and action. Like a modern computer, we process information in parallel, i.e. we perform different cognitive tasks at the same time. In some ways, however, the mind is *not* like a computer. We are slower at processing information and we make more mistakes; we are, however, much better than a computer at making guesses. Nonetheless, we can think of the brain as a piece of hardware and our experiences and learned responses as software. One branch of cognitive psychology, known as computational cognitive science, focuses on modelling cognitive processes as we believe they take place in the mind on a computer.

Pure and applied cognitive psychology

The cognitive approach dominates modern psychology. To understand why it has been so influential, we need to consider the distinction between pure and applied cognitive psychology. Pure cognitive psychology is a huge area of theory and research in itself. This involves achieving a better understanding of how we perceive, remember and think, etc. However, the cognitive *approach* can also be applied to understanding other areas of psychology. For example, in this chapter we consider attribution theory, a cognitive approach to understanding an important social process. Attribution theory aims to explain how we deal with information about people's behaviour to form impressions about the causes of that behaviour. This in turn allows us to make judgements about the nature of individuals based on their actions. Cognitive principles have also been applied to understanding and treating mental disorder. We know, for example, that people who are suffering from depression tend to attend to the negative aspects of a situation and remember unhappy events much more than do the rest of us. Cognitive therapies work by altering these patterns of information processing.

Attribution theory

Whenever we interact with other people we constantly process information about their behaviour. According to German psychologist Fritz Heider (1958), one of the key things we are looking for when we analyse this information is why people behave as they do. The cognitive processes whereby we try to judge why people behave as they do are called **attribution**. **Attribution theory** is the general term used to describe a group of explanations for how we make attributions. The most important judgement we have to make in the attribution process is to what extent the person's actions are a direct result of their character and to what extent they are a consequence of the situation. Whenever we judge that a person did something because of the type of person they are we make an **internal** attribution. Say for example that we see someone we know behaving in a grumpy manner. We might think 'that Rick really is a crabby chap'. On the other hand, we might make an **external** attribution and judge Rick's grumpiness to be the result of his situation. For example, he might be tired or ill, or the room might be excessively hot. In some circumstances we can make attributions based on a single behaviour. However, we can also use information about people's behaviour over time to arrive at more valid conclusions.

Correspondent inference theory

Sometimes we can make judgements about people's character (i.e. internal attributions) based on a single incident. This process is called **correspondent inference** because we are making an inference (i.e. a judgement) that the behaviour corresponds to the person's character. Jones and Davis (1965) suggested that in order to make an internal attribution from a single behaviour three criteria must be met. These are:

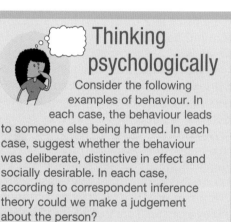

Thinking psychologically

Consider the following examples of behaviour. In each case, the behaviour leads to someone else being harmed. In each case, suggest whether the behaviour was deliberate, distinctive in effect and socially desirable. In each case, according to correspondent inference theory could we make a judgement about the person?

1 A man punches an 80-year-old woman to the ground and runs away with her handbag.
2 A boxer punches an opponent so hard that he collapses unconscious.
3 A man fails to put his handbrake on fully on a hill and his car rolls down the hill, hitting and injuring a child.

Consider what other key factors might differ in each of these scenarios other than the three factors in correspondent inference theory.

1   The behaviour must be deliberate; if it is accidental we cannot use it as a basis to judge someone's character.
2   The behaviour must have distinctive effects; if a behaviour has several possible consequences then it becomes unclear why it might have been done.
3   The behaviour should be low in social desirability; behaviour that simply follows social norms reveals little about a person's character.

Evaluation of correspondent inference theory

There seems to be little doubt that the three factors outlined by Jones and Davis can be of use in deciding when to make internal attributions. However, more recent studies have revealed other factors that can affect when we make correspondent inferences. One important factor appears to be group membership, i.e. we make different inferences depending on whether the person committing the behaviour is in the same social groups as ourselves. Vonk and Konst (1998) tested this in a study of 149 employees in an organisation. They were read descriptions of either socially acceptable or unacceptable behaviour by a fellow employee. These descriptions were accompanied by information to suggest that the behaviour was influenced by character or situation. It emerged that when the target person was an in-group member, participants were more likely to make external attributions for socially unacceptable behaviour and internal attributions for more positive behaviour. The opposite effect was found for out-group members. In other words, we make excuses for poor behaviour provided the person shares our group membership. However, we are more damning of poor behaviour than correspondent inference theory would suggest if the person is not 'one of us'.

One way in which we all categorise others and ourselves is by gender. The phenomenon described above in which we make more negative attributions about the behaviour of out-groups appears to apply to men and women. One consequence of this is that people tend to see crimes very differently according to whether they are committed by the same or the opposite sex. Workman and Freeburg (1999) read 638 students a story involving a date rape, showed them photographs of the victim and asked them to attribute responsibility to the victim, the perpetrator or the situation. Men were significantly more likely to attribute responsibility to the victim than were women, who tended to blame the man.

Another limitation of correspondent inference theory in its original form is its failure to take into account cultural factors. There appear to be some cultural differences in the tendency to make internal and external positive and negative attributions. Stander et al. (2001) carried out a cross-cultural study comparing the attributions made by American and Chinese husbands and wives towards one another. Chinese couples were found to make more internal attributions for positive behaviour and external attributions for negative behaviour to their spouses than did American couples. It is hard to know from a single study like this whether this generosity of attribution is specific to husband–wife relationships or whether it characterises Chinese culture in general. However, it does show that cultural factors are important – not something taken into account in correspondent inference theory.

Covariation theory

Correspondent inference theory provides a partial explanation for when we make internal attributions based on single behaviours. However, when we are judging someone we know in a situation we are familiar with, we generally have the opportunity to make use of rather more information than a single behaviour. Kelley (1967) proposed a model of how we make attributions when we have information about the person's past behaviour and about other people's behaviour in the same situation. Given this sort of information we can judge how an action **covaries** with their own and others' behaviour based on three criteria:

1 Consensus: whether other people also act in the same way in the same situation.
2 Consistency: whether the person we are judging always acts that way given the same situation.
3 Distinctiveness: whether the person behaves similarly across a range of situations.

The way this information can be used to make an attribution is shown in Table 4.1.

Note that consistency of behaviour has to be high before any sort of attribution can be made. In other words, we cannot make good use of behaviour that takes place irregularly and unpredictably to make any sort of judgement. Where consensus and distinctiveness are low (i.e. the behaviour is unusual and takes place in a range of situations), then we can make an internal attribution. If it takes place only in a particular situation or it is common behaviour among other people as well, then we cannot attribute the behaviour to the character of the person.

If you are a psychology student you may have had the experience of being late for lessons. This is a real-life example of where the covariation process is likely to be used by your teachers! For example, if Lana is always late (high consistency) to all lessons (low distinctiveness), and other students are generally on time (low consensus), then a teacher is likely to attribute the lateness to Lana's character. However, if all students are late to these lessons (high consensus) but on time to other teachers' lessons (high distinctiveness), then it is likely to be the situation (i.e. psychology lessons!) that is the problem.

Glossary

correspondent inference: a judgement that a behaviour reflects the character of the person.
covariation: the extent to which behaviour covaries with typical behaviour of that person and with the behaviour of others.

	Consensus	Consistency	Distinctiveness
Internal attribution	low	high	low
External attribution	high	high	high

Table 4.1 The covariation model

Evaluation of covariation theory

Using the above example of the psychology student who was late, we can see that the covariation principle can explain some of the judgements we make in real-life situations. This has important practical applications. For example, McKnight and Sutton (1994) used the covariation principle to understand better the causes of suicide in young offenders institutions. Where consensus was high and distinctiveness high, it was possible to attribute suicide to the environment. However, where consensus and distinctiveness were low, i.e. only one inmate made suicide attempts and they had a history of this type of behaviour, it was more likely that the behaviour could be attributed to their personal characteristics than to the environment. This sort of information is useful in deciding when it is necessary to change an environment like this.

Yet there is also evidence that although we *can* make use of covariation information when it is provided, this is *not* actually the sort of information we seek when looking to make an attribution. This was shown in a study by Ahn *et al.* (1995). They gave participants a scenario in which a fictional character called Kim was involved in a car crash the previous night. They asked participants what information they wanted in order to make sense of the situation. Covariation

Box 4.1
Attribution biases

One of the limitations of correspondent inference and covariation theories is that they assume we are fairly logical in our judgements about people. Of course, in reality this is not entirely true. There are a number of common errors or biases in the attribution process. Perhaps the most obvious and important is the **fundamental attribution** error (or FAE). This is our tendency to over-emphasise the character of the person and de-emphasise the situation, meaning that we tend to make incorrect internal attributions. A topical example of the FAE at work is in attribution of obesity. In reality, a range of factors, including genetic predisposition, affects body type. However, there is a strong tendency to attribute obesity to character flaws in the individual. This effect can be seen even in young children. Musher-Eizenman *et al.* (2004) asked 42 children of average age five years to describe other children of different body type and about their beliefs about the explanations for different body types. The children tended to make internal attributions for being overweight, the most negative descriptions of overweight children being from the children making internal attributions.

Another attribution bias is the **actor–observer effect**. This takes place when the person exhibiting a behaviour makes a different attribution from that made by people who observe it. Usually, the actor tends to make external attributions for socially undesirable behaviour and internal attributions for desirable behaviour. Observers tend to do the reverse. Stewart (2005) demonstrated the actor–observer effect in a study of 321 car crash survivors. When surveyed, the survivors overwhelmingly attributed accidents to the behaviour of other drivers. In other words, when it came to judging their own driving they made external attributions, but when it came to the driving of other behaviours their attributions tended to be internal.

theory would predict that they would ask questions about consistency, consensus and distinctiveness. These might include 'Does Kim often have accidents?' or 'Were there a lot of accidents last night?' However, people asked rather different questions, for example, 'Was Kim drunk?' and 'Was the road icy?' Ahn and Bailenson (1996) suggest that people are more interested in basing their judgements on the details of what happened rather than on background information, as is suggested in the covariation model. They call this a '**mechanisms approach**' to attribution.

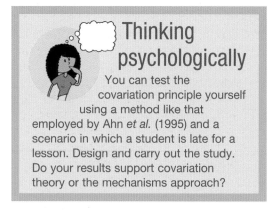

Thinking psychologically

You can test the covariation principle yourself using a method like that employed by Ahn *et al.* (1995) and a scenario in which a student is late for a lesson. Design and carry out the study. Do your results support covariation theory or the mechanisms approach?

Applying the cognitive approach to therapy

The cognitive approach to psychology has a number of practical applications. One of the most important is in understanding and treating mental health problems. Thinking back to our key assumptions of the cognitive approach we can apply these to mental health.

Mental processes

A basic assumption of the cognitive approach is that to understand human psychology we need to understand the nature of mental processes such as perception, attention, memory and thinking. It seems that many of the symptoms of mental disorder can be understood in terms of these processes. For example, it is now well documented that people with a tendency to think negatively are more vulnerable to depression. We can think positively or negatively about the world, the future or ourselves. The link between negative thinking and depression was demonstrated by Grazioli and Terry (2000). They assessed cognitive vulnerability in 65 women in the third trimester of their pregnancy and looked at who suffered post-natal depression. They found that those with high levels of negative thinking were more likely to suffer post-natal depression. Depression is also associated with particular patterns of attention.

Perez *et al.* (1999) compared selective attention in sufferers of depression with non-depressed participants in whom a sad mood had been induced by playing sad music and recalling unhappy memories. Participants were given a Stroop task involving unhappy stimuli. The Stroop task involves naming the ink colour in which each of a sequence of words is written. The task requires paying attention to ink colour rather than to the words. However, people find this difficult and the words people focus their attention on can reveal much about their state of mind. The major depressive group, but not the sad-mood participants, paid significantly more attention to unhappy words in the Stroop task, showing that attention works differently in depression.

Glossary

depression: a mental disorder characterised by a sad and/or irritable mood.
post-natal depression: depression occurring in a mother shortly after giving birth.
Stroop task: a procedure to assess selective attention, in which participants have to name the ink colours of words, ignoring the word meanings.

Information processing

One of the very important cognitive tasks we perform whenever we process information about people is attribution. There is now considerable evidence to suggest that attribution works differently in people suffering particular mental disorders. In one study, Yost and Weary (1996) compared 58 depressed and 57 non-depressed university students on a standard correspondent inference task like that used in the 1998 Vonk and Konst study (see page 59). It was found that the depressed group had much less of a tendency to make internal attributions. This is important because it shows that depressed patients are significantly more likely to see people as victims of circumstance. This encourages a helpless attitude. On the other hand, when it comes to making self-attributions it seems that depressed patients are much more likely to judge negative behaviours and events as due to their personal shortcomings. This was demonstrated by Wall and Hayes (2000), who assessed depression and attributions in 160 clients of a university counselling service. It emerged that depressed patients, unlike others, tended to make internal attributions for anything that went wrong in their lives.

The aim of cognitive-behavioural therapies

The psychological therapies based on a cognitive understanding of mental disorder are collectively known as cognitive-behavioural therapies (CBT). They are called '**cognitive-behavioural**', rather than just cognitive, for two reasons. First, they are based on the belief that if we alter cognition this will result in a change to patients' behaviour. Second, cognitive techniques are often used alongside the behavioural techniques discussed in Chapter 2. Although it is possible to train in a single 'pure' cognitive-behavioural therapy, most modern CBT involves combining techniques from a number of therapies. Two of the most important of these are Albert Ellis's rational emotive behaviour therapy (REBT) and Aaron Beck's cognitive therapy (CT).

So how do cognitive-behavioural therapies work? All therapies have the ultimate aim of making patients feel and function better. However, different therapies have different **mediating aims**, i.e. what they seek to directly alter. Whereas behavioural therapies have the mediating aim of changing behaviour and psychodynamic therapies have the mediating aim of improving emotional state, the mediating aim of CBT is to alter the ways in which people think. This is based on the idea that how we think affects our emotional state and our behaviour.

Rational emotive behaviour therapy

Albert Ellis (1977) applied cognitive principles to understanding how people respond to negative events. Specifically, he believed that how we respond emotionally when something goes wrong is based on the beliefs we have about such events. To Ellis, mental health is dependent on stoicism. Stoicism is the ability to remain emotionally stable in the face of difficulty. Ellis believed that stoicism stems from a healthy set of beliefs about the world. Beliefs that are overly negative or which put pressure on us to function perfectly at all times predispose us to over-react when something goes wrong. This in turn leads to anxiety and depression. This idea was crystallised in the ABC model. In this model A = the activating event, B = beliefs and C = (emotional) consequences. Table 4.2 shows the ABC model applied to understanding the effects of failing an exam (from Palmer and Dryden, 1995).

Although Ellis originally trained in psychodynamic therapy, he came to believe that it was quicker and more efficient to tackle the symptoms of mental disorder by challenging people's irrational beliefs and so make them more stoical. He called this rational emotive behaviour therapy (REBT). The name comes from the idea that if people can be made more rational in their thinking then their emotional state and behaviour will also normalise. Two types of irrational belief are particularly challenged in REBT.

● '**Musturbation**' is the belief that we *must* be perfect and successful at all times.

● '**I-can't-stand-it-itis**' is the belief that we cannot cope when something does not go smoothly.

Glossary

musturbation: beliefs phrased in musts, e.g. 'I must be perfect.'
I-can't-stand-it-itis: belief that difficulty or discomfort is unbearable.
utopianism: belief that the world should be a perfect place.
outcome study: study into the effectiveness of a therapy.

'Musturbation' makes us extremely sensitive to any kind of failure. 'I-can't-stand-it-itis' makes even the most minor problems and setbacks seem disastrous. Both refer to beliefs we might have about ourselves. But what about our beliefs about the world? REBT therapists use the term 'utopian' beliefs to describe the belief that the world is meant to be fair and easy to live in.

REBT involves vigorous argument with the patient in order to challenge irrational beliefs like 'musturbation', 'I-can't-stand-it-itis' and utopianism. REBT therapists may also ask patients to keep diaries of thoughts and events so that the therapist can show them evidence of how irrational their beliefs

A	Activating event	Failing an exam
B	Beliefs	'I should have passed' 'There shouldn't be exams like this' 'I can't bear not passing'
C	Consequences	Depression

Table 4.2 An example of the ABC sequence – after Palmer and Dryden (1995)

were. If patients are to tolerate this sort of attack on their beliefs, it is essential for them to trust and respect the therapist. In order to be successful, a therapist using REBT must be able to form a good relationship with the patient quickly.

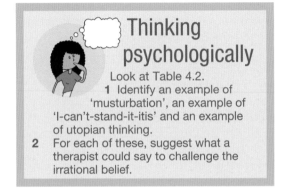

Thinking psychologically

Look at Table 4.2.
1 Identify an example of 'musturbation', an example of 'I-can't-stand-it-itis' and an example of utopian thinking.
2 For each of these, suggest what a therapist could say to challenge the irrational belief.

Evaluation of REBT

There is a large body of research to show that REBT can be effective in treating the symptoms of mental disorder, in particular anxiety problems. Engels *et al.* (1993) carried out a meta-analysis of 31 outcome studies and concluded that REBT was the most effective treatment for anxiety. More recently, REBT has been applied to treating a wider range of symptoms. In one recent study, Adelman *et al.* (2005) tested the effectiveness of REBT in anger management for 541 adolescents in residential behavioural health care. It was found that although anger levels, as measured by a standard clinical scale, remained slightly above average, for 17 of the 20 months of treatment they were significantly below the levels recorded at the start of treatment. This suggests that REBT is effective for anger management.

Although there is good evidence for the effectiveness of REBT, it is controversial and

has never become as influential in the UK as it has in the USA, where it developed. Reasons for this lack of popularity were explored in a survey of cognitive-behavioural therapists by Trower and Jones (2001). The main problems the therapists identified were that REBT was under-researched in comparison with other branches of CBT and that it was too *directive*. By this we mean that people objected to the idea of telling patients how to think. Neenan (2004) suggests that the highly aggressive way therapists using REBT techniques challenge their clients is incompatible with British politeness. Moreover, REBT requires clients to change their philosophy of life. As well as being difficult to achieve, this raises important ethical issues. Clients do not come to therapy to have their political or social views forcibly altered, yet this can happen in REBT.

web watch

Go to http://www.rebt.org/WhatisREBT.htm Read the questions and answers on this page. How convincing do you find the answers put forward here to defend REBT?

Cognitive therapy (CT)

Like Ellis, Aaron Beck was trained in psychodynamics, but (also like Ellis) he looked to develop a faster, more efficient way of tackling psychological symptoms. Whereas Ellis was interested in the role of irrational beliefs in stress, Beck was more concerned with the role of negative thinking in depression. Beck (1976) identified three types of negative thinking that characterise depression. The

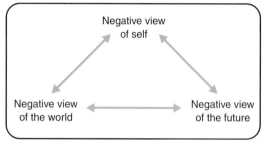

Fig. 4.2 Beck's cognitive triad

first of these is negative automatic thinking. This comes in the form of the **cognitive triad** of a negative view of self, negative view of the world and negative view of the future. Beck described these thoughts as 'automatic' because they occur spontaneously. The cognitive triad is shown in Figure 4.2.

The second type of negativity identified by Beck results from a distinctive pattern of selective attention. He noted that depressed people tend to attend to the negative aspects of a situation and ignore the positive aspects. This leads them to over-estimate the 'downside' of any situation. The classic example of this is the seeing of a half-full glass as half empty, rather than half full. Once we attend to negative aspects of a situation we inevitably reach negative conclusions about it.

Beck's final form of negative thinking involves the activation of **negative self-schemas**. Cognitive psychologists use the term 'schemas' to describe packets of information in which our knowledge of each aspect of the world is contained. Our self-schema contains all the information, beliefs, etc. we have that relate to ourselves. According to Beck, we acquire a set of beliefs, about ourselves through early experiences, in particular experience involving our parents. If these experiences are negative, then so will be our self-schemas. We interpret new information relevant to ourselves in the light of our existing self-schemas. Once we have a negative self-schema, it becomes difficult for us to interpret any new information about ourselves positively.

Like REBT, cognitive therapy aims to change the sort of cognitions that predispose us to psychological problems. In CT, however, there is less emphasis on aggressive argument against negative beliefs and more emphasis on testing and disproving them. Patients in CT are therefore given tasks to carry out. For example, a depressed patient might typically say that they had not been going out lately because there was no point as they would not enjoy it. A cognitive therapist might respond to this by setting them the task of going out with friends and recording whether they had enjoyed it. In the next session they would have to admit they had enjoyed going out, and this would help change their negative beliefs about the world.

Evaluation of cognitive therapy

There is more evidence to support the theoretical basis of CT than REBT. For example, a recent study by Parker *et al.* (2000) supports the link between early experience and cognitive vulnerability. The study assessed 96 depressed patients on their early experiences and responses to situations that might activate a self-schema. A significant relationship emerged between reports of negative early experiences and the existence of maladaptive self-schemas, which were in turn associated with the experience of depression. This suggests that early experiences can induce cognitive vulnerability and that this cognitive vulnerability may indeed make people more vulnerable to depression.

There is also evidence to support the effectiveness of cognitive therapy, at least for those who complete it. In one recent study for example, Cahill *et al.* (2003) assessed the severity of symptoms after each therapy session of 58 patients receiving CT for depression. By the end of the therapy, which lasted 12–20 sessions, 71 per cent of the patients who completed their therapy experienced a significant reduction in their symptoms. However, it was also found that 23 of the 58 patients did not complete their course of therapy. Of those who did not complete their course of therapy only 13 per cent improved significantly. This is clearly less encouraging and suggests that the headline figure of 71 per cent improvement over-estimates the benefits of CT.

Cognitive-behavioural therapy (CBT)

It is important to understand that in real life, most CBT involves a mixture of techniques from REBT, CT and other newer therapies. Most research into the effectiveness of CBT has looked at this blended technique. The evidence base for CBT is huge, making it overwhelmingly the most recommended psychological therapy in current National Health Service guidelines. CBT may be used alongside drugs as well as in isolation, increasing their effectiveness. In one study, Fava *et al.* (1998) assigned 40 patients with recurrent depression to one of two conditions. In the first, they received drug treatment alone. In the second, they received drugs and CBT. The group who received drugs plus CBT showed greater reduction in symptoms. At two-year follow-up, 75 per cent of this group were still free of symptoms, whereas this was true for only 25 per cent of the group who received only drugs.

Because of this huge evidence base, there is tremendous enthusiasm from many psychologists about CBT. However, this is not to say that there are no concerns. Harrington *et al.* (1998) point out that several published reviews of studies of CBT have inexplicably failed to mention studies in which CBT was found not to be effective. There are also some cases in which CBT has been found to be inferior to other psychological therapies. For example, in one study looking at alcohol dependency, Sandahl *et al.* (1998) found that at 15-month follow-up significantly more patients were abstaining from alcohol after psychodynamic therapy than after CBT. At the time of writing, CBT is increasingly being used instead of other psychological treatments throughout the NHS. However, it remains to be seen whether this is the shape of therapy to come or a short-term trend.

web watch

 Go to http://www.mind.org.uk/Information/Booklets/Making+sense/MakingsenseCBT.htm
Using the information here, prepare your own leaflet that you might use to promote CBT.

Where are we now?

The cognitive approach has dominated psychology for the last half century. One reason for this has been its wide range of application to understanding areas of psychology as different as person perception (as in attribution theory) and cognitive behavioural therapy. The emphasis in this chapter has been on applied cognitive psychology. There is in addition a massive body of research into the processes of perception, attention, memory, language and thinking. At the time of writing, a growth area in the cognitive approach is *cognitive neuroscience*, the study of cognitive processes in the brain. This has only now become possible with recent developments in technology. It seems likely then that the future of cognitive psychology is integrated with the biological approach.

Although cognitive psychology has been a dominant force in psychology and in some form will probably continue to dominate, this is not to say that it is without problems. One common criticism concerns **cognitive reductionism**. This is the tendency to think that we can understand and sort out any situation by reference to cognition alone. This way of thinking ignores factors that operate outside the mind. An employee *might* feel stressed at work because they have maladaptive beliefs, such as 'I-can't-stand-it-itis'. However, it is just as likely that their stress is caused by problems in their work environment, such as excessive workload and bullying. Of course, cognitive reductionism is a problem with the way some psychologists *use* the cognitive approach. It is not a reason to abandon cognitive psychology, just to be aware of its limitations.

Summing it up

- The major assumptions of the cognitive approach are an emphasis on **mental processes**, seeing the mind in terms of its processing of information and an understanding of the mind by comparison with a computer.

- How the mind processes information is important in its own right and is studied within the field of pure cognitive psychology. However, the cognitive approach can also be applied to understanding other areas of psychology. This is applied cognitive psychology.

- An important area of applied cognitive psychology is **attribution theory**. We make attributions when we decide why someone behaved as they did. In particular, attribution theorists are concerned with how and when we make judgements about someone's character based on their behaviour.

- We can make **correspondent inferences** about someone (i.e. judgements about their character) based on a single behaviour. However, this requires that the behaviour is deliberate, socially undesirable and has a single distinctive effect.

- When we have access to information about multiple behaviours by different people in a variety of situations we can make attributions by the **covariation principle**. This states that we can make an internal attribution when someone consistently acts differently to others across a range of situations.

- Both correspondent inference and covariation models represent ways we *can* make judgements about people based on their behaviour. However, research shows that in reality we also use other sources of information.

- We can apply the emphasis on mental processes and how the mind processes information to understanding mental health problems. Cognitive behavioural therapies aim to alter faulty or unhelpful cognitions.

- REBT does this by vigorous argument, in particular challenging beliefs that make us more sensitive to failure or difficulty. CT focuses more on testing and disproving patterns of negative thinking.

- CBT is very popular at present and has a large body of evidence to support its effectiveness.

- Most CBT therapists use techniques from a variety of pure therapies, including CT and REBT, although the latter has never become as influential in the UK as in the USA.

What have I learned?

1   Outline the main assumptions of the cognitive approach.

2   Describe how the cognitive approach has been applied to one theory in psychology. Suitable examples would include correspondent inference theory and covariation theory.

3   Describe how the cognitive approach has been applied in one form of therapy. Suitable examples would include REBT and CT.

4   Evaluate the strengths and weaknesses of the cognitive approach.

5   Compare and contrast the cognitive and biological approaches to psychology.

Reading around

■ Bond, F. W. and Dryden, W. (eds.) (2004) *Handbook of Brief Cognitive Behavioural Therapy*. Chichester: Wiley.

■ Forsterling, F. (2001) *Attribution.* Hove: Psychology Press.

■ Jarvis, M., Putwain, D. and Dwyer, D. (2002) *Angles on Atypical Psychology*. Cheltenham: Nelson Thornes.

■ Pennington, D. C., Gillen, K. and Hill, P. (1999) *Essential Social Psychology*. London: Hodder Arnold.

Core studies

What should I know?

- The procedure used by Asch (1955).
- The findings and conclusions of Asch (1955).
- A critical evaluation of Asch (1955).
- The procedure used by Milgram (1963).
- The findings and conclusions of Milgram (1963).
- A critical evaluation of Milgram (1963).

In addition I should be able to:

- identify strengths and weaknesses of laboratory experiments
- comment on the usefulness of quantitative and qualitative data
- interpret line graphs and frequency distributions
- assess ethical issues in psychological research
- understand issues of ecological validity in laboratory research.

Introducing research in the social approach

The social approach is concerned with how people interact with one another and how we are affected by the presence and behaviour of others, both individuals and groups. Almost every imaginable way in which people affect or respond to each other has been studied somewhere by social psychologists. Social psychologists use a variety of research methods, including experiments conducted in the laboratory and under more natural conditions.

The two core studies in this chapter are both carried out under controlled conditions. They are:

- **Asch (1955) Opinions and social pressure**
  Asch, S. E. (1955) 'Opinions and social pressure.' *Scientific American,* 193: 31–5.

● **Milgram (1963) Obedience to authority**
Milgram, S. (1963) 'Behavioural study of obedience.' *Journal of Abnormal and Social Psychology*, 67: 371–8.

Solomon Asch has been credited with largely shaping modern social psychology. His great contribution was to recognise that our social behaviour is not so much a response to the world as it really is but to how we see it. Asch famously demonstrated this when he asked students to respond to political statements like 'a little rebellion is a good thing'. He found that students were much more sympathetic to statements like this when they were told they came from respected American politicians like Thomas Jefferson, as opposed to feared foreign leaders like Lenin. In other words, students' perceptions of the statement affected their judgement rather than what was actually said. Asch's other notable work included studies of person perception, in which he demonstrated the importance of first impressions.

Asch was intensely interested in applying social psychology to real-life problems, in particular to resolving and preventing conflict. He was part of a network of psychologists who pursued a psychological understanding of the Holocaust. Perhaps Asch's best-known contribution to psychology was his work on conformity, examined in detail in this chapter. In this he demonstrated that a significant minority of people were willing to say that a line was the same length as another line of blatantly differing length, as long as other people had identified it as the same. This can be seen as a test of the '2+2=5' idea, first put forward in George Orwell's 1949 novel *Nineteen Eighty-Four* and revived more recently as a song ('2+2=5') by Radiohead.

Stanley Milgram worked with Solomon Asch from 1959 to 1960 and was influenced by him in both his interests and his general approach to psychology. Most psychologists in the 1960s rarely emerged from their laboratories to apply psychology to real life. Milgram had a very different outlook and was fascinated by the idea of using psychology to understand real-life situations. (Famously, when asked by his mother-in-law why New Yorkers no longer gave up their seats on public transport, he immediately designed a study with his students and sent them to find out.)

Like Asch, Milgram was interested in the social psychological factors that contributed to the Holocaust. Whereas Asch focused on conformity, Milgram's research was aimed at better understanding human obedience. More specifically, Milgram was concerned with **destructive obedience**, in which individuals follow orders from an authority figure in the knowledge that following those orders will cause harm to others. Milgram's aim was to set up an experiment that replicated the situations in which people in the Holocaust followed destructive orders. Before running the study, Milgram had intended to go to Germany to see whether Germans were uniquely obedient. However, this plan soon became redundant when he discovered how willing Americans were to follow destructive orders!

Asch (1955) Opinions and social pressure

What did Asch do?

The participants in the study were 123 male student volunteers from four American universities. Each participant was told that they

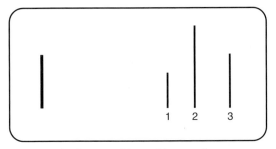

Fig. 5.1 The lines used in Asch's procedure

were taking part in a psychological experiment, but were given no details. They joined a group of between seven and nine young men sitting around a table. The group was together presented a task in which they had to match the length of a line with one of three alternatives. An example of the lines is shown in Figure 5.1.

Box 5.1
Procedure summary

Method: lab experiment.
Design: repeated measures.
Independent variables tested: accuracy of stooges' line matching, group size, presence of a dissenter.
Dependent variables measured: percentage of correct line matches.
Participants: 123 male students.

Only one participant in each group was genuine (technically called a 'naïve participant'). The others were 'stooges' working for Asch. They were asked to say in turn which of the three lines matched the length of the target line. This was intended to be a straightforward task. In the first two trials, the stooges identified the correct line, as did the naïve participant. However, in the third trial the stooges all identified the incorrect line.

The idea was to see whether the naïve participant would conform to the majority view or name the correct line in defiance of the group. If the naïve participant turned out at this point to be not so naïve and realised they were being manipulated, the experiment was stopped. Each participant took part in 18 trials and in 12 of them the stooges named an incorrect line.

Several conditions were tested. In a control condition the stooges always identified the correct lines. This was to ensure that any mistakes made by the naïve participants were due to conformity effects and not difficulty in the task. Asch also varied the size of the groups from two to 14 members in order to see what effect the size of the majority had on conformity. He also tested the effect of introducing a dissenter who identified different lines (not necessarily the correct ones) in defiance of the majority.

What did he find?

In the control condition in which stooges identified the correct line each time, the naïve participants succeeded in spotting it 98 per cent of the time. In the standard experimental condition where the group identified a different line, this dropped dramatically to 63.2 per cent. The size of the majority group also made a difference. In particular, when the group was very small, rates of conformity dropped. Figure 5.2 shows the percentage of participants identifying the wrong line in different-sized groups. Once the size of the group reached three, the effects of increasing its size became much more modest.

Having a dissenter in the group who identified a different line in defiance of the majority reduced the number of errors

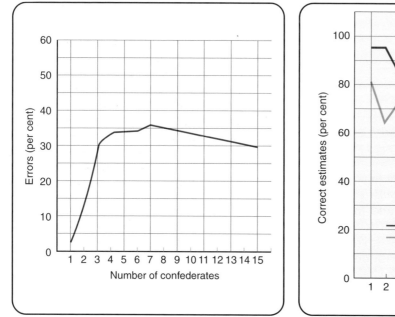

Fig. 5.2 *Effect of group size (from Asch, 1955)*

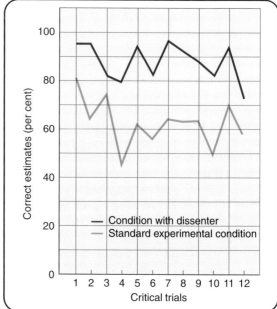

Fig. 5.3 *Effect of a dissenter (from Asch, 1955)*

sharply to only 9 per cent. Results across each trial are shown in Figure 5.3.

What did he conclude?

Asch concluded that the tendency for conformity is a powerful influence on our behaviour. As he put it: 'That we have found the tendency to conformity in our society so strong that reasonably intelligent and well-meaning young people are willing to call white black is a matter of concern' (1955: p. 5). In spite of his concern over his findings, Asch remained optimistic about human nature, noting that all the participants he had questioned believed that independence is more important than conformity.

web watch

Tired of reading about studies like this? You can get an audio file featuring some top psychologists discussing the Asch study at http://www.bbc.co.uk/radio4/science/mindchangers1.shtml

If, however, this has just whetted your appetite and you want to read about this in more detail you can read the full text of Asch's 1955 paper here: http://www.wadsworth.com/psychology_d/templates/student_resources/0155060678_rathus/ps/ps18.html

What were the strengths of this study?

Asch's study was carried out under controlled laboratory conditions. This had the advantage that he could control conditions completely. Because he was testing the participants in a range of conditions, this degree of control was particularly important. The range of conditions used was a strength, including the control condition. This successfully allowed Asch to say that the inaccurate answers given by the participants were due to conformity, not to difficulty with the lines.

Asch used a good sample size of 123 people, which is quite large for a laboratory experiment of this type. The fact that the stooges were similar in age, sex and socio-economic status to the naïve participants added realism to the study – in real-life situations it is our peers with whom we conform. The fact that the stooges were giving such blatantly wrong answers and still eliciting conformity is important. If a substantial minority will effectively say that 'white is black', as Asch put it, how much more conformist are we where the situation is more doubtful? The study is highly relevant to real life. It illustrates how

Where are we now?

Asch himself posed the question as to whether conformity is culture-specific. This was addressed in a meta-analysis by Bond and Smith (1996). Meta-analysis involves combining the results of smaller studies in order to analyse a large sample size. This particular analysis involved the results of studies comparing conformity in individualist and collectivist societies. Individualist societies are those, like the USA and Britain, where the emphasis is on the freedom of the individual. Collectivist societies, including China, Japan and Africa, place more emphasis in their culture on people's dependence on and obligations to one another. Bond and Smith concluded that conformity is greater in more collectivist societies.

Research continues into how conformist people are and under what circumstances. Conway and Schaller (2005) carried out a study with implications for both conformity and obedience. Eighty Canadian students were each asked to take the role of an employee with responsibility for choosing between two computer network systems for their company. They witnessed other employees agreeing unanimously that 'Wobblenet' was the better option. In two conditions they were ordered by their boss to choose 'Wobblenet'. In one of these he remained the boss and in another he left. Where the boss gave the order, most participants assumed that this was the reason for the pro-Wobble consensus among the others. They tended not to conform and chose the alternative network. This phenomenon, where we fail to conform because of an order, is called ironic deviance.

Have you ever watched a show featuring a panel of judges like *The X–Factor* or *Strictly Come Dancing* and wondered whether each judge conforms to the decisions the others have made? A study by Boen *et al.* (2006) may shed light on this. In the study, 27 judges were divided into panels of up to five and asked to judge the same 30 videotaped skipping performances. In one condition the judges were aware of each other's judgements and in the other they were not. There was significantly more agreement when they heard each other's feedback, suggesting that they did tend to conform to the judgement of the panel.

easy it is to influence people but also how important minority opinions can be.

What were the weaknesses of this study?

Although Asch used a reasonably large sample, the sample characteristics are another matter altogether. All were young, male, American students. It is unclear from a study of this type to what extent the findings can be applied across ages, sexes, socio-economic groups and nationalities. Like much of mid twentieth-century American psychology, this study falls foul of the criticism that it just describes 'the psychology of the middle-class American'. In fairness to Asch, he did acknowledge this and proposed further research to discover to what extent high levels of conformity are a cultural phenomenon.

Other psychologists have criticised Asch for the nature of his task. It is quite far removed from the sort of conformity-independence choices we make in real life. This, however, was deliberate, as Asch was setting out to see whether people would say that 'white is black'. The task also raises ethical issues. Participants were deceived and made to feel uncomfortable when they disagreed with the stooges. Finally, not all replications have yielded findings like those of the original study. For example, when Perrin and Spencer (1980) carried out exactly the same procedure on British students, only one in 386 participants conformed. It is unclear whether this means there is something wrong with the original experiment. It may be simply that the cultures of 1950s' America and 1980s' Britain were radically different.

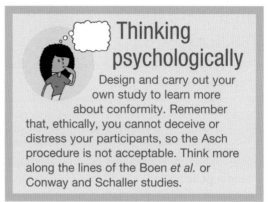

Thinking psychologically

Design and carry out your own study to learn more about conformity. Remember that, ethically, you cannot deceive or distress your participants, so the Asch procedure is not acceptable. Think more along the lines of the Boen *et al.* or Conway and Schaller studies.

Milgram (1963) Obedience to authority

What did Milgram do?

Milgram advertised for male volunteers to take part in an experiment on learning for a fee of $4.50. Forty participants aged between 20 and 50 took part. They were a mixture of manual workers, white-collar staff and a minority (22 per cent) of professionals. The location of the study was important. Both the reputation and physical environment of Yale University lent the procedure respectability. When they arrived at the university, each participant was told they would be either a teacher or a learner. An apparently random (but fiddled) selection procedure followed, so that in each case the participant ended up as the teacher. He was then introduced to a mild-mannered and pleasant 47-year-old man as a fellow participant. In fact, he was a stooge working for Milgram. He had been chosen for his highly likeable manner.

Box 5.2
Procedure summary

Method: lab pre-experiment.
Independent variable tested: orders from an authority figure.
Dependent variable measured: percentage of participants giving 450 volts.
Participants: 40 adult, working males.

The stooge learner was then strapped into a chair and wired up to a shock generator. The generator was demonstrated by giving the participant a mild shock. The stooge and the participant were positioned on either side of a screen so that they could hear but not see each other. The teacher participant then gave him a memory task involving remembering pairs of words. Every time the learner made a mistake the experimenter ordered the participant to give him an electric shock. Following each mistake the level of the 'shock' appeared to increase by 15 volts. The shock levels on the machine were labelled from 0–450 volts and also had signs saying 'Danger severe shock' and, at 450 volts, 'XXX'.

In fact, no real shocks were given. However, the stooge simulated pain and distress. As the voltage increased he gave a set series of responses. These included shouting, screaming, begging to be released and pointing out that he had a heart condition. Eventually, at 300 volts, he went silent, apart from knocking faintly on the screen. Participants were told to keep giving shocks in spite of this. The experimenter, who was in the same room as the participant, gave a series of verbal prods whenever participants protested:

- Prod 1: 'Please continue' or 'Please go on.'
- Prod 2: 'The experiment requires that you continue.'
- Prod 3: 'It is absolutely essential that you continue.'
- Prod 4: 'You have no choice, you *must* go on.'

In answer to any questions about the learner's wellbeing, participants were informed that the shocks were painful but not capable of causing permanent damage.

When the procedure was completed the participant was introduced to the stooge learner and reassured that he had come to no harm. Milgram debriefed each participant in depth and ensured that they were not distressed when they left.

What did he find?

Both quantitative and qualitative data was gathered. Quantitative data came in the form

Voltage	Number of Ps giving this as a maximum
15–60V	0
75–120V	0
135–180V	0
195–240V	0
255–300V	5 (at 300V)
315–360V	8
375–420V	1
420V+	26

Table 5.1 Distribution of maximum voltages given by teacher participants

of numbers of participants for whom each voltage was the maximum they would administer under orders. These are shown in Table 5.1.

A clear majority of participants administered the whole 450V. All gave at least 300V. Of those who refused to go the whole way, almost all stopped between 300 and 330V. This was the point at which the learner went silent.

Thinking psychologically

Turn to page 189 to find out about frequency histograms. Draw a frequency histogram to show the distribution of scores shown in Table 5.1.

If we look only at the quantitative data, we might be tempted to conclude that the participants were responding in a cold and uncaring manner. However, the transcripts of their speech and the observations reveal a very different picture. The majority showed signs of stress: protesting, sweating and striding about the room in agitation. Some became visibly angry; others wept. This striking contrast between people's actions and their feelings about those actions was very important in helping Milgram put together an explanation for his findings.

What did he conclude?

Milgram concluded that ordinary people are shockingly obedient to destructive orders. In fact, these results suggested that, under orders, most people would kill a stranger. Milgram also noted that people were well aware of the significance of their actions and were in no way shielded from their emotional consequences. People apparently obeyed, but not because they wanted to or because they didn't care about the consequences. On the contrary, people suffered considerable distress but, crucially, felt that they had no choice but to obey orders.

web watch

Go to http://home.swbell.net/revscat/perilsOfObedience.html

You can find transcripts here of some of the most interesting conversations Milgram had with his participants over the several studies he ran.

1 Which participant behaves in the way Milgram expected most people to? How obedient are they?

2 What is unusual about Mr Batta's behaviour? How might you explain this?

What were the strengths of this study?

Milgram's study was carried out under controlled laboratory conditions. The major advantage of this is that all conditions are fully under the control of the experimenter. The art of a good laboratory experiment is to create a situation under these controlled conditions that effectively mirrors a real-life situation. Several aspects of Milgram's procedure were quite effective in achieving this mirroring. Remember that Milgram's ultimate aim was to understand the Holocaust. The experimenter himself was a figure of legitimate authority, as long as he was in his lab directing an experiment. In keeping with this role, the experimenter wore a scientist's lab coat. This use of a uniform to symbolise legitimate authority mirrors the use of military uniforms to symbolise the legitimate authority of military leaders who give orders during atrocities like the Holocaust. The gradual increase in electric shocks so that participants found themselves on a 'slippery slope' mirrors the typical situation in which communities build up to genocide. This might start by socially excluding a target group, escalating to vandalism and small-scale violence and only then to systematic attempts to wipe them out. A further strength of Milgram's study is its relevance to real life. This was clearly a study worth carrying out, because it tells us something important about human nature. Atrocities in which ordinary people commit mass murder on the orders of their military, politicians or community leaders still take place. Milgram's findings are as important in understanding such events as they were 40 years ago.

What were the weaknesses of this study?

Milgram carried out his study under laboratory conditions and gave his participants a task that they would not normally come across in everyday life. This means that the situation in which Milgram's participants found themselves was in some ways quite artificial. As we have said, Milgram was clever in some of the ways his procedure mirrored real-life atrocities. However, some features of Milgram's procedure differed from the situations in which destructive obedience takes place in real life. For example, the experimenter reassured participants that the shocks were painful but not dangerous, and so the learner would come

to no real harm. This is quite different to, say, the position of a Nazi concentration camp guard who could have no doubt that inmates would die as a result of his actions.

Psychologists have also criticised Milgram on the basis of the ethics of his studies. Participants did not give informed consent to take part in a social psychology experiment. They were deceived in several ways. They believed the study concerned memory rather than obedience, that the stooge was another participant, that the shocks were real and that they were hurting or even killing the learner. They were also subjected to distress and, most seriously, denied the right to withdraw from the study. In response to these criticisms, Milgram's membership application to the American Psychological Association was suspended. However, he was admitted after an investigation. This concluded that he had taken great care to check the welfare of each participant following the procedure and that his work was sufficiently important to justify his methods.

Thinking psychologically

Locate a set of ethical guidelines for carrying out psychological research. You can find one such at http://www.theatp.org/ in the 'Publications' section. Evaluate the ethics of Milgram's procedure using these guidelines.

Variations on the original procedure

Over the next few years after the original study, Milgram carried out a series of follow-ups to test the effect of a range of different conditions on the rates of obedience. He found, for example, that when the study was moved from a prestigious university to a run-down office block, the number of people willing to give 450–volt shocks dropped to 47.5 per cent. When the teacher had to force the learner's hand down on to an electrode and strap it down, the percentage fell to 30 per cent. When the experimenter telephoned orders from a different room, only 20.5 per cent gave the full 450 volts.

Where are we now?

Milgram and numerous other social psychologists have replicated his classic study with a range of variations in the procedure. Luttke (2004) summarised the findings of these studies and concluded that destructive obedience is greatest when certain conditions are met. These are:

- when the victim is physically removed from participants
- when co-participants or stooges display obedience rather than rebellion.

According to Luttke, some of Milgram's own variations in his procedure have not generally yielded as much effect when replicated independently by other researchers. For example, the appearance of the experimenter and the location of the study generally make only minor differences to obedience rates.

In the Nuremberg trials of Nazi criminals, Adolph Eichmann famously said that he was only following orders and thus was not responsible for the consequences of his actions. This has since become known as the 'Nuremberg defence'. In a series of studies, Thomas Blass investigated people's attributions of responsibility when destructive orders are followed. In one study Blass (1996) showed students a film of Milgram's procedure and asked them about the relative responsibility of Milgram and his participants for administering the shocks. Participants attributed responsibility for hurting the learner to Milgram, not to the participants who followed his orders. In a follow-up, Blass and Schmitt (2001) showed students the same footage and questioned them about why Milgram had such power over his participants. They identified his expertise and his legitimate position as a scientist directing an experiment as the main factors. This is important, as it highlights the way the experimental situation mirrors real-life situations in which people are faced with orders from people claiming expertise and legitimate authority.

Obedience research has important implications in other areas, such as accident prevention. In 2002, a Russian airline pilot, Alexander Goss, was faced with an order from Swiss Air Traffic Control to dive to avoid a head-on collision. His own instruments told him to climb. He followed the orders of the controller and hit the other plane, killing 71 people. According to Tarnow (2000), many accidents of this sort occur because people in a crisis situation tend to follow orders from those in authority who have poor information on which to base their orders. Often, as in the Goss case, people receiving the orders have much clearer information and are in a better position to make the decision. Tarnow analysed the records from 37 plane crashes and suggested that 25 per cent of them were the direct result of pilots following inappropriate orders from the ground. In all these cases, the pilots had enough information to see that the orders were mistakes.

Summing it up

Asch (1955)

- This was a laboratory experiment with several conditions.
- The aim was to test whether students would conform to the obviously wrong judgements made by a group.
- Participants sat in a group of peers and each person in turn identified which of three lines matched a target line.
- The group was composed of stooges who regularly identified the obviously wrong line.
- In a control condition where the stooges gave the correct answers the participants got 98 per cent of the lines correct.
- In the experimental condition when stooges gave the wrong answer, participants were correct only around two thirds of the time.
- The **conformity effect** was sharply reduced when one of the stooges broke ranks and named a different line.
- Asch's study was carried out under controlled conditions, used a control condition and had a good sample size.
- On the other hand, his sample was unrepresentative and the task used to test conformity was not realistic.

Milgram (1963)

- This was a laboratory pre-experiment. The initial study had one condition, although later variations were true experiments, comparing obedience under different conditions.
- The aim was to see how many people would obey orders to give potentially fatal electric shocks to a stranger.
- Participants were told they were teachers in a learning experiment. Their task was to administer a memory task to a stranger and give him electric shocks every time he got an answer wrong.
- There were no real shocks and the other participant was in fact an actor who simulated pain and distress.
- As the voltage of the shocks increased and the actor simulated increasing distress, most participants objected, but Milgram gave them a series of verbal prods to encourage them to continue.
- 100 per cent of participants gave the actor 300 volts or more. 65 per cent gave the maximum voltage, although most showed signs of stress.
- Milgram's study was highly relevant to understanding real-life atrocities like the Holocaust. It also included a number of features that made it quite life-like.
- On the other hand, Milgram's procedure raises serious ethical issues, and some features were not effective in mirroring real life.

What have I learned?

1   What is a repeated measures design? Why can Asch's study be described as a repeated measures design?

2   What is a naïve participant? Why was it important that participants in both Asch's and Milgram's studies were naïve?

3   What is a control condition? What control condition did Asch use?

4   What did Asch mean when he said that people would say that 'white is black'?

5   Why is it important to replicate studies? How have Asch's and Milgram's conclusions stood up to replications of the procedure?

6   Give an example of one way Milgram's procedure mirrored real-life situations in which people give destructive orders.

7   What is quantitative data? Give an example of the use of quantitative data in this chapter.

8   What is qualitative data? Give an example of the use of qualitative data in this chapter.

Reading around

■ Asch, S. E. (1955) 'Opinions and social pressure.' *Scientific American,* 193: 31–5. Available online at: http://www.wadsworth.com/psychology_d/templates/student_resources/0155060678_rathus/ps/ps18/html

■ Gross, R. (2005) *Key Studies in Psychology.* London: Hodder & Stoughton.

■ Hock, R. (2004) *Forty Studies that Changed Psychology*. New York: Prentice Hall.

■ Milgram, S. (2004) *Obedience to Authority: an experimental view*. New York: Harper.

6

Studies in physiological psychology

What should I know?

- The procedure used by Rahe, Mahan and Arthur (1970).
- The findings and conclusions of Rahe *et al.* (1970).
- A critical evaluation of Rahe *et al.* (1970).
- The procedure used by Sperry (1968).
- The findings and conclusions of Sperry (1968).
- A critical evaluation of Sperry (1968).

In addition I should be able to:

- provide examples of correlations and questionnaires
- evaluate correlations and questionnaires in terms of their strengths and weaknesses
- understand issues relating to reliability and validity
- provide illustrations of control conditions
- understand scattergraphs
- explain ethical issues relating to informed consent.

Introducing research in the physiological approach

You will recall from Chapter 1 that the physiological approach is about the biological processes underlying our emotions, cognition and behaviour. In this chapter, we are interested in the impact of stress on health and in the role of different brain regions and, specifically, what we can learn about the left and right sides of the brain by separating them.

The two core studies in this chapter are:

- **Rahe *et al.* (1970) Stressful life events**
  Rahe, R. H., Mahan, J. L. and Arthur, R. (1970) 'Prediction of near-future health change from subjects' preceding life

changes.' *Journal of Psychosomatic Research,* 14: 401–6.

- **Sperry (1968) Split-brain patients**
  Sperry, R. W. (1968) 'Hemisphere deconnection and unity in conscious awareness.' *American Psychologist,* 23: 723–33.

The first study we will look at in the physiological approach is about stress. Rahe *et al.* (1970) is one of many studies which have explored the observation that when people experience significant events in their lives they are more likely to be ill than during times when their lives are relatively socially stable.

Through the 1950s, many studies indicated a relationship between stress and health. One such study was Rosenman and Friedman (1958), who found a link between stress and coronary heart disease. Their work was based on an initial observation of patients with heart conditions in a waiting room. Unlike typical patients, who relax comfortably in easy chairs, these individuals tended to leap out of their seats, apparently unable to sit still and wait. The wear on the chairs was telling – the fronts of the seats and arms had been damaged by the impatient behaviour of this particular group. Rosenman and Friedman concluded that such individuals (whom they called 'Type A personalities') experienced higher levels of stress and were more likely to suffer ill health related to heart disease. What was not clear was why they were more likely to be ill. Was it because they found life more stressful or because their personality tended to expose them to more stressful experiences? Further research has established a link between stress and ill health.

Many of the early studies were conducted using participants in hospital, i.e. those whose illnesses (both physical and mental) were severe, so the findings were not necessarily rel-

evant to the effects of more typical life stressors. Furthermore, any judgement of the stress level leading up to their illness would necessarily be retrospective and this was a problem for many studies (e.g. Greene, 1954; Greene *et al.*, 1956; Rahe *et al.*, 1964). This is an issue as, if we look back on sources of stress from the perspective of being ill, we are unlikely to be fair judges. Rahe *et al.* measured exposure to stress of the crew of three ships. These individuals, being isolated from other people but in one environment, were exposed to the same weather, general levels of work stress and infectious agents. They also all reported to the same medical facility, which was well used and kept detailed records. As a consequence, the situation was well controlled; any differences in health were likely to be due to differing vulnerability to illness rather than any environmental factors. Holmes and Rahe (1967) were therefore able to look for a correlation between stressful life events and subsequent illness.

Glossary

epilepsy: a disorder affecting approximately one in 130 people in the UK that is characterised by recurrent seizures (fits).

cerebral hemispheres: two roughly symmetrical halves of the brain on the left and right sides. Each consists of an outer layer of cerebral cortex beneath which are other brain structures.

seizure: a disturbance to normal brain activity caused by a sudden burst of excess electrical activity that leads to a temporary disruption in communication between neurones.

retrospective studies: these rely on the ability of participants to remember events in the past, such as times when they experienced stress.

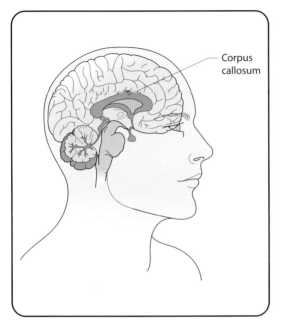

Corpus
callosum

Fig. 6.1 Location of corpus callosum

The second study we will explore from the physiological approach is Sperry (1968). This is one of many investigations of the role played by a structure that lies between the two halves of the brain, the corpus callosum. It is the largest of several structures joining the left and right cerebral hemispheres (see Figure 6.1). Earlier research on animals (e.g. Myers, 1961; Sperry, 1967a, b) and humans (Akelaitis, 1944) had shown that no key functions are lost if the corpus callosum is cut – providing that no other brain areas are damaged. The effects of damage to many other brain areas are generally obvious and frequently major.

This paper aimed to provide systematic evidence about the effect on humans of operations which cut the corpus callosum. It can tell us not only about the role of the corpus callosum but also that of the individual hemispheres. The 'split-brain' procedure is occasionally used with patients with severe epilepsy for whom drug control is insuffi-

cient. It aims to stop epileptic seizures by preventing the spread of electrical disturbances across from one side of the brain to the other. Although rarely used, it is remarkably successful; seizures become less frequent and less severe.

Sperry had to develop ingenious tests to demonstrate the losses associated with split-brain operations, because the problems are not apparent in day-to-day observation. To understand why these elaborate procedures were necessary, you will need to know some details about how different information is channelled through the brain.

- Movement **instructions** (or 'motor' messages) on one side of the body are sent from the opposite side of the brain (e.g. commands directing the right arm come from the left side of the brain). This is not disrupted by a split-brain operation.
- **Touch information** comes from each side of the body to the opposite side of the brain (e.g. the sensation of feeling a prickly holly leaf in the left hand is sent to the right side of the brain). This is not disrupted by a split-brain operation.
- **Visual information** comes into the nervous system from the eyes. In each eye, half the scene is to the left of a central point (this is called the 'left visual field') and half is to the right of that point (the 'right visual field') – see Figure 6.2. Importantly, information from the left visual field of both eyes is directed to the right hemisphere. Similarly, right visual field of both eyes is directed to the left hemisphere. So, half of the information from each eye stays on the same side of the head and half swaps to the opposite side of the head. This crossover of information occurs at the optic chiasm. This is *not* cut by the split-

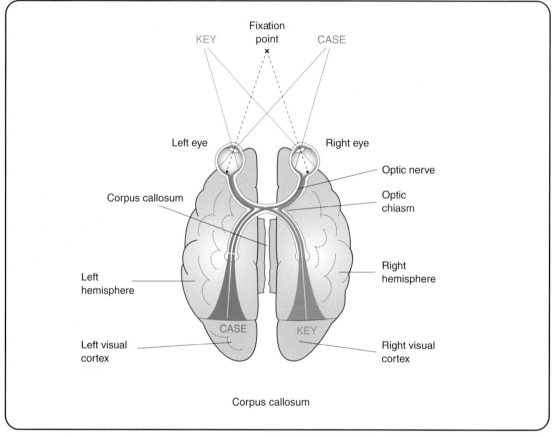

KEY Fixation point CASE

Left eye Right eye

Corpus callosum

Optic nerve

Optic chiasm

Left hemisphere

Right hemisphere

CASE KEY

Left visual cortex

Right visual cortex

Corpus callosum

Fig. 6.2 Right and left visual fields

brain operation. However, the connection between the visual areas of the cortex (which lie at the back of the head) through the corpus callosum *is* severed in a split-brain operation.

These routes are important in comparing the reactions from the right and left sides of the brain. For most individuals, whether right- or left-handed, the left hemisphere appears to be dominant.

Rahe, Mahan and Arthur (1970) Stressful life events

What did Rahe, Mahan and Arthur do?

This was a prospective study into the effect of stress on illness. A total of 2,684 naval men of varying ranks were asked to complete a 'Schedule of Recent Experiences' (SRE). This questionnaire was used to assess the stressful life events each individual had experienced over four consecutive six-month periods running up to their deployment on one of three navy cruisers. Each stressful experience recorded on the SRE was assigned a life change unit (LCU), a weighting that indicated the severity of that source of stress. The allocation of weightings had been previously established using a group of American civilians and had been found to be consistent when compared with other samples. A total LCU score for each participant was calculated for each of the four six-month periods in the two years prior to disembarkation.

The sample represented between 90 and 97 per cent of each ship's crew and fell by less than 10 per cent due to transfer off the ship. The average age was 22.3 years, approximately two thirds of the men were high school graduates and they ranged in experience from apprentice seamen to high-ranking officers with 30 years' naval service.

Once on board, any illnesses (even minor ones) were recorded by the ship's medical facility. When the data on health was analysed, any sickness believed to be motivated by a desire to shirk work was excluded, as were any reports of pre-existing conditions. The remaining information on the number, type and severity of new health problems was used to produce an illness criterion. Neither the participants themselves, nor the ships' medical departments, were aware of the design of the study.

Box 6.1
Procedure summary

Method: prospective investigation.
Design: correlational.
Variable 1: estimate of illness during 6–8 months' deployment on board ship, based on the ships' health records.
Variable 2: estimate of life change units from the preceding two years, assessed using the SRE questionnaire.
Participants: 2,864 US naval crew members from three ships of whom 2,664 contributed to the results.

Life events	Life crisis units
Death of spouse	100
Divorce	73
Marital separation	65
Jail term	63

Table 6.1 Extract from Schedule of Recent Experiences
Source: Holmes and Rahe (1967). Holmes–Rahe life changes scale. First published in Journal of Psychosomatic Research, 11: 213–18

web watch

You can try an updated, online version of the Holmes and Rahe 'Schedule of Recent Experiences' at: http://www.geocities.com/beyond_stretched/holmes.htm

Why do you think it has been necessary to change the test since it was first devised and to continue to do so periodically?

LCU bands included in group	Mean illness rate
1 and 2	1.405
3, 4 and 5	1.541
6, 7 and 8	1.676
9 and 10	2.066

Table 6.3 Mean illness score for all participants (with LCU scores in each of four different bands)

What did they find?

The relationship between stress and illness scores was investigated by testing for correlations between the individual's LCU totals for

LCU band	Mean illness rate
1	1.434
2	1.377
3	1.583
4	1.543
5	1.498
6	1.685
7	1.651
8	1.693
9	2.083
10	2.049

Table 6.2 Mean illness score for all participants (with LCU scores in each of ten different bands)

each of the four six-month periods and the illnesses reported by each man. The only significant relationship was between the LCU total for the six months immediately prior to departure and the illness score ($r = 0.118$). This indicates a positive correlation between the crew members' pre-departure life-change intensity and the illnesses they reported while at sea. Only the data relating to the final six pre-departure months was used in subsequent analyses.

Overall totals were calculated by putting the participants in order of lowest to highest total LCU and dividing the list into ten bands (each one tenth of the ship's crew). The illness ratings were then compared between bands. When divided up in this way, two of the ships showed large differences, one not so great. Therefore, when the data for all three vessels were combined, the differences between the ten bands were obscured. The only big differences were at each end of the scale (see Table 6.2). To overcome this, the grouping was changed, combining some of the ten bands to make four bigger groups. This data is shown in Table 6.3. As you can see, the higher the LCU band, the higher the mean illness rating.

The results were finally analysed to look at the nature of the link between LCU and

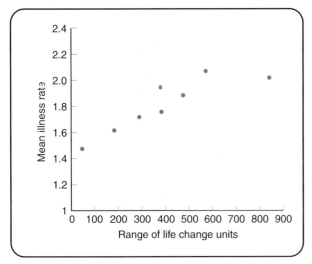

Fig. 6.3 Mean illness rates are related to life changes

What did they conclude?

The findings suggest that higher LCUs relating to the six months prior to departure are associated with higher illness rates on board ship. There is a clear pattern. When the pre-departure life changes are low, so are on-board illness rates. However, this relationship can be masked by stressful on-board experiences because this increases the illness rate for the entire crew. Furthermore, the link was stronger for older men (over 21 years of age) and married ones than for younger, single men.

What were the strengths of this study?

This was a prospective study. The reporting of stress cannot, therefore, have been affected by the experience of illness, as is potentially the case in retrospective studies. The prospective method is thus more valid. Furthermore, the participants did not know that their illness rates were going to be used, so their reporting cannot have been biased by expectations about the study. Similarly, the medical staff were unaware of the design of the study and were accustomed to keeping full records, so would not have recorded illnesses any differently than normal.

The choice of samples confined on board ship was beneficial for several reasons:

- It was customary for crew members to report even minor illnesses so the report rate would have been high.
- It ensured that all incidents were recorded in the same way.
- Individuals would have been exposed to similar pathogens and have received similar food and general health care.

illness rates. To do this, the men's LCU scores were re-grouped into numerical ranges on LCU score (i.e. LCU 0–99, 100–199, 200–299, etc. up to 600+). These results, plotted against mean illness rates, are shown in Figure 6.3. The graph shows a linear relationship between exposure to life events and ill health.

One final piece of evidence related to the nature of each ship's mission, which differed in work level and exposure to combat stressors. For example, two ships were on military missions off the coast of Vietnam. The relationships between the LCU and mean illness rates were strongest in the two ships judged to have the easiest missions. It is possible that higher current stress levels on the other ship obscured any differences that may have been caused by preceding stressful life experiences.

These control measures all improved the validity of the study as they increased the likelihood that any differences in illness were due to the individuals' previous life events rather than to any other factors. The sample itself was large and included crew members of differing ages, ranks and educational levels, representing a demographic spread. The findings were therefore likely to generalise beyond the sample itself.

The original version of the SRE (Hawkins, Davies and Holmes, 1957) has been revised many times to improve its validity and reliability. Rahe *et al.* used a military version of the SRE, based on Holmes and Rahe's (1967) updated SRE, so it was specific to this context. The reliability of the SRE has been tested, e.g. by Mendels and Weinstein (1972), who evaluated the LCUs allocated to each event and found a high correlation between the findings of Holmes and Rahe (1967) and their own results, from a sample which differed in both age and educational level. Furthermore, Mendels and Weinstein's correlation remained high when the sample was re-tested a year later. However, more recent studies have questioned the reliability of self-reporting of stress. Raphael *et al.* (1991) asked women to report stressful events each month over a ten-month period. When asked to recall the events again at the end of the study period, only a quarter of the originally reported categories appeared. Nevertheless, the findings in relation to Rahe *et al.* (1970) are supported by both earlier, retrospective studies (e.g. Rahe *et al.*, 1964) and subsequent prospective ones, such as Gupta and Gupta (2004), who found a significant correlation between stress and skin disorders.

web watch

You can find out more about the history of research into stress and illness on the internet:

● http://annals.high wire.org/cgi/content/full/124/7/673 – this catalogues the work of Holmes, who developed the first version of the SRE.

● Read Holmes's view on the success of the SRE at: http://www.garfield. library.upenn.edu/classics1982/A198 2PJ13900001.pdf

● Read Rahe's explanation of the difference between SRE, SRRS and LCUs at: http://www.psychosomatic medicine.org/cgi.reprint/40.2.95.pdf

What were the weaknesses of this study?

The correlation coefficients found by Rahe *et al.* were quite low (e.g. $r = 0.118$). Many of these results were nevertheless significant as the sample was so large. However, a correlation tells us only that there is a relationship. Just because two factors vary together, we cannot conclude that one causes a change in the other. Even in this prospective study, it is still possible that both the illnesses and the stressful events were caused by a third factor. Ill health is not necessarily dependent upon previous trauma. Indeed, not all studies that have looked at life events and illness have found a link (e.g. Theorell *et al.*, 1975; Vidal *et al.*, 2006).

The SRE is a self-report measure (i.e. the participants fill in the questionnaire themselves). In this situation, individuals may give biased responses, such as offering socially desirable answers. In a question asking about minor violations of the law, participants may choose not to report events that had in fact happened. This may be especially so for this particular sample of participants; military personnel about to go into combat may feel they should answer in a particular way.

The sample, while large and varied in some respects, consisted only of American males and represented a somewhat narrow occupational field. Women respond to stress in rather different ways from men, for example in the coping strategies they adopt. The findings may not, therefore, generalise from one gender to the other. Similarly, cultural differences in responses to stress have also been identified (e.g. Frydenberg et al., 2003). Occupational choice may also be an important factor in sensitivity to stress. For example, it is possible that those willing to go to war, or to spend time away from their families on board ship, are more resilient to stressors than those who choose against such a profession. This possibility is supported by the difference found by Rahe et al. in the strength of the link between stress and illness in older, married men compared with younger, single ones. The potential influence of such factors again limits the extent to which the findings may be applied to the wider population. Other differences could clearly exist, e.g. in the response of individuals to the death of their partner, which would depend on the nature of the preceding relationship; or to divorce, which for some may be seen positively. Furthermore, the life events are assumed to be independent of each other, whereas in reality they may not be. For example, marriage, a change of job and of residence may commonly coincide.

An ethical issue was raised as, although the participants were aware that they had filled in the SRE, they were unaware that their illness records were going to be used. They had not therefore given informed consent for their health to be monitored.

web watch

The Welsh Assembly has launched an initiative to combat stress at work, by tackling both the causes of stress (through the employers) and the effects of stress (on the employees). Look at its website and identify some causes of stress and their consequences: http://www.healthymindsatwork.org.uk/index.php?option=com_frontpageandItemid=1

Where are we now?

The Social Readjustment Rating Scale (SRRS) continues to be a widely used tool in health research. Clearly, not all illnesses are related to stress, but many are. As a consequence, of those investigations using life events as a measure of stress, some find a link to ill health, others do not. For example, Vidal et al. (2006) found no relationship between life events and inflammatory bowel disease, whereas Gupta and Gupta (2004) found that life events were significantly related to the deterioration of skin disorders (such as scalp itching). These studies illustrate the importance of being able to establish the role played by stress in physical disorders. Where a link exists, parties such as clinicians and employers, as well as the individual themselves, are better prepared to resolve the problem.

Thinking psychologically

Look back to the findings in Table 6.3.

1. a What graphical representation is appropriate for this data?
    b Plot these results; label the axes carefully and give the graph a title.
2. Explain why it is important that the mean, rather than the total illness ratings, is given in this table, whereas it would have been acceptable to use either in Table 6.2.
3. The relationship shown in Figure 6.3 is a linear one because the graph is a straight line. If the pattern of the graph had risen sharply at the end, what would this have indicated about the relationship between stress and illness?

Sperry (1968) Split-brain patients

What did Sperry do?

Sperry, in collaboration with several other researchers, devised an elegant procedure for testing the effects of hemispheric deconnection (see Figure 6.4). This had several key aspects:

● The left and right halves of the visual field could be stimulated together or separately.
● Tests could be combined with additional auditory, visual or other inputs.
● Unwanted stimuli could be eliminated.

The participants were 11 patients who had received surgery for epilepsy which cut the

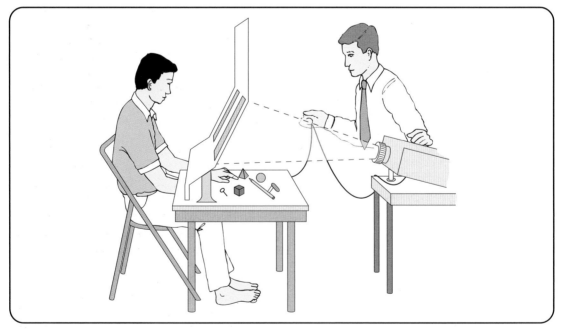

Fig. 6.4 Apparatus for studying lateralisation of visual, tactile, lingual and associated functions in the surgically separated hemispheres (from Sperry, 1968)

corpus callosum. When testing vision, the participant fixated their eyes in the centre of a screen on which visual stimuli appeared briefly (one tenth of a second or less). When we look at an object, our eyes make fast movements called 'saccades'. However, these saccadic movements take about 200 milliseconds to begin. The central fixation and brief presentation therefore ensured that the participants would not have time to move their eyes before the stimulus disappeared. This guaranteed that no information intended for one visual pathway accidentally entered the other. Figure 6.2 shows the route taken by the two streams of information from the left and right visual fields to the visual cortex. The

vertical midline on which the participant fixates is surprisingly precise: there is no significant overlap or gap between the visual fields. This equipment could thus be used to test whether split-brain patients had two independent visual experiences, one for the left brain and one for the right. This would indicate whether there was any communication between the two sides of the brain.

In different experiments, the apparatus was used to perform the following tests:

1   An object is flashed to one visual field (e.g. the left) and the same object is presented again to either the same or the opposite visual field. The participant indicates whether they recognise the object.

2   Items are presented either to the dominant hemisphere or to the non-dominant hemisphere. For a typical left-hemisphere dominant, right-handed participant, images presented to the right visual field reach the dominant hemisphere. Images presented to the left visual field reach the non-dominant hemisphere. The participant reports what they have seen using either speech or writing.

3   Two different figures are flashed simultaneously and separately to the left and right visual fields (e.g. '$' to the left and '?' to the right). The participant draws what they have seen using the left hand, which is covered up.

4   Word combinations are shown such that half appears in the left and half in the right visual field (e.g. 'key' to the left and 'case' to the right – see Figure 6.2). The participant is asked to respond in a variety of ways.

5   An object is placed in one hand and the participant is asked to identify it in one of the following ways:

Box 6.2
Procedure summary

Method: experimental procedure for presenting stimuli to the left and right visual fields either together or separately.
Design: individually, tests were of a repeated measures design because in any series each participant was compared on both left and right hemisphere responses. Most stimuli were presented as a tenth of a second flash to either the left or right visual field.
Independent variables tested: the main variable being assessed was the ability of the left compared with the right cerebral hemisphere.
Dependent variables measured: participants indicated awareness of stimuli by:
● verbal report
● written response
● pointing or choosing.
Participants: 11 patients who had received surgery for epilepsy which cut the corpus callosum.

a verbally

b by physical retrieval of the object with the same hand

c by physical retrieval of the object with the opposite hand (cross retrieval).

6 Symmetric hand pose: the participant begins with hands apart, not touching and out of sight. The experimenter moves one into a different position (such as in a fist, or with the fingers crossed). The participant replicates the position with the other hand.

7 Test of crossed topognosis: the participant has their hands in front of them, but not visible. The tip or base of one finger is lightly touched. In the control condition, the participant touches the same target point with the thumb of that hand. In the 'crossed' test, the participant must mirror the target point with the opposite thumb and hand. For example, if the experimenter touches the tip of the participant's left index finger, the control condition response is to touch the left thumb to the tip of the left index finger, but the 'crossed' response would be to touch the right thumb to the tip of the right index finger.

8 Using a picture of a hand presented only to the left or right visual field, a target point is identified by a black spot. The participant's task is to touch that location on their own hand with their thumb, either on the same side as was shown (e.g. left visual field and left hand) or the opposite.

9 A different object is placed simultaneously in each hand. They are then removed and jumbled up with other objects. The felt objects are then searched for by touch.

10 The participant is asked to write a spoken word, or copy a written word, with their left hand.

11 An outline sketch of a hand posture is flashed to one hemisphere. This must be mimicked with either the same-side or opposite-side hand.

What did he find?

The results of the different tests in Sperry's study were as follows:

1 The participant will recognise the object only if it is presented to the same visual field again – there seems to be no communication of the experience between the left and right hemispheres. The two visual fields of a split-brain participant appear to lead to independent trains of visual images and memories.

2 When asked to write or say what they have seen when it has been presented to the right visual field (left hemisphere), participants report accurately. When asked about items presented to the left visual field, they will report nothing. However, when asked to report by pointing or choosing a corresponding object with the left hand (i.e. using the right hemisphere), they can accurately indicate their memory for the object they have just denied seeing.

3 Using the left hand, hidden from view, the participant reproduces what they have seen in the left visual field (e.g. '$'). If then asked what they have drawn – without looking at it – they will report what was presented to the right visual field (e.g. '?') because only this figure has reached the verbal left hemisphere.

4   In the word combination tests (example 4 above), a participant might respond by reaching with the left hand for a key from a selection of objects. With the right hand, however, they would respond by writing the word 'case'. They would give this as a verbal response too. To a question about what kind of 'case' they were thinking of, a participant would be equally likely to say 'case of beer' or 'the case of the missing corpse' as 'key case'.

5   Objects in the right hand, information about which is transferred to the left hemisphere, are readily identified using speech or in writing. Objects held in the left hand, in contrast, cannot be named. The participant may even be unaware that an object is present. When the task is to identify objects previously held in the left hand by retrieving from a group of other items they can see or hold within a bag, the participant can readily perform the task with the left hand. The participant will

fail, however, to retrieve the correct object with the other hand.

6   Participants generally fail at symmetric hand pose tasks. Some very simple replications, such as of making a fist or lying the hand flat, could be achieved.

7   Split-brain participants were able to perform the control, within-hand tasks successfully but were typically unable to achieve the 'crossed' tasks. Some individuals, after practice, could achieve simple 'crossed' tasks, but even here their responses were much slower than for normal individuals.

8   On same-side pairing (e.g. presentation of the hand image to the left visual field and touching the left hand), split-brain patients perform normally. They are, however, unable to make an appropriate response with the opposite hand. If the image was presented to the left visual field, they would be unable to form the correct position with the right hand.

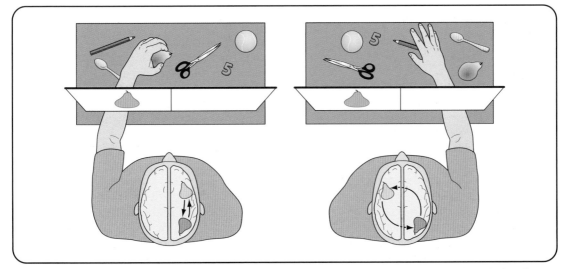

Fig. 6.5 An object flashed to the left visual field can be retrieved by the left hand but not the right hand

9   Each hand searches independently for the object it felt; the object held by the other hand will be rejected if it is encountered.

10 Participants can generally copy a written word with their left hand but are unable to write the same word if it is spoken to them.

11 Motor control of the limbs when one hemisphere is directing the opposite hand is fairly good. When expected to direct the hand on the same side of the body, control is poor in some patients.

One interesting observation Sperry made of these results related to instances where the participant repeatedly succeeded at 'right hemisphere' tasks of which they felt they had no awareness. When the contradiction was pointed out to them, typical responses were to 'explain' their successes as guesses or as the result of unconscious responses.

What did he conclude?

One hemisphere doesn't know what the other one has been doing

The findings suggest that the corpus callosum acts as a bridge between the left and right cerebral hemispheres. Without this bridge, the two areas appear to function as separate units. This enabled Sperry to identify some of the similarities and differences between the two sides of the brain. The left hemisphere, being far superior in terms of language, may appear to be dominant (see Figure 6.6). However, when appropriately accessed, for example by means such as pointing, the right hemisphere can perform identification and memory tasks. The testing of a split-brain patient shows that they have two independent streams of consciousness, i.e. that the oper-ation appears to produce *two* brains. While this view is reinforced by observations of the relatively non-linguistic properties of the right hemisphere, it is clearly also contra-dicted by the findings. In many ways, the commissurotomy demonstrates that there is great similarity in functional ability of the left and right hemispheres. So, it would be more accurate to think not of separating the brain in half but of doubling, i.e. creating two inde-pendent brains. This perspective is supported by the observation that such patients do not report any sense of 'missing' information. They engage in activities such as watching television and reading books without com-plaining of any distortion.

Are two half brains better than one whole one?

So, are commissurotomy patients advantaged by having two brains? In some simple situ-ations, the answer is 'Yes', for example when given left and right hemisphere tasks that would normally be difficult to attend to simultaneously. Here, unsurprisingly, com-missurotomy patients perform better than average. This is because they do not experi-ence the interference that a normal participant suffers. However, this advantage is lost when task complexity increases. Split-brain patients show a number of deficits, such as short-term memory impairment and fatigue in reading and other intellectually demanding tasks.

Are the two halves different?

The left hemisphere seems, from Sperry's findings, to be almost exclusively responsible for verbal tasks, be they spoken or written. The mental life of the right hemisphere seems to be somewhat different from this. It can perform:

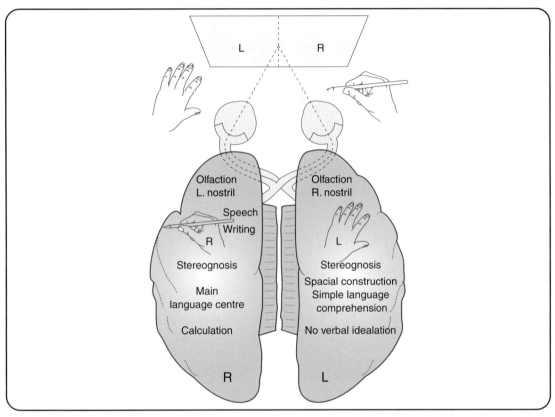

Fig. 6.6 An outline of the lateralisation seen in behavioural tests of split-brain patients (from Sperry, 1968)

- tasks that require a transfer of understanding from one sensory form (e.g. visual) to another (e.g. identifying by touch). For example, if an image of a cigarette is presented to the left visual field the participant can select the same item from choices which are out of sight (using the left hand). Note that if the right hand is allowed to feel the objects instead of the left, it can identify them and the corresponding hemisphere (the left) can name them out loud. This, of course, is of no use to the left hand, which is trying to identify the object, as the right hemisphere controlling it does not understand the spoken words
- similar transfers between other sensory modalities, including hearing and olfaction (smell)
- tasks similar to those described above, but where the participant is required to find an item that 'goes with' the one they have seen. For example, a participant presented with the visual stimulus of a wall clock to the left visual field can use the right hemisphere to select a corresponding item such as a toy wrist watch (by touch with the left hand). Here, the task is not merely one of

matching visual images but of finding related concepts

- tasks using abstract symbols. Participants may be presented with two numbers, either visually as written numerals in the left visual field, or as plastic block numbers in the left hand. Four out of the six participants tested could indicate the sum of two numbers. The right hemisphere could either point to it in a column using the left hand, or write it (with the left hand hidden)
- simple tasks based on verbal and written words. If the name of an object is presented to the left visual field the participant can then find this object from a physical array. In response to the word 'eraser', the right hemisphere can instruct the left hand to select an eraser from a group of items using touch alone. Of course, the participant cannot name the item they have selected (as the left hemisphere is unaware of the choice). It does show, however, that the right hemisphere understands the written word and could respond appropriately. The same applies to spoken words. If the participant is asked to find a piece of cutlery, they may choose (with the left hand) a fork from a selection of items. When asked to verbalise what has been chosen, the response from the left hemisphere, which is unaware of the choice made by the left hand, is as likely to be 'knife' or 'spoon' as 'fork'. While both hemispheres heard and understood the instruction, only the right hemisphere, which cannot respond verbally to the question, knows the correct answer. It is interesting to note that the right hemisphere can cope with fairly complex concepts in tasks like this, such as 'shaving instrument' (for razor) and 'dirt remover' (for soap).

Is hemispheric specialisation particularly human?

The tasks described above are of interest because they appear to be exclusively human. Although the right brain is animal-like in its virtual absence of spoken or written language, it is certainly human in other aspects of its mental capacities.

Sperry reports that further tests have identified a right-hemisphere ability to sort items into categories on the basis of shape, size and texture. The right hemisphere is also superior in some tasks such as tests of spatial relationships.

Finally, Sperry showed that the right hemisphere can process emotional information. When a nude is presented to the left visual field among other images, the participant may respond by blushing or giggling. They are, however, unable to explain their reaction. This is also illustrated in tests of olfaction. In response to an unpleasant odour introduced to the right nostril (there is no crossing over of olfactory information), a participant will grunt or exclaim 'Phew!', but cannot verbalise whether it is garlic or cheese. This affective understanding is further evidenced by facial and gestural responses when the left hemisphere 'guesses' out loud. The right hemisphere, hearing the answers and knowing they are wrong, may trigger head shaking, frowning or wincing. The right hemisphere gives the impression of being 'annoyed' by the errors made in vocal responses.

It appears, therefore, that although the left hemisphere is dominant for speech – a human characteristic – the right hemisphere also has particular abilities. These include spatial awareness, the ability to categorise and the ability to engage in emotional expression.

web watch

Read about Sperry being awarded a Nobel Prize for his work: http://nobelprize.org/ educational_games/ medicine/split–brain/ background.html

http://nobelprize.org/nobel_prizes/medi cine/laureates/1981/sperry–lecture.html

What were the strengths of this study?

In order for any differences to be exhibited between normal and split-brain patients, many controls must be implemented. The need for these illustrates how readily, under normal circumstances, impairments experienced by split-brain patients are hidden. To ensure that the participants could not compensate for the absence of communication across the corpus callosum via some other (external) sensory medium, the following controls were used.

Controlling for visual compensation

- When presenting visual stimuli, Sperry used timed presentations of less than one tenth of a second. This ensured that the material would be restricted to the intended visual field, longer presentations would allow eye movements to begin and therefore to allow detection by both hemispheres.
- In tests of manual stereognosis (identifying an object by touching it without looking at it), visual cues were eliminated.
- In testing the detection of smells, the non-tested nostril had to be closed and visual cues eliminated.

Controlling for auditory compensation

- In many tests, the left hemisphere must be prevented from 'talking' to the right, i.e. giving away the answer in a verbal response, so touching or pointing were used.

Controlling for non-verbal compensation

- In tests of the left hemisphere, it is important that the right hemisphere cannot give either implicit or overt signals to the left hemisphere (such as reaching with the left hand).

What were the weaknesses of this study?

Clearly, there are questions about whether the brains of people with epilepsy so severe that it cannot be controlled with drugs are good models for the general population. There may be differences underlying the cause of the epilepsy, or damage arising from seizures, that make these individuals atypical and unrepresentative.

Although there were clearly consistencies between the participants' responses, there were also some differences. One example is the ability to compute and report mathematical calculations using the right hemisphere alone. The small samples involved (six participants in this instance, only four of whom could perform the task correctly) mean that the generalisability of the findings is low. It is not clear whether the abilities of the majority fairly represent the division of labour between the left and right hemispheres in the general population. Indeed, Sperry stresses the extent to which individual differences between patients are apparent.

Many other factors in ordinary life ensure that the two halves of the brain have near-identical experiences. By necessity of being in the same body, the two hemispheres go to the same places, meet the same people and do the same things. The matching eye movements of the left and right eyes mean that the two hemispheres will centre and focus on the same objects, so attention is likely to be directed at the same events. It is therefore difficult to ascertain the importance of the part played by the corpus callosum, compared with contiguous experience, in normal individuals.

web watch

- Enter 'split brain' and 'Sperry' into a search engine. Find text and illustrations that illustrate what you have learned about Sperry's research. In particular, try to find other examples of conflict between the two hands, such as described in the 'Thinking psychologically' box on page 103.

- Look at this site: http://www.uwm.edu/~johnchay/sb.htm and use the functions to explore different combinations of presentations to the left or right visual fields and responses of the left and right hands. Record them in a table. You should be able to predict what will happen.

Where are we now?

Following on from Sperry's research, there have been extensive studies into the roles of the left and right hemispheres. While the general pattern evident from Sperry's research holds true, the situation is more complex than it at first appeared. One reason for this is the phenomenal development in techniques for investigating the brain. Since the 1960s, many brain-scanning procedures, such as Positron Emission Tomography (PET), functional Magnetic Resonance Imaging (fMRI) and Single Photon Emission Computerised Tomography (SPECT), have enabled researchers to 'watch' the activity of very specific brain areas during cognitive processing. Although we are still a long way from being able to trace the progress of a thought through the brain, these techniques offer a new dimension to the research begun by Sperry.

Current research into the roles of the cerebral hemispheres suggests that they may differ in the 'scale' of their processing. Presented with a complex stimulus, we can either process it at a global level (i.e. as a whole), or at a local level (i.e. for the characteristics of individual parts). Many studies have found that the right hemisphere is associated with processing globally, the left locally. Marshall and Halligan (1995) found that this was the case in patients with brain injury and Fink et al. (1996) found the same pattern in normal participants using PET scanning.

Research with split-brain patients that followed on from Sperry's also revealed some interesting findings. Le Doux et al. (1977) began investigating the motivational aspects of the left and right hemispheres with a patient who happened to be very linguistically competent in the right hemispheres. Using Scrabble letters to spell out answers to questions such as what job he would like to do, the left hemisphere spelled out 'draughtsman' but the right hemisphere answered 'automobile race'. This 'dual consciousness', and its reliance on language, has been the subject of much debate.

Ultimately, however, current research focuses not on the differences between hemispheres but on the systems upon which the brain operates. The brain, like most biological structures, is mirrored on the left and right sides. While there are some differences, there are many more similarities between the left and right hemispheres. Speculation on the reason for the duplication suggests that it is biologically sound – it is less susceptible to damage if the mechanisms on one side can take over the functions of the other.

Thinking psychologically

1 You can easily reproduce some of the tasks Sperry used to test his split-brain patients. Choose two and find or make suitable stimuli. Working in pairs, act as participant and experimenter and, for each test, role-play either a normal participant's or a split-brain patient's responses.

One finding from split-brain patients shows that there is sometimes conflict between the actions of each side of the body. For example, one man reported that he had to restrain his left hand with his right as the left one was attacking his wife, while the right was trying to defend her.

a Explain, in terms of the roles of the left and right hemispheres:
   i what instructions were being sent to each hand
   ii where each instruction was coming from.
b If you have studied the psychodynamic approach, consider how a Freudian might interpret these actions in terms of the id, the ego and the superego.
c If you have studied psychosurgery in the physiological approach, suggest what deficits might be expected in patients who had damage to:
   i the left cerebral hemisphere
   ii the right cerebral hemisphere.
2 The right hemisphere can match visual images on concept, for example by finding the 'pair' for a visually presented item on the basis of function. What would the right hemisphere choose as a match in each of the following cases:
   ● stimulus: dollar sign. Choices – fish, 30c piece, nail?
   ● stimulus: picture of hammer. Choices – fish, 30c piece, nail?

Summing it up

Rahe, Mahan and Arthur (1970)

● This was a prospective correlational study, looking for a link between current stress and future illness.

● Over 2000 naval servicemen completed a Schedule of Recent Experiences, a questionnaire of stressful life events, for the two years prior to a period at sea, during which their health was closely monitored.

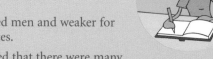

- A positive correlation was found between the number of life change units (an indicator of stressful events) experienced in the preceding six months and illness rating.

- This relationship was stronger for older, married men and weaker for those serving under more stressful circumstances.

- Using a confined sample of a ship's crew ensured that there were many controls. However, the sample was also limited, e.g. by being exclusively male.

- The participants were unaware that their health would be monitored, which raises ethical issues, although it did ensure that their reporting of illness was unbiased by their participation in the study.

Sperry (1968)

- This was an experimental study looking at the differences between the responses on specific cognitive tests of normal participants and individuals who had undergone surgery for epilepsy.

- The split-brain surgery separated the left and right cerebral hemispheres by cutting through the corpus callosum.

- The effect of this operation is to prevent the transmission of information between the left and right cerebral hemispheres. As a result, information entering through the left visual field only reaches the right hemisphere (and vice versa for information presented to the right visual field).

- Carefully designed tests allowed for presentation of stimulus material to only one hemisphere and through only one sensory modality (e.g. by presenting information very briefly, to one visual field, by displaying information to only the left side of the participant's fixation point and preventing them from using other cues, such as hearing or touch).

- Such tests, in a variety of combinations, showed that following the operation, patients could not transmit information from one hemisphere to the other: each appeared to have an independent stream of consciousness.

- When written or other kinds of information entered the left hemisphere the stimulus could be described verbally. This was not the case for information entering the right hemisphere. However, the right hemisphere (governing the left hand) could indicate an understanding of concepts and simple questions, for example by instructing the selection of a matching item by the left hand.

- The tests were precisely designed to exclude any possibility of information entering both hemispheres, thus the effect of any particular stimulus on either the left or right hemisphere could be ascertained with certainty.

- The participants Sperry used may not be representative, as their epilepsy was so severe it could not be controlled by medication: they were thus very unusual. This would affect the validity of generalisations to other people.

- Although there were clear consistencies between the results of Sperry's participants, there were also some differences. This casts some doubt on the reliability of the findings.

What have I learned?

1   In Rahe *et al.*'s study:

   a How and when was stress measured?

   b How and when was illness measured?

2   What makes Rahe *et al.*'s study 'prospective'?

3   a Which measure of central tendency was used by Rahe *et al.*?

   b Why was this the most appropriate choice?

4   a What operation had the participants in Sperry's study undergone?

   b What effect does this have on the transmission of information in the brain?

5   a In general, it is difficult to identify any obvious problems for patients who have had their corpus callosum cut. Why is this?

   b Describe how Sperry avoided visual information entering both hemispheres when he was presenting stimuli to participants.

6   What did Sperry's findings suggest about the differences between the roles of the left and right hemispheres?

Reading around

■ Gazzaniga, M. S. (1970) *The Bisected Brain*. New York: Appleton-Century-Crofts.

■ Springer, S. P. and Deutsch, G. (1998) *Left Brain, Right Brain: perspectives from cognitive neuroscience*. Basingstoke: Freeman and Co.

7

Studies in cognitive psychology

What should I know?

- The procedure used by Loftus and Palmer (1974).
- The findings and conclusions of Loftus and Palmer (1974).
- A critical evaluation of Loftus and Palmer (1974).
- The procedure used by Gardner and Gardner (1969).
- The findings and conclusions of Gardner and Gardner (1969).
- A critical evaluation of Gardner and Gardner (1969).

In addition I should be able to:

- provide examples of laboratory experiments and laboratory observations
- evaluate laboratory experiments and laboratory observations in terms of their strengths and weaknesses
- understand issues relating to validity and provide examples of controls
- use bar charts and histograms
- use systematic recording in observations.

Introducing research in the cognitive approach

You will recall the details of the cognitive approach from Chapter 4. In essence, it is about the way people (and animals) acquire and use knowledge and the way that they process this information.

The two core studies in this chapter are:

- **Loftus and Palmer (1974) Leading questions**
  Loftus, E. F. and Palmer, J. C. (1974) 'Reconstruction of automobile destruction: an example of the interaction between learning and memory.' *Journal of Verbal Learning and Behavior*, 13: 585–9.

- **Gardner and Gardner (1969) Teaching language to a chimp**

Gardner, B. T. and Gardner, R. A. (1969)
'Teaching sign language to a chimpanzee.'
Science, 165: 664–72.

This first study we will explore in the cognitive approach is one of many that Loftus and her colleagues have conducted on eyewitness testimony, that is, the reliability with which we can report the events that occurred at the scene of a crime. People are notably poor at recalling details such as faces, weapons and speed. The accuracy of eyewitnesses is important because their testimony can be vital to the conclusions of a jury and the outcomes of court cases. This particular study is

Glossary

post-event information: things arising after the encoding of a memory that can affect that memory on retrieval.

repeated reproduction: a technique in which participants recall the same learned material on several occasions separated by time delays. This exposes the effects of internal processes on the accuracy of memory.

schema: an internal framework for information that can affect the way incoming material is interpreted, stored and retrieved, so can introduce errors.

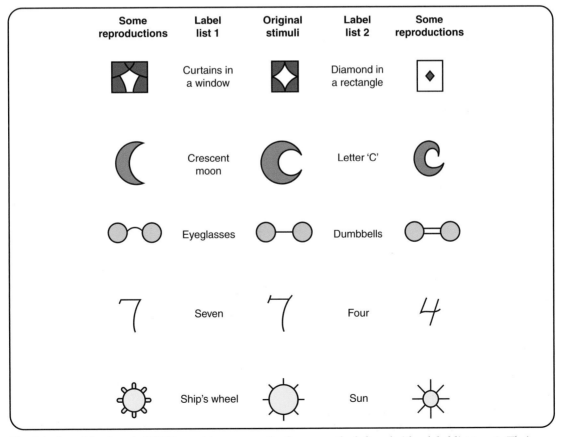

Fig. 7.1 Carmichael et al. (1932) participants saw the figures on the left and either label list 1 or 2. Their reproductions of the figures were affected by the words that they had seen (see figures alongside label lists)

about the way that the memory of an event is influenced by the form of questions that follow the formation of that memory. Prior to this study, research had shown that verbal labels given at the time of encoding (learning) could alter memory. Carmichael *et al.* (1932) found that presenting participants with identical figures but different accompanying words influenced the way that they reproduced the images (see Figure 7.1). This suggested that information is not simply saved and regurgitated, but memory is 'rebuilt' from stored elements as it is retrieved, i.e. that it is *reconstructed*. This reconstruction process can be affected by other sources of information, such as the verbal labels in the study by Carmichael *et al.* Another early approach to research, repeated reproduction, employed by Bartlett (1932), helped to identify other factors that influence the reconstruction of memory. He showed that when participants heard and attempted to reproduce an unfamiliar story, it became shorter, simpler and more coherent. Essentially, the participants were required repeatedly to retell a culturally unfamiliar folk tale called 'The War of the Ghosts'. In the absence of a context in which to understand the story, the participants found this very difficult, hence their errors. Thus it appears that both external information received during or after a memory is formed, and pre-existing knowledge or beliefs, can influence the way a memory is recalled. These factors, respectively, are referred to as 'post-event information' and 'the effects of schema'.

The second study we will be exploring from the cognitive approach is Gardner and Gardner (1969) which records their attempt to teach language to a chimpanzee. It is a study about language acquisition that is trying to find out whether there is something special about the minds of humans that means that we can learn to use language, whereas animals cannot. Early researchers such as Hayes and Hayes (1951) attempted to teach chimpanzees to use spoken English. Their chimpanzee, Vicki, was raised in the human household and was rewarded for noises that sounded like speech. However, after considerable training, she mastered only four words: 'mama', 'papa', 'cup' and 'up'. The inability of chimps such as Vicki and others (e.g. Gua, raised by Kellogg and Kellogg, 1933) can be accounted for by the difference between ape and human vocal tracts. Structural differences between the lips and larynx make it impossible for chimpanzees to make the range of speech sounds available to humans. This is compounded by the context of their spontaneous vocalisations. Chimpanzees tend only to use sound to communicate in situations of danger or excitement. Furthermore, they may be hindered by a reluctance to imitate speech sounds. Although these studies were unsuccessful in their attempts to teach chimpanzees to speak, there was some indication of a capacity for language. Gua, for example, learned to recognise approximately 100 spoken words, suggesting that her limitation was at least in part one of language production.

Following the lack of success in earlier studies, Gardner and Gardner used American Sign Language (ASL) rather than speech. This

web watch

Try reading 'The War of the Ghosts' for yourself. Bartlett's participants read it twice, then recalled immediately, and over time delays extending to several years. The story can be found at: http://cla.calpoly.edu/~dlvalenc/PSY30 7/LINKS/GHPSTWAR.HTM

is more suitable as chimps have a considerable capacity for manual dexterity and for physical imitation. This is a complete language, using a large vocabulary of gestural signs which can be combined to express complex ideas. Thus any limitation in the development of language could be isolated to the chimpanzee's cognitive ability (i.e. its capacity to understand), rather any physical restraints upon reproduction of the elements (i.e. speech sounds or signs).

Loftus and Palmer (1974) Leading questions

What did Loftus and Palmer do in Experiment 1?

This study included two separate but related experiments which aimed to investigate the influence of leading questions (i.e. ones that, in their content or form, suggest what answer should be given). In Experiment 1, 45 students, in groups of various sizes, watched seven film clips of traffic accidents lasting between 5 and 30 seconds. For each group, the order of the film clips differed. Following each film clip, participants were given a questionnaire that first asked them to describe the collision and then had a series of specific questions, including one about the speed of the vehicles involved in the collision (the critical question). The critical question was: 'About how fast were the cars going when they ... each other?' Five different verbs were used ('smashed', 'collided', 'bumped', 'hit' and 'contacted'), each being given to nine participants.

Box 7.1
Procedure summary

Experiment 1
Method: lab experiment.
Design: independent measures.
Independent variable tested: verb used in critical question ('smashed', 'collided', 'bumped', 'hit' or 'contacted').
Dependent variable measured: estimate of speed (in mph).
Participants: 45 students.

Verb	Mean speed estimate (mph)
'smashed'	40.5
'collided'	39.3
'bumped'	38.1
'hit'	34.0
'contacted'	31.8

Table 7.1 Speed estimates from Experiment 1

What did they find?

The results show that questions containing verbs such as 'smashed' that suggest greater speeds and impact of the accident produced significantly higher estimates. Four of the films were staged events, in which the accidents took place at 20, 30 and 40 mph (two clips). These produced average estimates of 37.7, 36.2, 39.7 and 36.1 mph respectively, indicating that people are not very good at judging how fast a vehicle is going. The actual

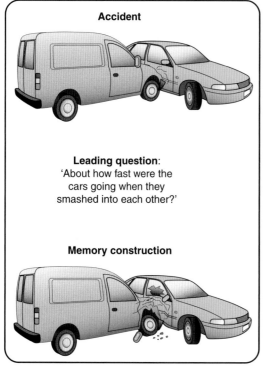

Accident

Leading question:
'About how fast were the
cars going when they
smashed into each other?'

Memory construction

Fig. 7.2 Reconstructive memory

speed of the vehicle in the film contributed little to the overall variance in participants' estimates.

What did they conclude?

The findings suggest that the form of a question, in this case the speed implied by a single verb, can systematically affect the answer a witness gives. There are two possible interpretations of these results. First, an individual who is uncertain about the speed (e.g. cannot decide between 20 or 30 mph) may base their decision on a response bias determined by the verb, so a more 'dangerous' sounding verb, such as 'smashed', would tend to bias them towards the higher guess.

Alternatively, the form of the question may actually alter the representation of the accident in the individual's memory, thus the memory of a participant exposed to the verb 'smashed' would be different, and more 'severe', than one whose question contained the word 'hit'. If this change in memory were the case, participants exposed to the verb 'smashed' would be predicted to falsely recall other details that would be expected in higher-speed accidents. Experiment 2 was designed to test this.

What did they do in Experiment 2?

In Experiment 2, 150 students in groups of various sizes watched a film lasting less than one minute which contained a multiple car accident that was shown for four seconds. After seeing the film, participants were given a questionnaire that first asked them to describe the collision and then had a series of questions. For 50 participants, this included the critical question: 'About how fast were the cars going when they smashed into each other?' For another 50 the question read: 'About how fast were the cars going when they hit each other?' The remaining participants were not asked about the speed of the vehicles. One week later the participants returned and were asked another ten questions about the accident, including the critical question 'Did you see any broken glass?', which they could answer either 'Yes' or 'No'. The position of this question was randomised. There was no broken glass in the film.

Box 7.2
Procedure summary

Experiment 2
Method: lab experiment.
Design: independent measures.
Independent variable tested: verb used in critical question ('smashed' or 'hit') or no question.
Dependent variable measured: reporting of broken glass.
Participants: 150 students.

Response	Verb condition		
	'smashed'	'hit'	control
'Yes'	16	7	6
'No'	34	43	44

Table 7.2 Answers to the question 'Did you see any broken glass?'

Verb condition	Estimated speed (mph)			
	1–5	6–10	11–15	16–20
'smashed'	.09	.27	.41	.62
'hit'	.06	.09	.25	.50

Table 7.3 Probability of replying 'Yes' to the critical question for different estimated speeds

What did they find?

The mean estimate of speed was significantly higher for the group exposed to 'smashed' (10.46 mph) than for those exposed to 'hit' (8 mph). Furthermore, participants were significantly more likely to report having seen broken glass if their question about the vehicle's speed used the word 'smashed' than following the same question using the word 'hit', or if they were not questioned about recalled speed.

Participants varied considerably in their estimates of speed in both verb conditions.

When classified by their speed estimates, it can be seen that participants who estimated higher speeds were more likely to report broken glass than those who estimated lower speeds. However, regardless of speed estimated, those participants exposed to 'smashed' were consistently more likely to report seeing broken glass than those exposed to 'hit'.

What did they conclude?

A leading question that implies more damage (i.e. 'smashed' compared with 'hit') results in both higher estimates of speed immediately afterwards and increased likelihood of reporting non-existent damage (broken glass) a week later. The finding that, regardless of estimated speed, exposure to the verb 'smashed' increased the likelihood of reporting broken glass compared with exposure to 'hit' suggests that the difference in the verbs is doing more than just affecting estimated speed.

One explanation of this effect is that the memory of a complex event is composed of two sources of information. First, information from the individual's perception of the original event (in this case from watching the films) and, subsequently, external information (such as presented by the experimenter in this study). Over time, these two sources of information become integrated and indistinguishable. In this study, the second source supplied the information that the cars smashed into each other, thus making the representation of the accident more severe than it actually was. Once the scene has been labelled as a 'smash', the individual is more likely to think that broken glass was present.

What were the strengths of this study?

As it was a laboratory experiment, it was possible to exert control over the independent variable so that the verb could be systematically varied to imply greater or lesser damage (hence the five verbs). It was also possible to control for potential extraneous variables that could have affected dependent variables, such as time allowed to encode and delay prior to recall. Most importantly, in Experiment 2 it was possible to separate the effect of the verbs used from the variation in participants' speed judgement to be sure that the verb was affecting memory of the accident directly, rather than only via the influence of recall of speed. These controls (and others, including use of standard film clips and questions) ensure that the findings are reliable. Furthermore, the findings of this study are supported by many other experiments into eyewitness testimony which confirm that leading questions distort memory (e.g. Loftus, 1975; Loftus and Zanni, 1975).

In Experiment 1 the order of the film clips was varied and in Experiment 2 the position of the critical question was varied. This randomisation helped to ensure that any differences in the dependent variable (estimated speed or reporting of broken glass) were due to the independent variable and not to order effects. In both experiments, the critical question was embedded within a series. This helped to disguise the aim of the study, so that the participants were less likely to identify this question as important and their responses would be unlikely to be affected by demand characteristics. These aspects of the design are important to the validity of the study. Furthermore, the study attempts to simulate the experiences of an eyewitness to a car crash and, since they could be asked leading questions in court, in this sense it has mundane realism.

What were the weaknesses of this study?

For eyewitnesses viewing a real car accident, there would be much greater motivation to observe and memorise the events than there would be for participants watching a film for a study. This lowers the ecological validity of the experiments, as the findings would be less likely to generalise to actual eyewitness memories.

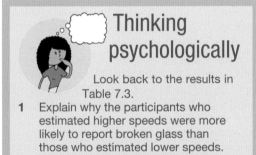

Thinking psychologically

Look back to the results in Table 7.3.
1 Explain why the participants who estimated higher speeds were more likely to report broken glass than those who estimated lower speeds.
2 If there had been little difference between the probabilities for participants exposed to 'smashed' and 'hit', how would the conclusions have differed and why?

Fig. 7.3 Participants forgot this scene if it was omitted from descriptions

Where are we now?

From Loftus and Palmer (1974) and many other of Loftus's studies, it has become clear that post-event information can be added to existing memories. More recent research has investigated whether such information can also be responsible for the loss of information from memory.

Wright, Loftus and Hall (2001) showed participants sequences of drawings of scenes in a restaurant depicting situations such as a guitar player by a table and a waitress taking an order (see Figure 7.3). They asked participants to read descriptions of the sequences from which critical scenes had sometimes been omitted. These descriptions, like the questions asked by Loftus and Palmer (1974), acted as post-event information. When the descriptions omitted critical scenes, participants were *less* likely to recall these events when subsequently tested. This effect can be understood in the context of previous research into the effect of leading questions as the memory is being affected by the integration of new information. In this case, however, this presents a situation in which information is absent and the memory is reconstructed without that original content.

The police have responded to the mass of evidence that shows the importance of leading questions. For example, in the Home Office Select Committee Report on Home Affairs (2001–2) Detective Chief Inspector Gareth Tinnuche states that police officers in South Wales receive training in the use of non-leading questions. However, it is evident that the use of leading questions by the police still occurs, for instance in the specific naming of suspects. (See http://www.publications. parliament.uk/pa/cm200102/cmselect/cmhaff/836/83604.htm#a7 for an example.)

web watch

Go to Elizabeth Loftus's website at: http://www.seweb. uci.edu/faculty/loftus/ There are many other studies on eyewitness testimony. Look at several (the earliest ones are likely to be the easiest) and explain the findings in terms of the way memory of an event is affected by information that follows the event.

Gardner and Gardner (1969) Teaching language to a chimp

What did Gardner and Gardner do?

Washoe, a female chimpanzee aged between 8 and 14 months at the start of the study, was the only participant. Her exact age was unknown as she was caught in the wild. This was essential as laboratory-reared chimps could not be obtained so young and this was important to the study as it aimed to investigate the mechanisms of language learning and genetic basis of these mechanisms, which required intervention beginning as soon as possible after birth. A chimpanzee was chosen as the species is both sociable and intelligent; sociability was essential as it is a key factor in human language learning.

Box 7.3
Procedure summary

Method: single participant experiment.
Variables: exposure to signing (ASL), models for imitation and reinforcement were all controlled. The incidence of new signs (i.e. vocabulary) was recorded, initially in detail and subsequently additional new signs that were used appropriately, spontaneously and on 15 consecutive days.
Participant: one chimpanzee (*Pan troglodytes troglodytes*), aged approx. one year at the start of the study.

A language based on movements rather than sounds was chosen for several reasons:

● Chimpanzee vocal communication is used for different purposes than that of humans.

- Previous studies had demonstrated that chimps could not acquire spoken language (e.g. Hayes and Hayes, 1951).
- Chimps are very dexterous, using their hands to manipulate objects in the wild. Even caged, laboratory animals spontaneously develop gestures such as 'begging' and those with extensive human contact develop a variety of such communicative movements.

Washoe was taught American Sign Language (ASL), a gestural language for the deaf. This is not simply finger-spelling of letters in English words but a language in which words and concepts correspond to precise manual patterns. As human and chimp hands are so similar, it would be possible for Washoe to replicate these easily. ASL signs are arbitrary, although some are more obvious than others. The sign for 'flower', for example, is made by extending the fingers of the signing hand, touching the finger tips together and holding them under each nostril as if sniffing a flower.

A social environment was created for Washoe in which all humans communicated exclusively in ASL, whether interacting with her or each other. This ensured that signing could not be perceived to have a lower social status than talking. Three techniques were used to train Washoe to use gestures:

- **Imitation** – a researcher would show Washoe a gesture and if she imitated it she was rewarded (e.g. with being tickled). Once Washoe had learned some signs, imitation could be initiated by making the sign for 'sign' or asking 'What is this?' in ASL.
- **Babbling** – human babies engage in vocal babbling (the production of random speech sounds) and it was anticipated that Washoe would produce similar manual 'babbling' which could be reinforced with positive feedback such as clapping and imitating, much as adults smile at babbling infants and babble back to them.
- **Operant conditioning** – it was possible to shape arbitrary movements in Washoe's behaviour by reinforcing closer and closer approximations to an actual sign, until Washoe reliably produced a correct sign when appropriate.

Situations such as games and outings were devised to maximise opportunities for signing and introducing new signs. Initially, a complete record of Washoe's signing was kept, but as her vocabulary expanded only new signs were recorded (from the sixteenth month). These were systematically recorded only if the sign:

- was spontaneous (i.e. arose without prompting)
- occurred in an appropriate context
- was recorded by three researchers independently
- was used at least once a day on 15 consecutive days.

As appropriate contexts for signs do not always arise, some additional, consistent signs were recorded, even though they did not fulfil the frequency criterion at 22 months.

What did they find?

Imitation	Washoe's teeth were brushed after every meal and, although she initially resisted this, she did submit. The sign for toothbrush was regularly used but Washoe had not imitated it. On seeing a mug of toothbrushes in a bathroom (at ten months) she signed 'toothbrush' spontaneously, suggesting that she had learned the sign and was using it purely to communicate (as it was unlikely that she was requesting to have her teeth cleaned). This is an example of 'delayed imitation'.
Babbling	Washoe did babble manually, although later than expected. As with human infants, she would sometimes make a gesture that resembled a sign, which was responded to as if it were correct and reproduced in an accurate form in an appropriate context. For example, in an imitation game, Washoe made a gesture like the sign for 'funny'. The sign for 'funny' was repeated by the researchers, accompanied by laughing and smiling. This sign was then used whenever something funny happened and Washoe eventually came to use it in appropriate circumstances. Other signs used by Washoe, such as 'hurry', may have arisen out of her own babbling rather than being imitative.
Operant conditioning	The sign for 'open' starts with the hands side by side, palms down, then 'opened' like a book, to palms up. Washoe's response to a closed door she wanted to get through – pounding with both palms on the door – provided a starting point for shaping this sign. When she placed her hands on the door spontaneously, they were lifted to complete the sign, and it was demonstrated for her to imitate. By prompting in this way, Washoe produced a version of the sign for 'open' and was reinforced by having the door opened. After training with three doors, this sign generalised to all doors and then to other objects that could be opened, such as cupboards, drawers, boxes and jars. Washoe also employed this sign to ask for taps to be turned on. This process, although using a combination of imitation and operant conditioning, also used guidance – training by placing the hands into the desired positions.

Table 7.4 Examples of the success of different language acquisition strategies

- **Vocabulary:** the following signs had met the criteria for acquisition by 22 months (in order of acquisition): 'come–gimme', 'more', 'up', 'sweet', 'open', 'tickle', 'go', 'out', 'hurry', 'hear–listen', 'toothbrush', 'drink', 'hurt', 'sorry', 'funny', 'please', 'food–eat', 'flower', 'cover–blanket', 'dog', 'you', 'napkin–bib', 'in', 'brush', 'hat', 'I–me', 'shoes', 'smell', 'pants', 'clothes', 'cat', 'key', 'baby', 'clean'.
- **Differentiation:** some signs became differentiated, e.g. Washoe used 'more' largely to mean 'do it again', e.g. for an action she could not name, and 'flower' to mean 'smell' (e.g. in response to the smell of tobacco). For this latter context, Washoe acquired a new sign for smell, although 'flower' was sometimes still used with this meaning.
- **Transfer:** signs such as 'more' and 'open' generalised readily from their original contexts to new ones. 'Flower' was applied not only to different flowers and contexts (e.g. indoors and outdoors) but

also to pictures of flowers, the same sign being used in each instance.

- **Combinations:** although the researchers signed in strings, no effort was initially made to train Washoe to do so: when she did, it was spontaneous (although this may have been inadvertently reinforced by responding more readily). However, as Washoe's vocabulary expanded, she combined signs more often. Some of these could not have been imitative (e.g. 'gimme tickle' before Washoe had ever been asked to tickle anyone else). Several signs were commonly used in combinations ('please', 'come–gimme', 'hurry', 'more', 'go', 'out', 'open' and 'hear–listen'), often as emphasisers (e.g. in 'please open hurry'), but this was not always the case (e.g. 'open key' to a locked door or 'eat listen' to the sound of a meal bell).

web watch

Explore the website of the Chimpanzee and Human Communication Institute:
http://www.cwu.edu/~cwuchci/index.html

This includes three 'chimpcams' and a link to the 'Friends of Washoe' site which provides a history of her life and that of other chimps in language projects with video clips of each chimp. Look at the biography of Loulis. In what key way was Loulis's acquisition of language different from Washoe's?

What did they conclude?

The findings suggest that sign language was a good choice for achieving two-way communication between humans and a chimpanzee. Washoe's expanding vocabulary, including nouns and verbs, her spontaneous transfer of meanings and rudimentary combinations of signs all suggest that she was intellectually capable of acquiring signs and using them to communicate.

What were the strengths of this study?

Washoe was provided with an appropriate language-learning environment in many ways. The use of different techniques for enhancing Washoe's learning of new words allowed for rapid acquisition of a wide vocabulary. The choice of ASL over a spoken language ensured that language acquisition was not limited by physical factors, such as the possible range of vocalisations: Washoe was readily able to make appropriate physical gestures and to detect differences in the gestures of others. Like a child learning language, Washoe was immersed in a language environment (in this case a signing one). This ensured that any important social cues and sources of motivation were present. This meant that Washoe was likely to exhibit any language she had learned as it was both familiar and would result in valued social rewards (such as tickling) as well as primary reinforcers (such as food). In addition to acquiring meanings, the use of language should result in the generation of novel utterances, i.e. it should be more than just reproduction. In the case of combinations such as 'gimme tickle', Gardner and Gardner suggest that this was the case for Washoe.

Fig. 7.4 Washoe with the researcher Roger Fouts

What were the weaknesses of this study?

Although Washoe developed a large vocabulary, this does not necessarily indicate the acquisition of language. Language use requires more than just the understanding of symbols, it also relies on syntax, i.e. a system of rules that determines the meaning of strings of symbols in relation to one another (e.g. by use of word order or word endings). Although Washoe did use combinations of words, there is little to suggest that in this usage any more meaning was added to multiple word utterances than that of the individual words themselves. For example,

would she have differentiated between 'Washoe tickle' and 'tickle Washoe'? Furthermore, although Gardner and Gardner reported novel combinations of words used by Washoe, there had been no systematic testing of Washoe's understanding of word combinations or word order at this stage.

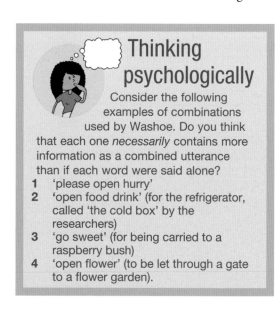

Thinking psychologically

Consider the following examples of combinations used by Washoe. Do you think that each one *necessarily* contains more information as a combined utterance than if each word were said alone?

1 'please open hurry'
2 'open food drink' (for the refrigerator, called 'the cold box' by the researchers)
3 'go sweet' (for being carried to a raspberry bush)
4 'open flower' (to be let through a gate to a flower garden).

Glossary

syntax: a system of rules in a language, e.g. that governs how words are combined to achieve different meanings.

Where are we now?

Further work on language has been conducted on many animals, including Kanzi, a Bonobo (pygmy chimpanzee). Kanzi uses a lexigram, a board with visual symbols representing words and concepts. He uses this extensively to communicate with humans and can ask and answer questions using it. For example, he can correctly respond to instructions such as:

● 'Put the pine needles on the ball.'
● 'Put the ball on the pine needles.'
● 'Get the ball that's in the group room' (when there was a ball next to him).
● 'Take the television outside.'

These findings begin to overcome the criticism of the Washoe project that chimps' use of word combinations is too simplistic to be called language. Tasks such as those given to Kanzi demand an understanding of the importance of word order in utterances. This is an important criterion in differentiating between mere replication of utterances, combined with trial-and-error learning, and a level of genuine linguistic competence.

web watch

You can find out more about Kanzi from:

● http://www.greatape trust.org/media/ video–research– savagerumbaugh.php – part of the website of the Great Ape Trust, Iowa (with several video clips of Kanzi).

● http://www.npr.org/templates/ story/story.php?storyId=5503685 – a radio programme with an accompanying funny video of Kanzi at a cook-out (under 'interactive' *social connection*).

● http://pubpages.unh.edu/~jel/ SGMonKanzi.html – a Kanzi article.

Summing it up

Loftus and Palmer (1974)

- There were two lab experiments with independent groups designs.
- The first compared the effects of five verbs (that sounded progressively more dangerous) in a question about car accidents that had been seen on film.
- This found that more 'severe' verbs resulted in a higher estimate of vehicular speed.
- The second tested whether people who had been asked about the speed of cars that 'smashed into' or 'hit' each other were more likely to report having seen broken glass.
- The 'smashed' group answered 'yes' more often to the question about broken glass, regardless of the speed that they had estimated the vehicles were travelling at.
- Information from the film and the subsequent questions seems to be integrated to form a single memory of the event, i.e. recall is distorted by post-event information.
- The experimental design allowed for control of extraneous variables, e.g. the reduction of the possibility of demand characteristics by embedding the key questions among others and controlling for individual differences in speed estimations.
- Although car-crash scenarios are realistic situations for individuals to witness, these would be in real life, not on film, therefore the experimental situation may not have produced realistic emotions or motivation to recall accurately.

Gardner and Gardner (1969)

- A single-participant experiment on a young, female chimpanzee who was immersed in a sign-language environment and actively taught ASL.
- Signing was encouraged by responding to manual babbling, offering opportunities for imitation, guiding imitation and reinforcement of gestures, including shaping.
- Suitable contexts to increase signing were provided, e.g. games and trips outside.
- Records of signs were at first detailed, then restricted to new acquisitions (i.e. signs that were spontaneous, made in an appropriate context, seen separately by three researchers and occurred at least once a day on 15 consecutive days).
- Responding to babbling, imitation and reinforcement were effective.
- Washoe's vocabulary comprised 34 words by 22 months, including nouns, verbs and emphasisers (e.g. 'flower', 'open', 'more').
- Washoe could differentiate between the use of signs for different contexts, e.g. between 'flower' (the source of a smell) and 'smell', which had similar signs.
- Many signs transferred their meaning successfully from their original context to new ones, e.g. using the same sign for 'flower' for different flowers, in different locations and for illustrations.
- Combinations of signs were produced, e.g. 'open key' in response to a locked door.
- The choice of signing over verbal speech ensured that Washoe was able to demonstrate that she could readily acquire symbolic meanings, an essential component of language.
- The extent to which Washoe generated novel utterances and combinations was uncertain.

What have I learned?

1 In Loftus and Palmer's first experiment, what were the IV and DV and how were they operationalised?

2 a Which measure of central tendency was used by Loftus and Palmer?

b Why was this the most appropriate choice?

3 a Plot a bar chart of the results in Table 7.1.

b Why is a bar chart the correct choice here?

4 a Plot a histogram for the results in Table 7.3 relating to the question, including the word 'smashed'.

b Why is a histogram more appropriate than a bar chart for this data?

5 How could Loftus and Palmer's study be criticised in terms of validity?

6 Gardner and Gardner avoided using speech as they '... reasoned that this would make it seem that big chimps talk and only little chimps sign, which might give signing an undesirable social status'. Why was this aspect of control important to the success of the study?

7 The sign for 'more' (fingertips together) was achieved through Washoe's tendency, when being tickled, to bring her hands together over the place she wanted to be tickled if the tickling stopped. By waiting until her hands were together to resume tickling, the researchers began to reward the use of the sign for 'more'. This version of the sign became reliable but was specific to requesting more tickles. Prompting Washoe by making the sign themselves, the researchers encouraged her to use this sign in other play contexts such as more 'pushing along the floor in a laundry basket' and more 'swinging by the arms'. Finally it transferred to wider contexts and was used spontaneously. Identify examples of the use of positive reinforcement, imitation and shaping in this example of the acquisition of a sign.

8 How did the process of guidance used by the Gardners differ from simple operant conditioning and imitation?

9 Washoe used the sign for 'dog' not only to photographs but also to the sound of a barking dog she could not see. Is this an example of differentiation or transfer?

10 What were the findings and conclusion of Gardner and Gardner?

11 What were the strengths of Gardner and Gardner's research?

Reading around

■ Aitchison, J. (1983) *The Articulate Mammal*. London: Hutchinson.

■ Bartlett, F. C. (1935) *Remembering*. Cambridge: Cambridge University Press.

■ Chomsky, N. (1957) *Syntactic Structures*. The Hague: Mouton.

■ Fouts, R. (1994) *Next of Kin*. New York: Morrow and Co.

■ Savage-Rumbaugh, S. and Lewin, R. (1994) *Kanzi: The Ape at the Brink of the Human Mind*. London: Doubleday.

■ Terrace, H. S. (1985) *Nim*. New York: Knopf.

What should I know?

- The procedure used by Bowlby (1944).
- The findings and conclusions of Bowlby (1944).
- A critical evaluation of Bowlby (1944).
- The procedure used by Gibson and Walk (1960).
- The findings and conclusions of Gibson and Walk (1960).
- A critical evaluation of Gibson and Walk (1960).

In addition I should be able to:

- identify strengths and weaknesses of laboratory experiments and interview procedures
- comment on the importance of sample size and sampling procedure
- interpret line graphs and frequency distributions
- assess ethical issues in psychological research
- understand issues of ecological validity in laboratory research.

Introducing research in the developmental approach

Developmental psychology is concerned with how we develop as we grow and age. Clearly, childhood is a period of intense growth and development; so much of the work of developmental psychologists has focused on childhood. A minority of developmental psychologists study adult development and older age. Psychologists study child development using a range of research methods. One approach is to use laboratory experiments. These involve testing children's abilities and behaviours under controlled conditions. Another approach is to interview children and adults about their childhood. The two core studies in this chapter use an interview and a laboratory method respectively. They are:

- **Bowlby (1944)**
  Bowlby, J. (1944) 'Forty-four juvenile thieves: their characters and home life.' *International Journal of Psychoanalysis,* 25: 19–52.

- **Gibson and Walk (1960)**
  Gibson, E. J. and Walk, R. D. (1960) 'The visual cliff.' *Scientific American,* 202: 67–71.

John Bowlby was a child psychiatrist and psychoanalyst who, in the 1930s and 1940s, worked at a London Child Guidance Clinic. He is largely responsible for the view (which we now largely take as common sense) that a child's relationship with their primary carer is extremely important in affecting their later development. Bowlby's interest in this area developed when, as a medical student, he volunteered at a residential children's home. Here he encountered children with disrupted relationships with their parents who displayed a range of abnormal behaviour. Bowlby became convinced that disruption to a child's first relationship (most commonly with the mother) was a major cause of psychological problems.

One of the issues Bowlby worked with at the Child Guidance Clinic was juvenile delinquency (i.e. criminal behaviour in young people). Bowlby was concerned that the modal age for appearing in court for theft was 13 years, suggesting that theft was a childhood condition. Bowlby compared theft to rheumatic fever, a condition that first appears in childhood or adolescence and recurs in adulthood. Bowlby's observations suggested that disruption to early relationships might be a factor in criminality. The 'Forty-four thieves' study was his first attempt to gather scientific data to investigate this link.

Our other core study is concerned with a very different aspect of developmental psychology, namely perceptual development. Psychologists have long been interested in the extent to which we acquire our visual ability through experience and the extent to which we are born able to perceive the world. The latter is called the 'nativist view' (not to be confused with naturist, which involves not wearing clothes). Eleanor Gibson and Richard Walk were particularly interested in whether depth and distance perception had to be learned. Early studies had involved rearing animals in the dark and seeing whether their lack of visual experience affected their ability to perceive distance normally. Lashley and Russell (1934) had reared rats in the dark and found that they could still jump the correct distance on to a platform. However, Gibson and Walk were unimpressed by this sort of test. Because the rats had to be trained to jump they could simply have learned to judge the distance correctly in the course of this training. Instead, Gibson and Walk (1960) developed a visual cliff technique.

The visual cliff has a glass top under which a real drop can be set up, clearly signalled by a pattern such as a check (as in Figure 8.1 on page 130). There is thus apparently a deep and a shallow side to the cliff. The glass top not only keeps the participant safe but also means that any clues to depth are visual and not available via the other senses. The visual cliff can be used to test depth perception in human infants as well as animals. The study reported here used both.

Bowlby (1944) Forty-four juvenile thieves

What did Bowlby do?

Between 1936 and 1939, 44 consecutive cases of children referred for theft were analysed. There was no systematic sampling procedure. All the suitable cases that came to the clinic within the period of the study were included in the study. They were compared with 44 cases who were also referred to the Child Guidance Clinic but who did not steal. The latter group was thus a **control group**. This allowed Bowlby to compare directly the characteristics of the children who stole with those who did not. The two groups were roughly matched for age and score on IQ tests. Half the children in each group were aged 5–11; the others were aged 12–16. Of the 'theft' group, 24 were referred by their school, eight by parents, three by the court and nine by the Probation Service. The sample was representative of cases seen by the Child Guidance Clinic, though not of those seen by the courts. Eleven of Bowlby's thieves were too young to be charged and most had long histories of theft.

On arrival at the clinic, each child had their IQ tested by a psychologist while at the same time a social worker interviewed a parent to record details of the child's early life. The psychologist and social worker made separate reports. A psychiatrist then conducted an initial interview with the child and the accompanying parent. The three professionals then met to compare impressions and read reports from school, courts, etc. The psychiatrist conducted a series of further interviews with the child and/or parent over the next few months in order to gather more in-depth information about the history and psychological characteristics of the child. Based on these sources of information each child was classified into one of six types:

- normal: no abnormal symptoms
- depressed: showing symptoms of depression
- circular: alternating symptoms of depression and over-activity
- hyperthymic: showing symptoms of over-activity
- affectionless: having no affection for others and no shame or sense of responsibility
- schizoid: withdrawn and lacking relationships with others.

What did he find?

Only two of the 44 thieves were classified as 'normal'. The classification of all 44 is shown in Table 8.1 overleaf.

Box 8.1
Procedure summary

Method: interview + psychometric testing.
Design: quasi experiment.
IV tested: juvenile theft.
DVs measured: psychiatric diagnosis, early separation.
Participants: 44 juvenile thieves and 44 matched controls.

Normal	2
Depressed	9
Circular	2
Hyperthymic	13
Affectionless	14
Schizoid	4

Table 8.1 Classification of the 44 thieves

Seventeen of the 44 thieves had suffered a prolonged or permanent separation from their primary carer in their first five years. Of these, 12 were classified as affectionless. Only two of the 14 affectionless children in the theft group had no such separation. There was thus a strong relationship between developing the affectionless character and having a prolonged or permanent early separation from the primary carer. Only two of the non-criminal control group had had a prolonged separation in their first five years. There was thus a strong relationship between theft and early separation experiences. These relationships are shown in Table 8.2.

What did he conclude?

The results supported Bowlby's belief that early relationship experiences are crucial to the developing child and that disruption to the relationship between a child and its primary carer can have serious psychological consequences. More specifically, Bowlby concluded that early prolonged or permanent separation from the primary carer dramatically increased the probability of involvement in theft. Such separation was especially strongly linked to the affectionless character.

What were the strengths of this study?

The study took place at a Child Guidance Clinic and worked directly with children and their families. There was thus nothing artificial about the environment or the tasks required of participants. Data was gathered in a number of ways from children and families, using a range of specialists. A large volume of information was gathered in each instance, including in some cases months of regular interviews. Bowlby was thus extremely thorough. His

	Number in theft group	Number in control group
Affectionless character	14	0
Prolonged early separation	17	2
Affectionless character and prolonged early separation	12	0

Table 8.2 Relationships between separation, affectionless character and theft

sample was representative of the cases seen by Child Guidance Clinics, and he used a control group who were well matched to the thief group in that they were of similar age and also attended the clinic. The study was also extremely relevant to real life, and remains so today. If criminality can be affected by early experiences then it is important that we understand these effects. Although modern research only partially supports the findings of this study, the relationship between early experience, family relationships and criminality is still an important area of current study.

What were the weaknesses of this study?

By modern standards this study suffers from a number of methodological problems. The sample of 44 was quite small, especially considering that it was divided into six groups. The sample was gathered by opportunity – consisting of the children who happened to be referred to the clinic where Bowlby worked. More could have been done to ensure that they were representative of juvenile thieves in general: for example, including some first-time offenders. There were also problems with Bowlby's assessment procedures. The labels he put on the children (circular, affectionless, etc.) were not all standard psychiatric diagnoses, and the study was conducted before standard interviews existed to ensure that different psychiatrists would reach the same diagnosis for the same patient. Most importantly, Bowlby himself was the assessing psychiatrist and he knew the aim of the study. When he was classifying each child he knew whether they were in the thief or control group. He may thus have unconsciously been biased in his judgement. It is now standard procedure to use a **double-blind** method in which the interviewer does not know the aim of the study. This helps to avoid bias.

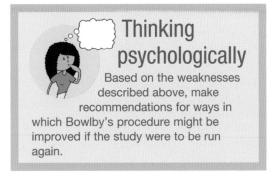

Thinking psychologically

Based on the weaknesses described above, make recommendations for ways in which Bowlby's procedure might be improved if the study were to be run again.

Glossary

double-blind: a procedure to avoid bias. Neither the participant nor the researcher who speaks to them knows the purpose of the assessment.
deprivation: experience of separation of a young child from its primary carer.
privation: the prevention of the formation of an attachment between infant and primary carer.

Where are we now?

The 'Forty-four thieves' study was conducted early on in the development of Bowlby's ideas. His early concept of **maternal deprivation**, the idea that separation from the primary carer has serious consequences for development, was later revealed to be rather too simple. Most psychologists would now make a distinction between deprivation and **privation**. Privation occurs when no attachment is formed between infant and primary carer. Deprivation takes place when a child is separated from an attachment figure after an attachment has been formed (Rutter, 1981). Modern research suggests that the serious problems Bowlby initially put down to separation are actually associated with privation.

In spite of these theoretical problems, modern research has continued to show a link between early separation, problems with early relationships and criminality. For example, in one recent study Maki et al. (2004) followed up 2,906 people in Finland who had been isolated at birth between 1945 and 1965 to protect them from tuberculosis in the family. On average they were separated for seven months. 12.1 per cent of males and 7.9 per cent of females who had experienced this type of separation had a record of violent offending. This compared with 7.1 per cent of male and 5.1 per cent of female controls. Statistically, the association here between criminality and early separation is rather more modest than that in the 'Forty-four thieves' study. Nonetheless, studies like this do support Bowlby's basic ideas.

Thinking psychologically

In the Maki et al. study infants were separated from their primary carer at the moment of birth and kept apart from them for an average of seven months. Is this an example of deprivation or privation? To what extent do these findings support maternal deprivation hypothesis?

Bowlby moved on from his early ideas about maternal deprivation to develop **attachment theory**. Attachment theory aims to explain how and why attachments develop between an infant and its primary carer, and the consequences of these attachments. Bowlby's colleague, Mary Ainsworth, went on to classify a number of attachment types. Most modern research into infant–primary carer relationships and criminality makes use of these attachment types. One such study comes from Smallbone and Dadds (2004). They assessed attachment to each parent and aggression, antisocial behaviour and sexual coerciveness (likelihood of forcing someone into a sexual act against their will) in 162 male students. Insecure attachment was associated with high levels of aggression, antisocial behaviour and sexual coerciveness. Interestingly, sexual coerciveness was most strongly associated with insecure attachment to the father. This suggests that Bowlby was wrong to place so much emphasis on attachment to the primary carer.

Another contemporary approach to investigating attachment-related problems involves the psychiatric diagnosis of reactive attachment disorder. Attachment disorder has been recognised as a mental disorder since 1980. It is diagnosed when insecure attachment has a severe effect on the functioning of an individual. In one such recent study, Seifert (2003) assessed the relationship between reactive attachment disorder, other psychological problems and violent crime. The records of 479 participants from the mental health and prison systems were analysed. Attachment disorder was found to be associated with criminality in general and in particular with violence.

Glossary

sexual coerciveness: likelihood of pressurising or forcing someone into sexual activity.
reactive attachment disorder: a psychiatric diagnosis made when an insecure attachment leads to abnormal behaviour.

web watch

Try visiting the Stony Brook Attachment Research Centre at http://www.psychology.sunysb.edu/attachment/ You can read various articles in full, including some by John Bowlby.

Box 8.2
Procedure summary

Method: laboratory experiment.
Design: repeated measures.
IV tested: depth cues.
DV measured: direction of crawling.
Participants: 36 babies and a range of infant animals.

Gibson and Walk (1960) The visual cliff

What did Gibson and Walk do?

The study involved 36 human infants aged between 6 and 14 months and their mothers. All the babies were able to crawl. Each child was placed in the centre of the visual cliff on a centreboard (see Figure 8.1). Their mothers then called to them from the cliff side and the shallow side. The aim was to see whether they would be less inclined to crawl across the 'cliff' than the shallow side. If they would not cross the 'cliff' this would suggest that their depth perception was intact as soon as they could crawl. This would in turn suggest that human depth perception is innate, supporting the nativist position.

It takes a few months before humans learn to crawl. It was possible therefore that if the babies tested in this study would not cross the visual cliff it was because they had had time to learn depth perception. To test this possibility, the researchers ran a similar procedure on a range of animal species including rats, chicks, lambs, kids, puppies and kittens. The procedure with the animals simply involved placing the neonate on the centreboard and seeing which way they would move. Particularly of interest were the chicks, kids and lambs because they could stand and so be tested within 24 hours of birth. They would thus have had no opportunity to learn to perceive depth.

A further test was carried out on the kids and lambs. An adjustable cliff was set up so that the apparently shallow surface could be lowered once the animal was on it. The idea was to test how the animal would respond to the visual cues suggesting that the depth of its surroundings was suddenly descending.

An additional condition was set up in which the pattern that displayed the depth cues was replaced by a uniform grey surface. This was to test whether it was the pattern that allowed the participants to perceive distance. If it were indeed the pattern that allowed the depth perception, it would be expected that the participants would no longer show a preference for the shallow side.

Fig. 8.1 This baby placed on the 'deep' surface freezes

What did they find?

Twenty-seven of the 36 human babies crawled off the centreboard. Of these, all 27 crawled on to the 'shallow' side at least once. By contrast, only three crawled on to the 'deep' side. In addition, many of them crawled away from the mother when she called to them from the deep side. Of the lambs, kids and chicks, none ventured on to the 'deep' side; all moved to the shallow side of the centreboard. When placed on the deep side they 'froze'. This is shown in Figure 8.1.

In the condition with the lowered surface, all the animals similarly adopted an immobile defensive posture when the visual surface dropped more than 12 inches from the top glass. The animals did not adapt when this procedure was repeated a number of times, but continued to freeze. Turtles, the species tested with the poorest eyesight, showed the poorest

depth perception as measured by the visual cliff. Seventy-six per cent of them crawled to the shallow side, but a number did crawl on to the 'deep' side. When the pattern was replaced by uniform grey, no animals showed no preference for the deep or shallow side.

What did they conclude?

All the species tested, including humans, showed intact depth perception by the time they could move independently. In some species this was within a few hours after birth. This suggests that their ability to perceive depth was present at birth. The nativist position was thus supported. The fact that in the 'grey condition' no species showed any preference for the shallow side allowed the researchers to conclude also that the innate mechanism for depth perception involved interpreting changes in patterns indicating depth.

What were the strengths of this study?

The major strength of the study was the ingenious design of the visual cliff. This was arguably the first successful procedure to be used for measuring depth perception in infants. The infants' movement was an easily identifiable measure of their perception. As well as allowing depth perception to be tested in relative safety, the design of the visual cliff allowed researchers to eliminate the role of other senses, such as touch. This ensured that what was assessed was *visual* perception. Previous research into depth perception in animals could be criticised on the basis that it was unclear how well the findings could be applied to humans. A strength of the Gibson and Walk study was that they were thorough in testing their procedure on a range of species, including humans. The consistency of findings across a range of species gives their conclusions particular credibility.

What were the weaknesses of this study?

Aspects of the study can be challenged on both methodological and ethical grounds. The sample size of 36 human infants was relatively small. Moreover the age range was rather large (6–14 months) considering that they were meant to be a sample of humans only just capable of crawling. It could even be argued that there was little point in including human babies in the study as humans have ample time to learn depth perception by the time they can crawl. However, the authors are clear that it is the combined findings from humans and other species that justify their conclusions. The validity of the measure of depth perception – the preferred direction participants moved from the centreboard – is open to question. It is hard to surmise from this sort of visible behaviour what is happening in the mind of the participant. Clearly, neither babies nor animals could tell the researchers whether they were motivated to avoid a drop. We should always be a little cautious about making judgements like this.

There are potential ethical problems with the procedure. The sight of the visual cliff may have distressed the babies even though they were in no danger of falling. They were not capable of giving real consent to risking distress, although their mothers did give consent for them. They did not have a right of withdrawal if they suffered distress. It is even conceivable that the babies might have been particularly distressed by their mothers appearing to persuade them to fall off a cliff! Fortunately, however, there is no evidence of this.

Where are we now?

Research continues to show the importance of texture patterning as a source of information about depth. Sinai, Ooi and He (1998) tested adults on their ability to judge distance up to seven metres. They found that when the ground was even, participants could use texture as a cue and judge distance very accurately. However, when other stimuli were put in the way, for example a ditch, the accuracy of their distance estimates declined. This shows the importance of texture patterns as a distance cue. Of course, patterns of texture are not the only cue. For small distances like those simulated in the visual cliff we can use binocular cues (i.e. those requiring both eyes) as well as monocular cues like pattern. Binocular cues include stereopsis, analysis of the differing information entering each eye. Evidence for the importance of binocular cues comes from a study by Backus *et al.* (2001), in which areas of the brain known to be sensitive to differences between two sources of information were seen to be active during depth perception tasks.

Other studies have continued to investigate the question of whether basic perception processes like depth perception are innate or acquired through experience. Tondel and Candy (2007) presented babies aged 2–5 months with the image of a fast-moving clown. Most of the babies were able to track the clown, even when it moved at speeds of 50 cm/second. This suggests that the ability to track moving objects is innate, in line with the nativist position. However, Pei, Pettet and Norcia (2007) have shown, using a range of different textures and patterns, that although human infants can make use of crude patterns like the squares in the visual cliff, they cannot detect more subtle differences in texture like adults can. It thus appears that, while some basic perceptual processes are intact at birth, more advanced visual perception does require experience.

Summing it up

Bowlby (1944) Forty-four juvenile thieves

- Forty-four children aged 5–16 were referred to a Child Guidance Clinic because of stealing.

- These and a matched control group were assessed by a psychiatrist and psychologist and classified according to their psychological symptoms.

- Bowlby was particularly interested in the affectionless category. Affectionless children had no close relationships and their criminality was characterised by lack of conscience.

- A social worker and then a psychiatrist interviewed parents for information about early experiences of separation between the child and their primary carer.

- Seventeen of the thieves and none of the control group were classified as affectionless.

- Twelve of the affectionless children had had prolonged or permanent separation from their primary carer in their first five years.

- Bowlby concluded that early separation can lead to the development of an affectionless character which in turn leads to criminality.

- The study has been criticised on the basis that Bowlby conducted psychiatric interviews himself and may have been biased in his assessments.

- Modern research continues to show relationships between criminality and privation and insecure attachment.

Gibson and Walk (1960) The visual cliff

- A visual cliff was set up. This involved glass covering a surface, the pattern on which displayed depth cues. One half of the surface appeared to have a drop while the other half appeared to be the height of the glass.

- Thirty-six babies aged 6–14 months took part in the study.

- They were placed on a board in the centre of the visual cliff. Their mothers called them over from the deep and shallow sides.

- Twenty-seven crawled on to the 'shallow' side at least once. Only three crawled on to the 'deep' side.

- The procedure was repeated using a range of animal species. In most species all crawled to the 'shallow' side and none to the 'deep' side.

- When the patterned surface was replaced with uniform grey the animals displayed no preference for either side.

- The major advantage of the study was the clever design of the visual cliff.

- The major limitation with any research of this sort is inferring from babies' behaviour what they are thinking or perceiving.

What have I learned?

1   Bowlby's design was a quasi experiment. Explain how a quasi or natural experiment differs from a true experiment.

2   Why were Bowlby's participants not representative of those seen by the courts?

3   How strong is the relationship between prolonged separation and the affectionless character? Explain your answer using the data in Table 8.2.

4   What does current research suggest about Bowlby's ideas?

5   What were the advantages of the visual cliff apparatus?

6   Why was it important for Gibson and Walk to use animals as well as human babies?

7   Why was the condition of the uniform grey surface used?

Reading around

- Eysenck, M. J. and Keane, M. (2006) *Cognitive Psychology: a student handbook.* Hove: Psychology Press.

- Flanagan, C. (1999) *Early Socialisation*. London: Routledge.

- Holmes, J. (1993) *John Bowlby and Attachment Theory*. London: Routledge.

- Jarvis, M. (2001) *Angles on Child Psychology*. Cheltenham: Nelson Thornes.

Studies in the psychology of individual differences

9

What should I know?

- The procedure used by Rosenhan (1973).
- The findings and conclusions of Rosenhan's study.
- An evaluation of Rosenhan's study.
- The procedure used by Buss (1989).
- The findings and conclusions of Buss's study.
- An evaluation of Buss's study.

In addition I should be able to:

- discuss the strengths and weaknesses of field research
- assess the usefulness of cross-cultural research
- understand the importance of sample size and sampling procedures
- use frequency data
- understand issues of validity in psychological research.

Introducing research into individual differences

As the title suggests, the field of individual differences is concerned with how humans differ from one another. The bulk of psychological research is more concerned with what we have in common than how we vary. Research into our physiology, cognition, social behaviour and development has mainly been concerned with establishing broad rules about human psychology, i.e. how we all function. The field of individual differences takes a contrasting approach and looks at how people differ from one another. We differ from one another in numerous ways, as a function of our age, sex and cultural, genetic and family background. Some of the most studied aspects of individual differences include intelligence, personality and mental health. The two studies in this chapter are concerned with mental health and sex differences. They are:

- **Rosenhan (1973)**
  Rosenhan, D. L. (1973) 'On being sane in insane places.' *Science* 179: 250–8.

- **Buss (1989)**
  Buss, D. (1989) 'Sex differences in human mate preferences.' *Behavioural and Brain Sciences,* 12: 1–49.

People have wrestled with the notion of mental illness since long before the birth of psychology. In the Middle Ages, people exhibiting eccentric behaviour or unusual psychological symptoms were liable to be burned as witches. More recently, it has been customary to diagnose 'mental illness' from a patient's symptoms in the same way that physical illness is diagnosed. The term 'mental illness' presupposes that mental disorders are essentially illnesses that have biological causes and which can be diagnosed and treated as such. This is actually an on-going debate, and many psychologists prefer more neutral terms like 'mental disorder' or 'mental health problems'. In 1948, the World Health Organisation published the first comprehensive system for classifying and diagnosing mental illness. This is the ICD (International Classification of the Causes of Disease and Death), now in its tenth edition (early 2007). In 1952, the American Psychiatric Association published its own system, the DSM (Diagnostic and Statistical Manual of Mental Disorder), now in its fourth edition (early 2007).

Although it is standard practice to make a diagnosis using one of these systems, there have always been concerns about their reliability and validity. In the late 1960s and early 1970s a number of researchers questioned the validity of psychiatric diagnosis. Validity is discussed in detail on page 168. Briefly, a procedure or measure is valid if it measures what it sets out to measure. Psychiatric diagnosis is thus valid only if those making the diagnosis correctly identify patients with a mental disorder. One way of studying this is to use 'pseudopatients', who do not really have a mental health problem. Pseudopatients are introduced into the mental health system without the knowledge of the professionals working there. If during diagnosis they are identified as faking their symptoms or simply as having nothing wrong with them, this suggests that diagnosis has good validity. If, however, they receive a diagnosis in spite of having no real condition this suggests that our procedures for diagnosis lack validity. A number of studies have used pseudopatients. The best known of these is the one by David Rosenhan (1973).

A very different issue in the study of individual differences concerns gender differences in mate selection (choosing a sexual partner). As long ago as the 1870s, Charles Darwin suggested that mate selection was a matter of evolution because it determined which members of a species got to reproduce and pass on their characteristics to future generations. More recently, psychologists have developed a whole field of evolutionary psychology. Evolutionary psychologists are interested in how behaviours like mate selection might be affected by instincts designed to maximise the chances of reproducing and passing on our genes. There are now a number of theories in this area.

Trivers (1972) proposes that one factor affecting mate selection is **parental invest-**

ment. In humans, females invest more time and energy in reproduction than men. Men (Child Support Agency notwithstanding) *can* invest as little as a few minutes of casual sex to impregnate a woman, who will then carry the child through pregnancy and typically take the bulk of responsibility for raising that child to adulthood. The fact that women invest so much more in reproduction means that they will tend to be fussier in their mate choice. It also means that women's selection of men should be influenced by their likelihood and ability to contribute to child rearing. Put bluntly, this theory predicts that women will favour ambitious, hard-working and rich men who are most likely to be able to look after them and their children.

Evolutionary psychologists have proposed other factors that affect mate choice. Fertility and reproductive value are two related factors. These primarily affect males' choice of females because for men, access to fertile females is the major factor affecting their chances of reproducing. **Fertility** is the probability of reproduction now. **Reproductive value** is the probability of reproduction in the future. Fertility in women peaks in late teens or early twenties and obviously the younger the woman, the longer she is likely to remain fertile. This whole approach therefore predicts that men will favour younger women. Because facial appearance gives clues to age and therefore to fertility and reproductive value, this approach also predicts that facial attractiveness in women will be very important to men.

A third line of research is based on the idea that we want to be sure that any investment we make in reproduction ensures that we pass on *our* genes to future generations. For women this is easy – unless there is an unfortunate mix-up in the maternity ward

there is little doubt that a woman's child is biologically her own. For men, on the other hand, it is much harder to know that a child is theirs. This line of thinking predicts that men, to a much greater extent than women, will value chastity (lack of sexual activity) in their partner (Dickemann, 1981).

Evolutionary psychologists are often interested in how behaviour varies across cultures. In general the more something holds true across a range of cultures, the more likely it is to be a result of evolution. In a major cross-cultural study, Buss (1989) tested a range of predictions from evolutionary theory about sex differences in mate selection. It was predicted that, regardless of culture, women would tend to prefer men who were ambitious, industrious (hard working) and financially well off. It was also predicted that men would prefer young, attractive and chaste women.

Glossary

fertility: the short-term probability of reproduction.
reproductive value: the long-term probability of reproducing.
chastity: lack of current sexual activity.

Rosenhan (1973) On being sane in insane places

What did Rosenhan do?

Eight pseudopatients took part in the study. Five were men and three were women. Three were psychologists, one a psychology student and one a psychiatrist. The others were not mental health experts; one was a paediatrician (a medical doctor specialising in treating children), another a housewife and the other a painter and decorator. All used false names so that they would not have a diagnosis on their own medical records after the study. The mental health professionals also gave false information about their occupation so that they would not receive any special treatment.

Twelve hospitals were targeted for the study. In one case, where Rosenhan himself was the pseudopatient, his identity and the purpose of the study were known to the hospital authorities. In all other cases the hospitals were entirely unaware of the study. A wide range of hospitals was deliberately chosen; one was private and one attached to a university. The others were all publicly funded. Some were new, others old. Some had much better staff–patient ratios than others.

Each pseudopatient phoned a hospital then attended an appointment where they reported hearing voices. In each case, the voice was the same sex as the pseudopatient and unfamiliar to them. The voices were sometimes unclear but the words 'empty', 'hollow' and 'thud' could be made out. Apart from the voices, they gave accurate descriptions of their mental state. Once admitted to the hospital psychiatric wards, they acted normally with staff and patients. They accepted (but did not take) medication from staff. When asked, they reported no further symptoms. In three hospitals, the pseudo-patients recorded the number of fellow patients who expressed doubts that they were genuine. In four hospitals, they attempted to ask doctors and nurses questions and recorded their responses.

A follow-up to the main study took place at another hospital, whose staff had expressed doubt that they would be fooled by pseudopatients. They were informed that one or more pseudopatients would present themselves over the next three months. Staff rated all new patients on a 1–10 scale for how likely each new admission was to be a pseudopatient. In fact, no pseudopatients approached them in this time; the idea was to record how many real patients were falsely judged to be pseudopatients.

Box 9.1
Procedure summary

Method: field study.
Design: pre-experimental.
IV tested: false symptoms.
DVs measured: admission to hospital, diagnosis.
Participants: eight pseudopatients and the staff and patients of 12 hospitals.

What did he find?

Quantitative and qualitative data was gathered. In 100 per cent of cases, the pseudopatient was immediately admitted to hospital. The length of stay ranged from 7–52 days (average 19 days). Eleven patients were diagnosed with schizophrenia and one with manic depression. While in hospital, no doctors or nurses questioned the genuineness of the pseudopatients. However, of the 118 patients in the three hospitals where patient responses were recorded, 35 (30 per cent) challenged the pseudopatients. In the four hospitals where staff responses to questions were recorded, in no case did they make an effort to answer the questions. Their responses are shown in Table 9.1.

Responses (per cent)	Psychiatrists	Nurses and attendants
Moves on, head averted	71	88
Makes eye contact	23	10
Pauses and chats	2	2
Stops and talks	4	0.5

Table 9.1 Staff responses to pseudopatient questions

Qualitative data was available in the form of notes taken by the pseudopatients and hospital staff. These illustrate how staff interpreted the behaviour of the pseudopatients in line with their beliefs that they were mentally disordered. One nurse recorded daily that her pseudopatient 'engaged in writing behaviour', seeing this as a compulsive behaviour (in fact the pseudopatient was keeping notes). Another interpreted the bored pacing of a pseudopatient as nervousness. One patient mentioned how in childhood he was closer to his mother but more recently had got on better with his father. In his notes this was presented as follows: '... manifests a long history of considerable ambivalence in close relationships, which begins in early childhood. A warm relationship with his mother cools in adolescence. A distant relationship with his father is described as becoming very intense.' This makes the normal ups and downs of family life sound dysfunctional.

Glossary

pseudopatient: a participant who fakes symptoms in order to enter the mental health system as a patient.
ambivalence: mixed feelings.

Further data came from the follow-up study. Over the three months of the study, 193 genuine patients and no pseudopatients were admitted. Forty-one were judged with a high level of confidence to be a pseudopatient by at least one member of staff. In 23 cases at least one psychiatrist, and in 19 cases a psychiatrist and another staff member, believed they were dealing with a pseudopatient.

What did he conclude?

The major conclusion of the study was that even experienced mental health professionals couldn't reliably distinguish between real and false patients. Faking a single symptom on a single occasion was sufficient to receive a psychiatric diagnosis. Furthermore, once in the mental health system, patients' normal behaviour was interpreted as symptoms of their disorder. This indicates that the validity of psychiatric diagnosis was poor. It is important to remember that Rosenhan did not use his data to criticise the competence or conduct of doctors or nurses. Instead he blamed the poor results on the 'system' of diagnosis.

web watch

You can read Rosenhan's paper in full at the following: http://www.walnet.org/llf/ROSENHAN-BEINGSANE.PDF

What were the strengths of this study?

This was a field study, carried out in 12 real hospitals. The doctors and nurses involved were not aware that they were taking part in a study (at least until the follow-up stage). These factors are important because they ensured that all doctors, nurses and patients behaved naturally. Although the study involved only eight pseudopatients and twelve hospitals, care was taken to ensure that the hospitals chosen were representative of the range available to the public. A good range of data was gathered, both quantitative and qualitative. From the quantitative data we get the headline figures – how many patients were admitted, how many pseudopatients were falsely identified, etc. From the qualitative data we get further useful information about the kind of things doctors and nurses said to and about the pseudopatients. Most importantly, this study was highly relevant to real life. It brought the important

issue of the validity of psychiatric diagnosis to public attention and led to major improvements in diagnostic procedures. If the study were repeated now, it is very unlikely that similar results would be found.

What were the weaknesses of this study?

In spite of its clear importance this is a controversial study. It raises both ethical and methodological issues. The ethical issues centre around consent and deception. The doctors, nurses and patients in the hospitals did not give consent to take part in a psychological study. In addition the pseudopatients set out deliberately to deceive them. There was a risk of stress to everyone involved, including the pseudopatients. A further problem is the effect the study had on public confidence in the mental health system. Obviously, on one hand the study flagged up weaknesses in the system of diagnosis used at the time. On the other hand, the publicity generated by the study may have done more harm than good if it discouraged people who were concerned about their mental health from seeking help. This is particularly true now, when diagnostic procedures have improved out of all recognition, but the study is still taught to thousands of psychology and sociology students. There is a risk of continuing to bring psychiatry into disrepute without just cause.

There are also important methodological questions about this study. Clearly, the study showed that it is possible to fool the system (at least as it was 30 years ago). However, does this really mean that the system does not work under normal circumstances? The study lacks mundane realism (see page 169 for a discussion) because the task of identifying fake patients is entirely different to the task of assessing real patients. There is also something of a gap between the data gathered, which actually paints quite a mixed picture of diagnosis, and the entirely negative conclusions reached by Rosenhan. For example, the fact that in 11 of 12 cases the same diagnosis was reached is a positive finding. It at least shows very good **reliability** (i.e. consistency) in psychiatric diagnosis. In addition it was noticed in every case (admittedly after varying time lags) that the patient no longer had symptoms and they were thus released from hospital.

Where are we now?

There have been important changes to systems of psychiatric diagnosis since Rosenhan's study. At the time, the standard system was the second edition of the DSM (DSM-II). We are now (early 2007) on the fourth edition with revisions (DSM-IV-TR). One of the major reasons for continuing to work on newer versions of systems like this is to improve the validity of diagnosis. One way that newer versions have tightened up on diagnosis is in specifying that symptoms must occur with particular frequency or over a particular period. For example, in the DSM-IV system, hearing voices must take place for over a month before they could be used as a basis for diagnosing schizophrenia.

This is not to say however that the issues surrounding the validity of psychiatric diagnosis and classification are all settled. In a more recent attempt to fool the system in 1999, novelist Ian McEwan submitted a false case study based on one of his novels to the *British Journal of Psychiatry*. This described a case of the fictitious De Clerambault's Syndrome, which involves sexual stalking and is named after the French psychiatrist who first identified it. The case report was never published, suggesting that the psychiatric establishment has become wiser since Rosenhan's day!

An alternative way to assess the validity of psychiatric diagnosis is to assess patients using different systems like DSM and ICD and see whether the two systems lead to the same diagnosis. This is an example of concurrent validity, which is discussed in detail on page 170. In a study of concurrent validity of diagnosis Andrews *et al.* (1999) assessed 1,500 people using DSM-IV and ICD-10. Overall, the agreement between the systems was 68 per cent. Very good agreement between the systems was found for the diagnosis of depression, substance dependence and generalised anxiety. However, there was agreement only 35 per cent of the time on post-traumatic stress, with ICD-10 identifying twice as many cases as DSM-IV. Generally, people were more likely to receive a diagnosis according to ICD-10 than according to DSM-IV. This study shows moderately good validity for psychiatric diagnosis.

Box 9.2
Procedure summary

Method: survey.
Design: cross-cultural comparison.
IV tested: sex.
DV measured: factors affecting mate preference.
Participants: 4,601 males and 5,446 females from 33 countries.

Buss (1989) Sex differences in human mate preferences

What did Buss do?

Thirty-seven samples were obtained from 32 countries covering six continents. Countries with separate populations such as Israel, Canada and South Africa that have more than one population had separate samples taken from each group. For example, separate samples of English- and French-speaking

Country	Sample size
Nigeria	172
South Africa	228
Zambia	119
China	500
Indonesia	143
Iran	55
Israel	582
Japan	259
Taiwan	566
Bulgaria	269
Estonia	303
Poland	240
Yugoslavia	140
Belgium	145
France	191
Finland	204
Germany	1083
Great Britain	130
Greece	132
Ireland	122
Italy	101
Netherlands	417
Norway	134
Spain	124
Sweden	172
Canada	206
USA	1670
Australia	280
New Zealand	151
Brazil	630
Colombia	139
Venezuela	193

Table 9.2 Sample size from each country

Canadians were taken. The total number of participants was 10,047. Of these, 4,601 were male and 5,446 were female. Their average age was 23.05 years. Sample sizes for each country are shown in Table 9.2.

Sampling methods varied from one country to another, but were generally either opportunity or self-selecting in nature. The New Zealand sample consisted of secondary-age school children. The Estonian participants were those applying for marriage licences in particular districts. A number of countries used university students. The German participants responded to newspaper adverts.

Two questionnaires were administered to all participants in their native language. The first measured the importance of factors affecting mate choice. Eighteen characteristics were assessed for importance. Some were irrelevant to the study, for example sociability. Others were the target variables of age, good looks, good financial prospects, chastity, ambition, industriousness and no previous sexual experience. Participants rated the importance of each factor on a 0–3 scale where 0 was irrelevant and 3 was indispensable. The second questionnaire asked participants to rank 13 factors affecting mate choice in order of importance. Within the 13 factors were 'good earning capacity' and 'physical attractiveness'.

Remember that evolutionary theory predicts that women will tend to prefer men who are ambitious, industrious and financially well off. It also predicts that men will tend to prefer young, attractive and chaste women.

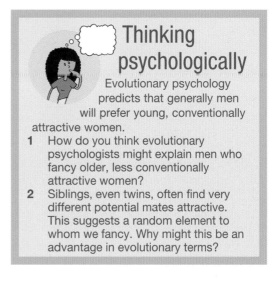

Thinking psychologically

Evolutionary psychology predicts that generally men will prefer young, conventionally attractive women.

1   How do you think evolutionary psychologists might explain men who fancy older, less conventionally attractive women?
2   Siblings, even twins, often find very different potential mates attractive. This suggests a random element to whom we fancy. Why might this be an advantage in evolutionary terms?

What did he find?

Broadly, the results were in line with evolutionary theory, although there were some cultural differences in mate selection priorities. In 36 out of 37 cultures, women placed significantly more importance on good financial prospects in a mate than men. The exception was Spain, where women placed only fractionally more importance than men on finance. In 34 of the 37 cultures, women placed more emphasis on ambition and industriousness than men, although the difference was great enough to be statistically significant in only 29 of the cultures. In three samples, Spanish, Colombian and Zulu South African, the position was reversed. Men rated ambition and industriousness in women as more important than women did in men. In all 37 cultures, the average age of men's ideal woman was significantly younger than their own age and that of women's ideal man. Similarly, in all 37 samples women's ideal man was older than themselves. The average age difference between the ideal man and the ideal woman was four years. This is shown in Table 9.3.

Men's ideal woman	24.83
Women's ideal man	28.81

Table 9.3 Ideal mate age

In all 37 cultures, men rated good looks as more important than did women. In 34 of the cultures, this difference was great enough to be statistically significant. Chastity and lack of previous sexual experience was the factor that varied most across cultures. Out of the Western European countries, only Ireland placed much emphasis on chastity. In only 23 of the 37 cultures was there a gender difference in the importance placed on chastity in a potential mate. However, the findings were still broadly in the direction predicted by evolutionary theory; overall, men placed more importance than women on chastity. In no culture did women place significantly more emphasis on chastity in a partner than men.

What did he conclude?

Buss concluded that there was support for all the predictions from evolutionary theory tested in the study. Across the 37 cultures tested, a strong trend emerged for men to choose mates based on age and attractiveness – and to a lesser extent chastity. Women, on the other hand, placed more emphasis on ambition, industriousness and earning capacity. These findings suggest that parental investment, reproductive value and paternal probability do play a role in mate selection in humans.

What were the strengths of this study?

This was the first study of its kind. This is sometimes called a **seminal study**. Many seminal studies are small in scale, being intended to raise questions and inspire large-scale research rather than to really answer research questions. If you have conducted any research of your own yet, the chances are you have worked with a dozen or two participants and perhaps not even left your school or college to find them. This certainly cannot be said of Buss! The scale of his study is very impressive, with over 10,000 participants taking part and 33 countries being represented. Buss was very thorough in representing every inhabited continent and a wide range of differing cultures.

The use of two separate measures to gather data about factors affecting mate preference is also a strength of the study. Whenever we use a single questionnaire it is hard to know what might affect people's answers. Using two different questionnaires reduced the chances of this. Finally, using a questionnaire method is the most direct way of finding out about mate preferences. Other studies, which use measures such as marriage records, have been criticised on the basis that they really measure mate selection. Local cultural factors such as arranged marriage affect mate selection as well as mate preference. Answers to questions are probably a more valid measure of mate preference.

What were the weaknesses of this study?

Although the scale of Buss's study is impressive, his sampling procedures were much less so, and he admits himself that the samples were not representative of the populations looked at in the study. Opportunity and self-selecting sampling are by definition not methods for obtaining a representative sample of people. The sample size in some countries was also quite small; for example only 28 men and 27 women represented Iran. Although the results were remarkably consistent across cultures, we cannot be entirely sure that they would have been so if more representative samples had been tested.

Glossary

self-selecting sample: a sample of volunteers.
opportunity sample: a sample made up of the most easily available participants.

Thinking psychologically

If you were to run Buss's study again, how could you improve on his sampling procedure?

Where are we now?

Since the time of Buss's study, evolutionary psychology has grown into an exciting and dynamic field of research. Mate preference and mate selection remain important areas of current research. Evidence has continued to mount from a range of sources that mate choice is influenced by instincts to maximise successful reproduction and child rearing. In a fascinating study, Pillsworth, Hasleton and Buss (2004) tested whether sexual desire in general and for long-term partners in particular increases when women are ovulating. A sample consisting of 202 female university students were questioned about how sexy they felt that day, both in relation to their partner and to other attractive men, and where they were in their menstrual cycle. It emerged that sexual desire peaked around ovulation in women with partners but not others. In addition, among the women with partners, women expressed more desire towards their partner relative to other men when ovulating. Moreover, there is evidence

that men rate women as more attractive when they are ovulating (Roberts *et al.*, 2004).

There is also some additional evidence to support the idea that there are universal sex differences in mating preferences. One of the important hypotheses has been that men, with their low parental investment, seek sex with a range of women, while women are choosier, seeking sex with fewer men. In a major cross-cultural study by Schmitt (2003), this was tested in 16,288 people from 53 countries. In every culture there was a significant difference on each of several measures between women's and men's preferences for variety in mates. In every case, men desired a larger number of mates.

Evolutionary psychology faces a number of on-going controversies. Bergstrom and Leslie (2000) challenged much of the existing research into mate preference and selection because studies generally look at men or women or both, in isolation. Asking people about their mate preferences in principle is quite different to assessing how they behave in real situations in which their potential partners are exhibiting attractive or unattractive behaviour. It may thus not be a valid measure of how we select mates. There have also been more serious challenges to the whole principles of evolutionary psychology. In direct opposition to the notion of instinctive sexual behaviour, social constructionists place their emphasis on the role of culture in affecting our social behaviour. The debate over culture versus evolution has been particularly bitter over the issue of rape.

Evolutionary psychologists believe that one of the instincts guiding our behaviour is to reproduce and pass on our genes. Thornhill and Palmer (2000) suggest that rape has evolved as a mechanism for sexually unsuccessful men to pass on their genes. For support, evolutionary psychologists can draw on examples of similar behaviours in other species. A number of species, for example mallards, use forced sex as a reproductive strategy. Rose and Rose (2000) have challenged this perspective, proposing instead that rape is actually a cultural phenomenon. They go on to suggest that the evolutionary perspective contributes to the social acceptability of rape by suggesting that it is inevitable and in some ways beneficial to the species. Instead of instinct, social constructionists emphasise how cultural practices benefit those with social power at the expense of those with less power. As most rape is carried out by men (who generally hold more social power than women) against women, a social constructionist view is that rape is a way for men to uphold their dominant social position over women.

web watch

You can read the Buss paper online at http://homepage.psy. utexas.edu/HomePage/ Group/BussLAB/ publications.htm

Try visiting this page as well for a general user-friendly and well-illustrated introduction to evolutionary psychology. This includes video material and links to more information on some key ideas and authors: http://salmon/psy.plym.ac.uk/year3/PSY339EvolutionaryPsychology/EvolutionaryPsychology.htm

Thinking psychologically

Although there is plenty of evidence for the ideas of evolutionary psychology, many psychologists (and even more sociologists) dislike it. Look at the argument between Thornhill and Palmer and Rose and Rose (above). You may want to do an internet search for the authors and find out more about their views.

1   How strong do you think the evidence is for an evolutionary basis to rape?
2   Is the Rose and Rose objection more about scientific evidence or political correctness?

Summing it up

Rosenhan (1973)

- This was a field study aiming to test how mental health professionals would respond to pseudopatients faking a single symptom on a single occasion.

- Rosenhan and a set of volunteers made hospital appointments. At the appointments they told doctors they heard voices.

- All were admitted to psychiatric wards where they stayed for between seven and 52 days.

- In 11 of 12 cases they were released with a diagnosis of schizophrenia in remission.

- Thirty per cent of fellow patients challenged the genuineness of pseudopatients but no doctors or nurses noticed there was nothing wrong with them.

- Normal behaviour in the pseudopatients was interpreted as symptoms of mental disorder.

- In a follow-up procedure, staff in another hospital rated all new patients for likelihood of being Rosenhan's pseudopatients.

- Forty-one of 193 new patients over the next three months were judged to be pseudopatients. In fact, all were genuine patients.

- The major strengths of the study were its real-life setting and importance to the mental health system.

- The major limitation is that the task of spotting fake patients lacks realism. This is not part of the day-to-day work of mental health professionals.

Buss (1989)

- This was a cross-cultural comparison of factors affecting mate preferences in men and women.

- The aim was to test the predictions of evolutionary psychology that men would prefer young, attractive, chaste women, while women would favour industrious, ambitious, high-earning men.

- A survey method was used, with two separate measures of preferred mate characteristics.

- 10,047 participants from 33 countries and 37 cultural groups were surveyed.

- In 36 of 37 samples, women placed more emphasis than men on financial prospects and in 34 samples they placed more emphasis on industriousness and ambition.

- In all 37 samples men placed more emphasis on attractiveness than women.

- In all 37 samples the ideal age men gave for women was significantly younger than that women specified for men.

- Attitudes to chastity varied widely between cultures.

- The greatest strength of the study was its scale. Over 10,000 people were surveyed.

- Its major limitation was the sampling methods, which varied from one country to another and were generally unrepresentative.

What have I learned?

1 Why was it important for Rosenhan's participants to give false names to the hospitals?

2 Which group of mental health professionals came out worst in terms of responding to patients?

3 Give an example of hospital staff interpreting normal behaviour as abnormal.

4 Give an example of quantitative and of qualitative data gathered in Rosenhan's study.

5 What is the basic idea behind evolutionary psychology?

6 Define parental investment and outline how it can explain human mating behaviour.

7 Why do evolutionary psychologists sometimes conduct cross-cultural studies?

8 Why is evolutionary psychology controversial?

Reading around

■ Buss, D. M. (2003) *The Evolution of Human Desire: strategies of human mating*. New York: Basic Books.

■ Cartwright, J. H. (2001) *Evolutionary Explanations of Human Behaviour*. London: Routledge.

■ Heller, T., Reynolds J., Gomm, R., Muston, R. and Pattison, S. (1995) *Mental Health Matters*. Milton Keynes: Open University.

■ Jarvis, M., Putwain, D. and Dwyer, D. (2002) *Angles on Atypical Psychology*. Cheltenham: Nelson Thornes.

Research methods in psychology

10

The range of research methods

0

-box

What should I know?

- The difference between qualitative and quantitative research methods, including:
  - laboratory experiments
  - field experiments
  - natural (quasi) experiments
  - correlations
  - observations
  - questionnaires
  - interviews.
- The strengths and weaknesses of qualitative and quantitative research methods.

In addition I should be able to:

- recall examples of studies that illustrate each of the research methods above
- understand what type of data is produced by these research methods.

Qualitative and quantitative data

Some investigations produce numerical data: this is called **quantitative data** as it indicates the quantity of a psychological measure (for example, the speed of a reaction time or the rating of a personality factor). These kinds of measures are most often associated with particular research methods, such as experiments and correlations. It is, however, possible to produce quantitative data from observations, questionnaires or interviews, for example by recording the number of times a behaviour is observed or by counting responses to closed questions. In Chapter 12 we look in more detail at the kinds of quantitative data that can be obtained and how they are analysed.

Qualitative data, in contrast, indicates the quality of a psychological characteristic and comes from research that generates in-depth, descriptive findings. This is typical of observations in which particular behaviours are the focus of an observer's detailed account or questionnaires and interviews in which responses to open questions elicit elaborate reporting of feelings, beliefs or opinions. For example, rather than counting the number of aggressive acts a child performs, these may be observed and described in detail.

Box 10.1
Qualitative and quantitative approaches to research

Quantitative approaches aim for objectivity in data collection. The researcher should be independent and unbiased in their observations. These features lead to greater confidence in the findings of the research. Qualitative research, in contrast, is concerned with deriving a fuller understanding of the meaning of the data, especially within its social context. A characteristic of such research is thus that the researcher aims to gain an internal perspective on the data. The researcher, rather than some inanimate tool such as a questionnaire, becomes the primary instrument for data collection. They therefore try to understand the participants' subjective perspective. To this end, participants in qualitative research may sometimes be included within the research team. In quantitative research, on the other hand, efforts are made to reduce the participants' knowledge of the aims of a study and they may even be deceived in order to achieve this.

Experiments

An experiment is a way to carry out an investigation in which one variable is manipulated by the experimenter and the effect of this

change on another variable is observed or measured. In this way the experimenter can see whether the factor they are manipulating *causes* the other variable to change too. If it does, there is said to be a cause and effect relationship between the two variables. The variable causing the change, the one being manipulated by the researcher, is called the **independent variable** (or IV). The variable being measured, that varies as a consequence of the changes in the IV, is called the **dependent variable** (or DV). An experimenter can be sure that it is only the IV that is causing a change in the DV as all other variables are closely controlled.

Glossary

dependent variable: the factor in an experiment that is measured by the researcher. Changes in this factor are predicted to be caused by (i.e. dependent upon) changes in the independent variable.

independent variable: the factor in an experiment that is manipulated, changed or compared by the researcher. It is expected to have an influence upon the dependent variable.

The independent variable of a study will exist in two or more forms, called 'levels' or 'conditions'. A simple example would be the measurement of performance under high- and low-stress conditions. The IV here is the stressor and two levels might be achieved by having a large or small audience present. The DV, of performance, could be measured as speed to perform a task such as assembling a simple jigsaw puzzle. Two more complex examples are from your core studies. In the first experiment in Loftus and Palmer's study (see page 109), there were five levels of the IV

(see page 109)

– five different verbs used in a leading question. The DV in this case was the participant's estimate of speed. Sometimes an experimental condition is compared with one in which the IV is absent; this is called the 'control condition'. In Asch's study (see page 75), accuracy of the participants' judgements was recorded both in the presence of an opposing majority and when the participants were not under pressure from the majority. As the influence of conformity is absent in the latter situation, it is described as a control condition. In this study, the DV was indicated by whether or not the participant denied his senses and raised his hand to agree with the majority judgement about line length or not.

Glossary

control condition: a condition in an experiment is characterised by the absence of the IV. It is used as a baseline to compare with an experimental condition.

experimental design: the way in which participants are allocated to levels of the IV.

practice effect: an improvement in participants' performance that arises because they have experienced an experimental task more than once. They may become more familiar with the task or recall their previous answers.

fatigue effect: a decline in participants' performance that arises because they have experienced an experimental task more than once. They may be bored or tired.

order effects: either practice or fatigue effects. In a repeated measures design they can produce changes in performance between conditions that are not due to the IV, so can obscure the effect of the DV.

If an investigation uses the experimental method, it will also have a **design**. This relates to the way that participants are allocated to different levels of the IV.

There are three different experimental designs:

- **independent groups** – a separate set of participants is used for each level of the IV (i.e. each condition is 'independent'). One problem with this is that any difference between conditions might be due to individual differences between the participants rather than the effect of the IV

- **repeated measures** – the same group of participants is used in every level of the IV (i.e. they 'repeat' the test but under different conditions). The main problem with this design arises because participants experience the experimental task more than once. As a result, their performance may improve (a practice effect) or worsen (a fatigue effect)

- **matched pairs** – pairs of participants are identified who share important characteristics for that particular experiment (e.g. age, gender, first language or dominant hand). One member of each pair is put in a group for each level of the IV. Difficulties with this design centre around problems with matching participants effectively.

The advantages and disadvantages of the different designs are explored in Box 10.2 overleaf.

Glossary

counterbalancing: a way to ensure that participants do not all carry out the different conditions in an experiment in the same order. This overcomes order effects by making sure that the levels of the IV are completed in different orders by different participants in a repeated measures design.

demand characteristics: features of an experimental setting that indicate to participants the aims of the study and so can influence their behaviour.

Box 10.2

The strengths and weaknesses of different experimental designs

Independent groups designs
Strengths:
- It limits demand characteristics as participants are tested only once, so are unlikely to work out the aims of the study.
- As each participant is tested only once, order effects cannot arise, so there is no need for counterbalancing.

Weaknesses:
- If there are important individual differences between participants in each condition, these could obscure the effect of the IV.
- More participants are needed than in a repeated measures design.

Repeated measures designs
Strengths:
- It limits the influence of individual differences, because a direct comparison is made between each participant's performance in different levels of the IV.
- Fewer participants are needed, so, with the same total number of participants, the findings may be more representative than other designs, as more results would be collected in each level of the IV.

Weaknesses:
- If the DV is measured in exactly the same way in each IV level, there is a risk of order effects, as the participant may become fatigued or practised.
- If measures such as the tests used in each condition are not identical, this may cause differences in the DV that are not due to differences between levels of the IV.
- Demand characteristics may have more influence than in an independent groups design, as participants are tested twice so have more chance to work out the aims of the study.

Matched pairs designs
Strengths:
- It controls for the effect of specific individual differences, i.e. the variables on which the participants were matched.
- There is a lower impact of demand characteristics than in independent groups as participants see the experimental setting only once so have less chance to work out the aims.

Weaknesses:
- Participants can only be matched on some variables prior to the study, but there may be others that are more important.
- Matching participants is time-consuming and often imperfect.

Thinking psychologically

1 What was the independent variable in Loftus and Palmer's first experiment?
2 What was the dependent variable in the study conducted by Carmichael *et al.*, described on page 108?
3 What was the control condition in Bowlby's study?
4 Identify the experimental design in each of the following:
   a Experiment 2 in Loftus and Palmer's study.
   b Asch's comparison of different group sizes.
   c A study of reaction to stress of males and females in which different-sex twins are used as participants. The female twin from each pair is in one group, the males in the other.

Reference?

Glossary

validity: whether a study is a true measure of the intended effect. If so, the findings should apply to situations other than that of the research setting itself.
reliability: whether a study produces findings that are consistent. This applies to both items within a set of data (e.g. questions in an interview) and over different occasions or with different researchers.

Laboratory experiments

A laboratory experiment is conducted in an artificial setting, i.e. the participants are in a situation that has been created for the

They will therefore be ... ticipating in a study ... aware of its aims). ... en readily manipu- ... variable to create two or ...ons and can measure the ... variable accurately.

The contrived set-up in a laboratory experiment is important, as it means that the researcher can control any extraneous variables that are thought to be likely to influence the DV. As a consequence, they can be sure that any changes in the DV can have been caused only by the IV. This certainty is important because it means that the **validity** of the study is high. The degree of precision that can be exercised also means that the measurement of the DV is very precise, increasing both validity and **reliability**. This is because any variation in participants' responses would be accurately recorded by changes in the DV, so the same results are likely to be produced if the study were to be repeated. This reliability is also due to having a standardised procedure. In addition, this means that replication is possible. Think about two ways to measure attention in class. You could do it either by timing how long is spent making eye contact with the teacher, or by counting the number of times students daydream. Time spent making eye contact will be very reliable as it can be measured exactly. A count of the number of times each student daydreams, however, depends on the observer's judgement of 'daydreaming' and it could not take into account the length of time they were not paying attention. Eye contact would also be a more valid measure if the students daydreamed for reasons other than a lack of attention.

Glossary

mundane realism: the extent to which an experimental task represents a real-world situation.

Field experiments

Field experiments are conducted in the participants' normal environment for the situation or activity being explored. For example, they might be conducted in the home for babies, in the park for dog-walkers or in court for eyewitnesses. As in a laboratory experiment, the researcher creates or manipulates the levels of the IV and measures the DV.

Participants in a field experiment are in a less artificial setting than those in a laboratory setting, so may be more likely to behave in true-to-life ways. If so, the study would be said to have higher **mundane realism**. The effect of demand characteristics would also be lower as the aims of the study would be less apparent. Furthermore, as participants may be unaware that the experiment is taking place, this is also likely to make their behaviour more realistic. However, not telling the participants about the experiment in advance has advantages and disadvantages in terms of ethics. On one hand, it means that they have not been given the opportunity to give their informed consent to participate (see Chapter 11), but on the other, there is no need to deceive them about the aims.

Natural experiments

It is not always possible for the researcher to actually manipulate the IV – it may not be possible or ethical to do so. This would be so in a study assessing people's stress levels before and after the building of a noisy road, or one comparing levels of aggression in children who have violent or non-violent parental models. In cases such as these, it may still be possible to use an experimental design by finding contrasting situations that already exist and taking measures of the DV in each instance. This is called a natural or 'quasi' experiment.

Of course, it is much more difficult to impose controls in a natural experiment than in either field or laboratory experiments. There is therefore less certainty that any observed changes in the DV have necessarily arisen as a consequence of the IV. However, if the contrasting situations are chosen carefully, there may be very few extraneous variables. For example, Charlton et al. (2000) compared the levels of children's aggression before and after the introduction of transmitted TV. It is highly unlikely that there were other, coincident changes that could have obscured or exaggerated the effect of the IV in this instance (see page 30).

As with field experiments, there are advantages in comparison to contrived situations. Since the difference is naturally occurring, it is less likely that demand characteristics will be apparent (although this will also depend on how obviously the measure of the DV is taken). In addition, the mundane realism of the situation is necessarily high, since the change or difference is a real one. It is likely, therefore, that the test will be a valid one and the findings will be highly representative. However, it is likely to be difficult or impossible to replicate a natural experiment.

Correlations

A correlation is a link between two variables. In a study with a correlational design, a measure is taken of two variables, each of which varies on a scale. The relationship between these two factors can be a:

- **positive correlation** – in which both variables increase together, e.g. hours spent watching TV and frequency of aggressive behaviour
- **negative correlation** – in which one variable increases as the other decreases, e.g. increasing stress and decreasing health.

Of course, it is also possible for there to be *no* correlation between two factors. The findings of a correlational study can be represented graphically, using a scattergraph. This is a graph with one variable along each of the axes with each data point (each participant's two scores) representing a single point (see also page 190).

A correlational design is useful in situations where variables can only be measured, rather than manipulated or compared, so an experimental design is not possible. This may be the case if changing the variables would not be practical, such as amount of pre-school exposure to TV, or would be unethical, such as increasing real-life exposure to violence. However, if a correlation is found between two variables, this tells us only that the two factors are related, it does not mean that one factor necessarily causes a change in the other. A correlation does not allow us to make judgements about cause and effect. Unlike in an experimental design, we cannot be sure that the changes in one variable are dependent upon the changes in another, either might be causing the effect or they may both be affected by another, different variable. This is illustrated by the example in Box 10.3.

Box 10.3
Can we tell if this pattern is causal?

Siân and Angharad have been selling friendship bracelets in the local market for over a year and are looking at the way their takings have varied. Siân looks at the pattern and it reminds her of an article in the local newspaper about thieving from shops in the town centre. When they look at the incidence of thefts and of their bracelet sales, there is a clear positive correlation. The more bracelets they sell, the higher the number of thefts. Angharad wonders whether they've made the bracelets wrong – the effect isn't one of friendship at all – they seem to be making people more selfish instead!

What is the most likely explanation for this apparent relationship?

Observations

In observations, data is collected by watching participants' behaviour. The findings can be analysed and interpreted in different ways, depending on the nature of the data collected. Initially, recordings tend to be non-focused: that is, the observer looks at the range of possible behaviours to investigate. Subsequently, in focused observations, a set of behaviours which have been clearly defined is used. Observations of these specific actions can be made using techniques such as:

- **time sampling** – the action being performed at preset intervals is recorded, e.g. watching one child in the playground and recording every ten seconds whether he or she is behaving aggressively, non-aggressively or is not interacting with others

- **event sampling** – a checklist of behaviours is drawn up and a tally is kept of an individual's performance of each of the items on the list.

Observations can therefore generate either qualitative or quantitative data. When detailed descriptions of events are gathered, qualitative data is produced. This could be done in non-focused observations or when long time intervals allow for in-depth recording. Alternatively, checklists or short-interval time sampling can generate quantitative data. This can readily be analysed using statistical methods and findings can be illustrated graphically.

In relation to the social setting the observer may be either:

- a **participant** observer – so is part of the social setting, such as a researcher investigating stress at work who is employed alongside the participants
- a **non-participant** observer – they are not involved in the situation being observed, such as a researcher who comes into a workplace once a week to record employee behaviour.

In addition, an observer may be:

- **overt** – their role as observer is obvious to the participants, e.g. when the researcher is holding a clipboard
- **covert** – the nature of the observer's role is hidden from the participants, such as if they are disguised as a member of the social group (such as the colleague described in the first example above) or if they are physically hidden (e.g. using CCTV).

The environment in which observations take place can be natural, such as in a familiar work environment, or contrived, e.g. in a university laboratory.

Glossary

inter-observer reliability: the extent to which two observers will produce the same records when they watch the same event.

self-report measures: data collection techniques, such as interviews and questionnaires, in which the participant is required to provide information about their experiences, e.g. their beliefs or feelings.

One advantage of the observational method is that in some situations it is possible to ensure that participants are unaware that they are being observed. This reduces demand characteristics as they cannot be affected by their expectations about the research. This is possible when the observer is covert, either as a participant or non-participant observer. For participant observers there is an added advantage that they become involved in the social experience so can gain insights into the emotions or motivation felt by participants. As a consequence, their findings may be more detailed and more valid. In self-reports, e.g. interviews or questionnaires, people may not describe their behaviour accurately. Observations may therefore be more valid than these methods.

There are also disadvantages to the observational method. Especially if they are participant, observers may become too involved in the situation and will thus produce subjective, biased records. A strict scientific approach would see this as problematic, although a more qualitative approach may not (see page 152). If an observer is covert but participant, it may be difficult for them to record their findings immediately, thus errors may arise as they have to remember events. If researchers attempt to overcome these issues or to increase the volume of data generated by having multiple observers, another problem may arise. Each observer does not necessarily arrive at the same record of behaviours after having viewed the same scene. This is described as having low **inter-observer reliability:** that is, the consistency between observers is poor. Finally, there are issues of privacy and consent, as participants may be unaware that they are involved in a study. This is particularly so in instances of covert observation, in which the observer's role is disguised.

Questionnaires

A questionnaire is called a 'self-report' measure, as participants provide information directly about themselves. They consist of a set of written questions that can use a range of different questioning techniques. These include:

- **closed questions** – these have a small number of fixed choices for answers such as 'Yes' or 'No', e.g. 'Did you have a holiday this year?'
- **open questions** – these can elicit longer, fuller answers, e.g. 'Describe a stressful aspect of your holiday' or 'How did your feelings change during the time you were taking medication?'
- **semantic differentials** – opposing pairs of words are placed at each end of a line along which the participant places a mark (see Box 10.4). They can be used to measure emotions
- **Likert scales** – a statement is presented and a range of simple responses is offered. The participant selects one from several choices (see Box 10.4). They can be used to measure attitudes.

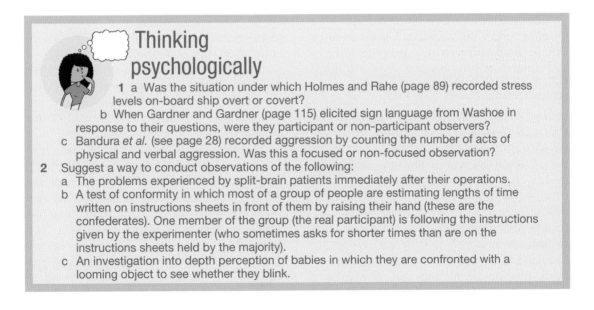

Thinking psychologically

1 a Was the situation under which Holmes and Rahe (page 89) recorded stress levels on-board ship overt or covert?

b When Gardner and Gardner (page 115) elicited sign language from Washoe in response to their questions, were they participant or non-participant observers?

c Bandura *et al.* (see page 28) recorded aggression by counting the number of acts of physical and verbal aggression. Was this a focused or non-focused observation?

2 Suggest a way to conduct observations of the following:

a The problems experienced by split-brain patients immediately after their operations.

b A test of conformity in which most of a group of people are estimating lengths of time written on instructions sheets in front of them by raising their hand (these are the confederates). One member of the group (the real participant) is following the instructions given by the experimenter (who sometimes asks for shorter times than are on the instructions sheets held by the majority).

c An investigation into depth perception of babies in which they are confronted with a looming object to see whether they blink.

Box 10.4
Examples of question types in questionnaires

Likert scale:

I am an easy-going person.	strongly agree	agree	don't know	disagree	strongly disagree
There isn't much that really bothers me at work.	strongly agree	agree	don't know	disagree	strongly disagree
People generally think I get wound-up too easily.	strongly agree	agree	don't know	disagree	strongly disagree
I feel sorry for people who are stressed.	strongly agree	agree	don't know	disagree	strongly disagree
I work best under pressure.	strongly agree	agree	don't know	disagree	strongly disagree

Semantic differential:

How did you feel during the robbery?

calm	I...I	tense
afraid	I...I	bold
confused	I...I	clear-headed
interested	I...I	fed-up

Questionnaires are important tools as they can be used to investigate people's feelings and thoughts, for instance their attitudes, beliefs or intentions. This is useful as these things cannot be investigated by observations alone. The method itself is very flexible, as the different questionnaire techniques provide a range of ways to obtain different styles of data. Closed questions produce numerical results that are easy to collate, score and compare and can be analysed statistically. Furthermore, because such questions are readily understood and answered, they tend to produce relatively reliable and replicable findings. In contrast, data from open questions provide detail and can give greater insight into the reasons behind people's responses, such as their attitudes or beliefs. In comparison with interviews, questionnaires have the advantage of being less threatening as the participant is not face to face with the researcher. People are therefore more likely to respond honestly to questions about socially sensitive issues such as stress, sexuality or drug use. Questionnaires are also cheaper and quicker than interviews because they do not require a specialist to administer them.

However, questionnaire techniques have disadvantages too. Closed questions offer a small number of possible answers, so may not allow participants to say exactly what they mean. If this is the case, the results may not reflect the individual's true opinions or feelings, thus lowering the validity of the findings. Validity may also be affected by participants' response biases. People tend to answer questions in rather set ways, preferring to make consistent responses such as always answering 'Yes'. Participants also tend to give the answers that they think people ought to; this is called a **'social desirability bias'**. Validity and reliability may be reduced because people may simply be unable to self-report accurately. They may not, for example, be able to recall how they felt about an event or know why they behaved in a particular way. Their responses may therefore not accurately reflect their emotions or behaviours. Further distortion of the results can arise if there is a sample bias. If a questionnaire has to be returned by post, for example, certain sorts of people may be more likely to put a stamp on the envelope and so contribute to the sample.

Glossary

sample: the members of the target population who become participants in a study.

Interviews

Unlike a questionnaire, the questions in an interview are direct, i.e. asked face to face (or sometimes over the telephone). In other ways, however, the methods are similar, for example employing open and closed questioning techniques. A good interview uses questions that are non-leading and clearly understandable. The language used should also be jargon-free and questions should avoid double negatives. The responses given by participants are organised by the interviewer and may be interpreted. Depending on the style of interview used, the sequence of questions may or may not be predetermined:

- In **structured interviews**, the wording of questions and their order are fixed.
- In **unstructured interviews**, the topics to be covered may be predecided but the

order and nature of questions tend to follow the participant's lead.

The structured interview technique enables researchers to elicit information about the same issues from many participants. As questions are consistent, the reliability is likely to be higher than in unstructured interviews. As the data produced is simpler, structured interviews are also easier to analyse than unstructured ones. However, unstructured interviews allow researchers to gather more detailed data and provide access to information that may not be obtained in inflexible structured interviews. For example, while it is easy to count up how many times an individual says 'Yes' to closed questions about sources of stress to which they are exposed, a researcher is more likely to understand how the individual is feeling from answers to open questions.

Unlike when responding to a questionnaire, participants being interviewed may be more likely to respond in socially desirable ways because they are face to face with another person. The interviewer themselves may also be affected by the social situation. They may have preconceived beliefs about what they expect to find, or about the individual, and this may bias the questions they ask or the interpretation they place on the answers. These are issues of subjectivity and are especially problematic in unstructured interviews where the questions can vary. The potential for differences between interviewers also lowers inter-interviewer reliability. Different researchers investigating the same topic with the same participants are less likely to gain the same results if they are using an unstructured technique than a structured one. This inconsistency in unstructured interviews also means that analysis, comparison and generalisation of the findings are more difficult than for structured interviews.

web watch

Search the internet for a site that reports a range of famous psychological studies. Write a list that very briefly describes what was done in ten different investigations. Identify which research method was used in each case. If you can, test a partner on your list – can they correctly identify the research method from your description?

Thinking psychologically

1 Would each of the following questions be open or closed?
   a Did you see any broken glass? (see page 110.)
   b Describe a stressful experience you have had in the last year.
   c Which line is the same length as line X, line 1, 2 or 3 (see page 75)?
   d Tell me about the symptoms you are experiencing.
2 a Design a Likert scale that would test which aspects of their psychology course students in your group are finding relatively easy or difficult.
   b Devise a semantic differential (with about five measures) that would help to assess whether a participant was distressed after leaving a study such as conducted by Milgram.
3 If you were planning an interview to explore the way that an individual feels after diagnosis with a mental health disorder, what interview technique and question styles would you use and why?
4 How would the following issues affect the validity of a study?
   a A questionnaire takes a long time to fill in, so people who are retired are more likely to fill it in than employed people.
   b In an interview about prejudice, participants don't want to look 'bad' in front of the interviewer so play down their racist views.
   c In a questionnaire about attitudes towards the criminal justice system, there are Likert scales with statements such as 'eyewitnesses are easily confused', 'cross examination in court aims to mislead people' and 'victims distort the way they recall incidents'. In each case, 'strongly agree' is on the left-hand side of the page.

Qualitative and quantitative methods compared

In general, quantitative data is relatively reliable. For example, the use of closed questions in an interview or a checklist in an observation is more likely to generate consistent findings than are open questions or non-focused observations. Numerical data is also easier to analyse. Numbers can readily be used in a mean, median or mode to indicate the 'average' score in a group. Such data can also be illustrated graphically, so sets of data can be easily compared. This would also help to show any trends or patterns in the results. Finally, only quantitative data can be used in statistical testing. This is important when a decision needs to be made about whether a particular pattern that can be seen in a data set could simply have arisen by chance (rather than being due to the IV, for example).

By contrast, qualitative data is more informative in terms of detail. It can provide both a depth and breadth of coverage of a topic that is likely to be absent in quantitative data.

As a consequence, it is possible that quantitative data may fail to identify the key issue in an investigation if that particular variable was not the focus of the study. For example, in an experiment there is likely to be only one (or a small number) of measured or manipulated variables – if the particular factors chosen for attention are not in fact the most important, the investigation may misrepresent the situation. The findings may attach greater significance to the particular factors that were tested than they really deserve. A similar distortion may occur in an interview or questionnaire using closed questions. In the absence of the opportunity to say what really matters, respondents would be forced to misrepresent their views or feelings. In these cases, qualitative data would be more likely to provide an accurate representation of the real world.

web watch

Find an online dictionary. Create a list of all the new words in this chapter and make yourself a research methods dictionary. Put the words and their definitions into a table so that you can cover up one side and test yourself on the meanings of the terms.

Summing it up

- **Qualitative data** is detailed and descriptive and can be obtained from self-report methods using open questions and from observations.

- **Quantitative** data is numerical and is obtained using methods that score variables, such as experiments, correlational studies, observations using checklists and self-report methods using closed questions.

- In an **experiment** an IV is manipulated and the effect on a DV is measured. Participants are allocated to levels of the IV in one of three designs (repeated measures, independent groups or matched pairs). Other possible variables are controlled.

- Experiments may be conducted in **laboratory** or **field** settings, the former giving greater control. The researcher can therefore be more certain that changes in the DV are the result of changes in the IV. **Natural experiments** utilise situations in which an existing change provides the different levels of the IV. Such situations are likely to be highly representative of the real world.

- A **correlational study** measures two variables. This is a useful technique when variables cannot be manipulated. These may correlate positively – both increase together – or negatively – one goes up as the other goes down. Alternatively, no correlation may be found. If a link is found this does not imply a causal relationship.

- **Observational studies** record behaviour by watching participants. The role of the observer in relation to the observed situation can vary, e.g. in the extent of their involvement and visibility. Records may be highly structured, e.g. using checklists, or less focused. Observations are useful when situations cannot be manipulated.

- Self-report methods include **questionnaires** and **interviews** and can investigate feelings or attitudes. Either can ask open or closed questions but only interviews are conducted face to face. Interviews may be relatively fixed in nature (structured) or unstructured. Questionnaires use additional techniques such as Likert scales and semantic differentials. These techniques allow researchers to access information such as feelings that cannot be seen by an observer.

- In general, qualitative methods produce rich and detailed data that is more meaningful and representative of the social context. They are less likely to overlook important aspects of the data which do not conform with prior theoretical expectations.

- In general, quantitative methods produce valid and reliable findings that can be replicated. They generate data from which general patterns can be established with certainty. In experiments, cause-and-effect relationships between variables can be deduced.

What have I learned?

1   Which of the following are quantitative and which are qualitative data?

   a   A correlation collecting data about hours of computer games played and number of school detentions for aggression.

   b   An interview that allows people to describe their attitudes to patients with schizophrenia.

   c   An observation in which nurses record details about a range of indicators of confusion in split-brain patients immediately post-operatively.

   d   A questionnaire that looks at the differences between men's and women's attitudes to relationships that offers yes/no answers to a range of simple questions.

   e   An experiment investigating eyewitness testimony in which the DV is measured by counting how many times participants are misled by questions.

2   Which method is being used in each of these situations? If it is an experiment, which design is being used?

   a   A study investigating the effect of interactive whiteboards on classroom behaviour that looks at the same classes before and after new boards are installed.

   b   A study comparing depth perception in kittens that have been raised in either a dark or an illuminated environment.

   c   An investigation in which a researcher uses his office to watch babies first interacting with their primary carers, then with a research assistant. He records indicators of the strength of the bond as new sights and sounds are presented.

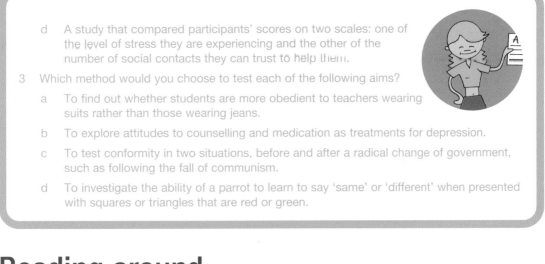

d   A study that compared participants' scores on two scales: one of the level of stress they are experiencing and the other of the number of social contacts they can trust to help them.

3   Which method would you choose to test each of the following aims?

a   To find out whether students are more obedient to teachers wearing suits rather than those wearing jeans.

b   To explore attitudes to counselling and medication as treatments for depression.

c   To test conformity in two situations, before and after a radical change of government, such as following the fall of communism.

d   To investigate the ability of a parrot to learn to say 'same' or 'different' when presented with squares or triangles that are red or green.

Reading around

● Hayes, N. (2000) *Doing Psychological Research: Gathering and analysing data*. Buckingham: Open University Press.

● Russell, J. and Roberts, C. (2001) *Angles on Psychological Research*. Cheltenham: Nelson Thornes.

Reliability and validity

In psychological research and practice we often have to measure things. In everyday life we use the term 'accuracy' when we are concerned with how well something is measured. For example, we would be worried if our electricity meter did not measure accurately how much electricity we used because we might end up paying too much in our electricity bill. When we are dealing with something like electricity consumption, defining accuracy is quite straightforward. Does the meter record correctly how much electricity we used?

However, the things we are trying to measure in psychological research are rarely this clear cut. All we can do is estimate how accurate our procedures and measures are. There are two ways of estimating accuracy: reliability and validity.

Reliability

In psychology, reliability means consistency. This is a slightly different meaning to how we use the term in everyday speech. For example, if a student is consistently late or consistently fails to do their homework, then to a psychologist their behaviour is reliable. However, 'reliable' is probably not the first word that their teacher would think of to describe them! A psychological procedure or measure is reliable if it consistently measures something Say, for example, that we test a person's IQ on two occasions. If the test is reliable we would expect them to achieve the same or very nearly the same score each time.

We can measure reliability in a number of ways:

- **Test-retest reliability** is the simplest way to assess reliability. As in the IQ example above, it only requires us to administer our test or procedure to the same people on two occasions. If there is a strong relationship between the results on the two occasions, this indicates good reliability.
- **Split-half reliability**. A slightly more complicated way to assess reliability is to split a test or procedure into two smaller tests. If the two halves of the test indicate the same thing, this is also an indicator of good reliability.
- **Inter-rater reliability**. Sometimes, a psychological test involves observing people and noting their actions. Alternatively, we might ask people questions. The information we obtain from observations and interviews can be used to classify people. If two or more observers or interviewers using a standard observation or interview schedule classify people in the same way, then this indicates good reliability.

Thinking psychologically

An important area in psychological and psychiatric practice is diagnosis of mental disorder. Here, it is important that the ways we carry out diagnosis are reliable. Below are the symptoms used to diagnose anorexia in the American Psychiatric Association system. Although symptom A is measured objectively by scales and weight charts, symptoms B, C and D are assessed by means of an interview.

A Refusal to maintain body weight at or above a minimal normal weight for age and height (e.g. weight loss leading to maintenance of body weight less than 85 per cent of that expected; or failure to make expected weight gain during period of growth, leading to body weight less than 85 per cent of that expected).

B Intense fear of gaining weight, or becoming fat, even though underweight.

C Disturbance in the way in which one's body weight or shape is experienced, undue influence of body weight or shape on self-evaluation, or denial of the seriousness of the current low body weight.

D Amenorrhoea (the absence of at least three consecutive menstrual cycles).

1 How could you assess the reliability of the diagnosis of anorexia using a test-retest method?

2 How could you assess the reliability of the diagnosis of anorexia using a split-half method?

3 How could you assess the inter-rater reliability of the diagnosis of anorexia? The reliability of psychiatric diagnosis has improved in recent years. Suggest one way in which this might have been achieved.

Validity

The other major estimate of accuracy of a psychological procedure or measure is validity. Put simply, a test or procedure is valid if it measures what it sets out to measure. Validity is a little more complex than reliability. There are various types of validity and various ways to measure them. We might be concerned with the validity of a study or procedure for carrying out a study, or we might be more concerned with the validity of a particular way of measuring a psychological variable.

Experimental validity

Experimental validity is a broad term meaning the extent to which an experimental study or method really investigates what it intends to and generates results that can be generalised to other people who did not participate. Experimental validity can be divided into internal and external validity.

> ## Glossary
>
> **experimenter bias:** the phenomenon in which researchers unconsciously influence their findings because they know what they wish to find.

Internal validity

This is the extent to which we can be sure that the results of a study are a product of what we think they are. In other words, can we be sure that the dependent variable (the thing we measure and which makes up our results) is a product of the independent variable (the thing that differs between the experimental conditions)? One factor that

can affect internal validity is the reliability of our measures. Another is **experimenter bias** – if we know what we expect or wish to happen in an experiment we can communicate this to participants and influence their results.

The design of a study is also important in affecting internal validity. If we use independent groups (an independent measures design) then we need to be sure that our groups of participants are very similar. Otherwise, it may be that any differences we observe between two conditions are due to differences in participant characteristics rather than our independent variable. If we use a repeated measures design, we need to ensure that participants do not score higher in the second condition because of practice or lower because of boredom. Table 11.1 shows some ways of dealing with these common threats to internal validity.

Threat to internal validity	Strategy to overcome threat
Reliability of measures	Use standard measures or several measures
Experimenter bias	Double blind method
Independent measures design	Match groups as closely as possible
Repeated measures design	Counterbalancing

Table 11.1 Maximising internal validity

External validity

This is the extent to which we can be sure that our results hold true once we are outside the experimental situation. Can we, for example, generalise our results from the laboratory to the real world, or from our small group of participants to the world at large? These questions are formalised in the terms 'ecological validity' and 'population validity'.

● **Ecological validity** is the extent to which we can be sure that results can be generalised from our experiment to real-life situations. There are two major factors that affect an experiment's ecological validity. One is its setting. A field experiment, which is carried out in a real-life setting, is *likely* to have better ecological validity than a laboratory experiment, which is by definition an artificial set-up. However, we also have to take into account how realistic the tasks are that participants carry out during a study. The technical term for this is the **mundane realism** of the study. A laboratory experiment can still have reasonable ecological validity if it has good mundane realism, whereas a field experiment with poor mundane realism can still be criticised for its ecological validity.

● **Population validity** is the extent to which we can be sure that results can be generalised from our sample of participants to the population at large: in other words, to other places, times and groups. In Chapter 5 we looked at two classic social-psychological studies: by Asch (1955) and by Milgram (1963). These were both carried out on men in

Thinking psychologically

Look back at Chapters 5–9, which deal with core psychological studies. Assess the ecological validity of each of the following studies by placing a tick or cross in each box.

Study	Natural setting?	Mundane realism?
Asch (1955)		
Milgram (1963)		
Loftus and Palmer (1974)		
Rosenhan (1973)		
Gibson and Walk (1960)		

Which studies appear to have the best and worst ecological validity?

the USA after the Second World War. We cannot assume that their results would necessarily apply to women, to people in other countries or to people in other historical periods. In fact, without a closer look at how they selected their participants (and also in Asch's case how he allocated them to conditions), we could not even be confident that results could be applied to other post-war US males!

Validity of psychological measures

Experimental validity refers to entire psychological studies or procedures that may form the basis of several studies. However, we should also consider the validity of the measures we use in psychological research and practice. For example, we use IQ tests to assess 'intelligence'. However, before we can measure intelligence we have to start with a definition of intelligence. We might also want to think about existing measures of intelligence and whether our IQ test says anything useful about how a person will perform in real life.

These questions are formalised as content, concurrent and predictive validity:

- **Content validity** is the extent to which we can be sure that our test or procedure measures the right things. For example, what cognitive abilities make up IQ? If an IQ test is to have good content validity it should measure all the components of IQ, but nothing else. A panel of experts can be used to assess content validity. For example, a team of IQ experts might be asked to name the mental abilities that a new IQ test should measure.

- **Concurrent validity** is the extent to which our test or procedure agrees with other measures of whatever variable we are assessing. For example, we can validate a new IQ test by giving people the new test and existing IQ tests. If our test has good concurrent validity, then people will score very close to the same IQ as they do on other IQ tests.

- **Predictive validity** is the extent to which the results of our test or procedure are associated with some aspect of a person's future behaviour or achievement. For example, sticking with our IQ test example, if an IQ test has good predictive validity, a score obtained from it should be able to predict how someone will get on in education or employment.

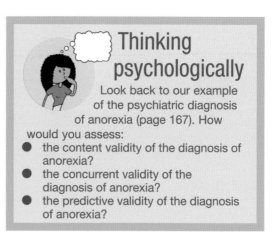

Thinking psychologically

Look back to our example of the psychiatric diagnosis of anorexia (page 167). How would you assess:
- the content validity of the diagnosis of anorexia?
- the concurrent validity of the diagnosis of anorexia?
- the predictive validity of the diagnosis of anorexia?

The relationship between reliability and validity

We have already said that for a study to have good internal validity it must use reliable measures. The same principle is true of valid measures. A psychological test cannot have good validity if it does not have reasonably good reliability. However, the picture is more complicated than this. We can usually increase reliability by tightening up on our measurements. For example, we might say that for a diagnosis of anorexia, a patient must go below 80 per cent rather than 85 per cent of body mass, or miss four rather than three periods. It will become slightly harder to get a diagnosis and those making a diagnosis will be more likely to agree. This will improve reliability of diagnosis, but what about validity? This will in fact be made worse because patients with slightly milder cases will no longer get a diagnosis. This is a problem, as it is likely to affect their receiving treatment. Similarly, when we mark your A-level exams, we can increase inter-rater reliability by accepting only one answer for each question. However, sometimes there is more than one correct answer, so if we accept only one answer we risk reducing validity. Often, then, there is a trade-off between reliability and validity.

Glossary

population: the group from which the sample is drawn.

Sampling

We have already said that for a study to have good population validity we must have a representative group of participants. The procedure by which we select our participants is called 'sampling'. The aim of sampling is to obtain a group of participants that are representative of our target population. The target population is the group you want to represent in the sample. There are two commonly used sampling methods that are unlikely to produce a representative sample.

- **Opportunity sampling** involves asking whoever is most easily available to take part. So participants might be classmates, friends, family members or whoever happens to be available in the college refectory or library. This is the most common method in student practicals. It is also used in professional research in studies where results are unlikely to be affected by age, education or socio-economic status. Many researchers rely on university students.
- **Self-selecting (volunteer) sampling** involves advertising for volunteers. Most people do not volunteer to take part in studies unless we actually approach and ask them. This is therefore guaranteed to obtain an unrepresentative sample! However, it is useful when we are looking for highly unusual people. For example, in parapsychology research we might particularly want to test the abilities of people who claim to be able to communicate by telepathy. We probably won't find many people who make such claims among our immediate circle, so advertising for volunteers is the best approach.

There is a range of ways we can obtain participants that are more representative of the target population:

- **Systematic sampling** involves selecting every nth person on a list. We can choose n by dividing the population size by the sample size. So if we have a school population of 1,000 and we want a sample of 50, $1{,}000/50 = 20$, so we could simply go down the list of pupils and select every twentieth person.
- **Random sampling**. The technical definition of a random sample is one in which every member of the target population has an equal chance of being

selected. You might think this is true in an opportunity or systematic sample. However, in an opportunity sample where you go to the school or college library for participants, those who never go to the library have no chance of being selected. Equally, if you are taking every *n*th person off a pupil list and there is a child with the name of Aardman, they will always be first on the list and probably always selected. A child with a name like Abacus will probably always be second on the list and never selected! Contrived, but true! Similarly, if you take every tenth student to walk through the front door at the start of the day, and there is a back entrance, or if some students come in late, they have no chance of being in the sample.

web watch

Traditionally we have obtained random samples by putting names in a hat or by giving every member of the target population a number and taking numbers from a random number table. However, this can all be done more quickly and efficiently online. Have a look at: http://www.mathsyear2000.org/explorer/randomiser/

There are several ways of randomising here. The 'random integers' and 'random items' functions are particularly useful for sampling.

● **Quota and stratified samples** are samples in which we try to be sure that as many proportions in the population as possible are represented by the proportions of the sample. So, if our

target population is 55 per cent female 45 per cent male, so will be our sample. If 20 per cent of our population is under-21, so will be 20 per cent of our sample. In a quota sample, provided the proportions are right, any members of the target population are acceptable. If you are stopped in the street to be interviewed, the chances are that you are part of a quota. If the interviewers ignore you it means that either you are not in their target population or that they have enough participants of your age and sex. In a stratified sample, there is a random element as well as a quota. The idea is that every member of the target population within the bounds of the quota has an equal chance of selection. To do this by hand is very complex and time consuming, and it is normally achieved using a computer.

Ethical issues in research

We have seen that there are lots of practical issues to think about when carrying out psychological research. However, we also need to think about ethical issues. Ethics is defined by Wikipedia as follows: 'a major branch of philosophy . . . the study of value or morality. It covers the analysis and employment of concepts such as right, wrong, good, evil, and responsibility' (2006np). In other words, it is about understanding systems of morality. Morality is absolutely central to psychology. The ultimate aim of all psychology is to make life better for people. We are fighting a losing battle in trying to achieve this if we make life worse in any way for the people we work with! These include clients with whom professional psychologists work and those who take part in our studies. This chapter is concerned with the latter.

The world's major professional psychological organisations publish extensive codes of ethical principles and guidelines. The following principles are based on a publication from the British Psychological Society (2006). The American Psychological Association and the Australian Psychological Society publish similar documents.

1   **Introduction**. It is important that the public can have confidence in the profession of psychology. How well researchers treat participants will affect public perceptions of all psychologists. All psychologists and psychology students at all levels should abide by the following principles and urge colleagues to do so.

2   **General**. Researchers should always consider the ethical implications of their research. Foreseeable threats to the well-being, dignity, health and values of participants should always be eliminated. The cultural values of participants should be recognised and responded to.

3   **Consent**. Researchers must take reasonable steps to obtain *real* consent from participants. Real consent is consent freely given from a participant who fully understands what they are agreeing to. Where children are being studied, a parent or adult in loco parentis is required to give consent. Where adults with impairments are being studied, consent should be obtained from another person who would reasonably be expected to know whether the participant would wish to take part. Researchers should not use payment or their position of power over participants to persuade them to consent to activities.

4   **Deception**. Deceiving participants should be avoided whenever possible.

Participants should be informed of the purpose of the investigation as soon as possible. It is not acceptable to deceive participants when it is likely that they will object or become distressed when debriefed. Where deception is an essential part of the design of a study the researcher has three obligations:

● to ensure that alternative procedures are not available
● to ensure participants are properly debriefed at the earliest opportunity
● to consult with colleagues about participants' likely responses when they discover the deception.

5   **Debriefing**. Whenever participants are aware that they have taken part in a study they should receive a full explanation of the research as soon as possible. Researchers should also ensure that the participants' experiences were not distressing and that they leave the study in at least as positive a mood as they entered it. Where a negative mood has been induced for the purpose of the study it is essential that a positive mood is induced during debriefing.

6   **Withdrawal**. Participants should be made aware of their right to withdraw from a study at any point. Payment does not alter a participant's right to withdraw. Where children are concerned, avoidance of the procedure should be taken as withdrawal and it should be ended. When debriefed, participants have the right to withdraw their data.

7   **Confidentiality**. Unless agreed with participants in advance, their individual results and any personal information obtained in a study should be completely confidential. Where it is likely that a participant would be identifiable following publication of

results, they must agree to this at the start of the study.

8 **Protection**. Participants should be protected from harm, including stress. This means that they should be exposed to no more risk than they would normally encounter in their usual lifestyle. Participants should be confident of confidentiality to prevent worry. Where the procedure does cause unexpected harm in spite of taking due care, the researcher is responsible for taking steps to rectify this, for example offering referral to another professional. Discussion of children's results with parents, teachers, etc. should be done with caution as there is a risk of influencing their opinion of the child.

9 **Observation**. Observational studies risk breaching privacy. In observations where participants are unaware they are being observed, they should be observed only in places and situations where they would expect people to observe them. The cultural norms of participants should be respected when deciding whether they would expect to be observed.

10 **Advice**. If a researcher sees signs of a physical or psychological problem that the participant is unaware of, but which might threaten their future well-being, they should inform them. Where participants seek professional advice, the researcher should be cautious. If they are not qualified to give the advice they should refer the participant on to an appropriate professional.

11 **Colleagues**. Where colleagues are conducting research that falls foul of

web watch

You can view several sets of ethical principles and guidelines online. Have a look at the following. What similarities and differences can you see?

Society	Web address
British Psychological Society (BPS)	http://www.bps.org.uk/the-society/ethics-rules-charter-code-of-conduct/code-of-conduct/code-of-conduct_home.cfm
American Psychological Association (APA)	http://www.apa.org/ethics/
Australian Psychological Society (APS)	http://www.psychology.org.au/aps/ethics/default.asp
Association for the Teaching of Psychology (ATP)	http://www.theatp.org/ Click on 'publications' and scroll down.

one or more of the above principles, it is important to inform them and to try to persuade them to alter their conduct.

Applying ethical principles to real research

You might think these principles are extremely reasonable. Indeed, in principle they are. No psychologist would wish to harm or distress their participants, or to deceive them unnecessarily. However, in reality there are many occasions when it is quite tricky to balance strict ethics against the importance of finding out what you want. Let us consider one of the studies we have already looked at in detail. Had Milgram not stretched the boundaries of what is ethically acceptable, his study would have suffered from poor internal validity. Note that the sort of ethical guidelines and principles we rely on today had not been developed when most of the core studies you have looked at were carried out.

The ethics of the Milgram study

You can read a full account of Milgram's study on page 78. Looking at the ethical principles outlined on page 173, some issues leap out from his procedure. First, his work is sufficiently controversial to risk altering public perceptions of psychologists. Participants did not give real consent because they believed they were taking part in a memory experiment rather than a study of obedience. They were deceived on several counts, including the purpose of the study, the status of the learner as a fellow participant, the fake shocks and, most importantly, that they might have injured or killed the learner. They suffered significant stress and, critically, they were denied their right to withdraw from the study. This all seems pretty damning. However, the procedure could not have been carried out without these features. In some

ways, Milgram paid close attention to ethics. For example, he informed participants of the purpose of the procedure at the earliest opportunity and went to considerable lengths to make sure they left the experiment in a positive frame of mind. When surveyed later, the vast majority of participants said they were glad to have taken part. We also need to consider the purpose of the study. It was and still is very important to understand better the participation of ordinary people in atrocities. The study was thus not performed casually, and the short-term stress suffered by participants must be balanced against the good that can come out of such a study. Banyard and Flanagan (2005) conclude that 'Milgram was a good guy' (p. 57).

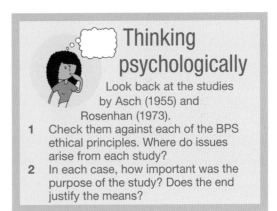

Thinking psychologically

Look back at the studies by Asch (1955) and Rosenhan (1973).

1   Check them against each of the BPS ethical principles. Where do issues arise from each study?
2   In each case, how important was the purpose of the study? Does the end justify the means?

Dealing with ethical issues

We have seen that ethical issues in psychological research are quite complex. Psychological researchers care deeply about ethics. However, they also have a job to do and there is a risk that if psychologists are too cautious about ethical issues they end up not tackling the most important issues. Unfortunately, it often seems that the more important a piece of research, the more ethical issues it can raise. Haslam and Reicher (2003) have used the term 'impeccable trivia' to describe the findings of studies where researchers have played too safe ethically and so not found really interesting, important results.

So how do psychologists steer the course between important findings with dodgy ethics and ethical cleanliness with pointless findings? One strategy is to define ethical principles. All major psychological associations have such ethical principles and periodically review and update them. Guidelines are also periodically published to cover particular areas of research that raise ethical issues, above and beyond the general

Box 11.1
Guidelines for televised studies

1   **Consent.** It is particularly difficult to obtain real consent from participants about to appear on reality TV. This is because, although participants can be warned about some of the things that will happen to them, some events are unpredictable, and people cannot know how they will feel about the things that will happen to them. A detailed consent form, explaining as many of the possible consequences of appearing as possible, is strongly recommended.

2   **Confidentiality.** Participants must be made fully aware of how much of their privacy they will lose by appearing on television. They must be aware of when their discussions with a psychologist are confidential and must be able to have confidential meetings with the psychologist.

3   **Responsibility.** Psychologists and TV companies must be clear about the precise role of the psychologist. The psychologist will work within their area of expertise and is likely to wish to involve or refer participants to another psychologist or other professional. For example, a personal space researcher

might be well qualified to design an environment like the *Big Brother* house, but they might not have any expertise in mental health. In this case, an agreement must be reached allowing them to involve a mental health expert if required.

4   **Follow-up involvement.** Psychologists will be aware of the emotional impact and possible long-term consequences for participants of appearing on reality TV. It is thus important to arrange with the TV company for extended access to participants after the end of the programme.

5   **Professional boundaries.** Psychologists are strictly limited to practising within their area of competence. A clinical psychologist should not comment or be asked to comment on a sporting performance and an educational psychologist should not comment or be asked to comment on adult mental health.

6   **Manipulation.** Reality TV involves putting people in particular situations to observe their response. Usually this is harmless, but psychologists involved in designing these situations should take account of the general ethical principles for research. For example, people should not be deceived and they should be aware of their right to withdraw.

ethical principles. An area of increasing concern is research broadcast as 'reality television'. Two recent examples of such research have attracted particular discussion. *Castaway* (McVey *et al.*, 2003) featured two groups of volunteers marooned on a Scottish island. *The Experiment* (Haslam and Reicher, 2003) featured a prison simulation. Both of these were serious psychological studies, although widely viewed as 'reality TV'. The British Psychological Society has issued additional guidelines to address the issues raised by this type of research. These are described in Box 11.1.

Of course, psychologists are often involved in reality TV, in shows that are intended as entertainment rather than research. If you are a *Big Brother* fan you may have watched *Big Brother's Big Brain*, in which psychologists and other professionals such as psychiatrists and psychotherapists discuss the psychology of what is happening to participants in the show. The ethics of this are controversial. Banyard and Flanagan (2005) have suggested that there should be an additional principle added to the current BPS ethical principles – 'don't talk bollocks to the media' (p. 56).

Consent

Consent is a particularly difficult issue for psychological research. We don't want to do things to people that they wouldn't wish us to. On the other hand if they know exactly what we are going to do and why, they probably won't act naturally and there is no point in using them. In some kinds of observational research we really need participants not to know they are being watched at all. Two kinds of consent thus become particularly important.

● **Presumptive consent.** In some situations psychologists may judge that they can presume that someone would consent to

being observed simply because they are in a situation where they are observed anyway. At one extreme, psychologists might analyse the content of TV viewing, looking at gender stereotypes in advertising or violence in cartoons. Here we are *usually* on pretty safe ground. By knowingly appearing on television you are by definition giving consent to be observed. At the other extreme, public toilets are technically public space, yet people using them would generally assume that they are not being systematically watched. We would definitely be unwise to presume consent to carry out an observation there!

● **Prior general consent.** Another approach to gaining consent without giving too much away is to ask participants for consent to take part in several types of research. Participants need not know in which area they are participating. A variation in this method is to ask for consent to several types of study including one *in which they will be misled about the purpose of the study*. As long as participants fully understand that this may happen and freely give consent, it may be acceptable to proceed. However, this requires caution, and bear in mind the rest of the ethical principles. In particular, remember that deception may not be used when it is likely that the participants will object once they are aware they were deceived.

Role-play

There are some situations where it would be ethically impossible to use naïve participants, i.e. participants who had little or no idea what was going on. For example, social psychologists have studied people's responses to being in a prison situation, both as a guard and as a prisoner. To use naïve participants would mean arresting innocent people unexpectedly and throwing them into a prison. This would clearly be unacceptable. What we *can* do though is ask people to role-play how they would act in a prison situation. This has been done, famously by Philip Zimbardo in the 1970s, and more recently by Haslam and Reicher (2003). Role-playing gets around some ethical issues, but by no means all. We can avoid deceit and have more in the way of real consent when we use role-play. However, once people are in their role they may still experience very strong emotional responses to the situation. Protecting the participants is therefore an issue.

web watch

You can read about Haslam and Reicher's prison role-play at http://www.psychology. ex.ac.uk/projects/ theexp/intro.shtml. Go to links and read the article in *The Times Higher Education Supplement*. What steps were taken to maintain good ethics in this study?

Ethics committees

A researcher operating on their own will find it hard to make the complex and subtle judgements required to judge the ethics of their own research. For this reason, it is standard practice to run details of our studies past an ethics committee before proceeding. Ethics committees consider the possible risks to participants' welfare and dignity. The British Psychological Society (2004) has published guidelines for how to conduct the process of gaining ethical approval. These are described in Box 11.2.

Box 11.2
Standards for ethical approval of psychological studies

- Ethical approval is required for all research by psychologists and psychology students.
- Once a procedure has been approved it is not necessary to re-approve it every time it is carried out. (This is why your student practicals may not all be assessed by committee.)
- Ethical approval must be by a committee. This can be a Department Ethics Committee, an Institutional Ethics Committee or an External Ethics Committee.
- All psychology departments conducting research should have an ethics committee.
- Under certain circumstances, a Department Ethics Committee should refer research to an Institutional Ethics Committee. This includes research into criminality, and other instances where the welfare of the researcher or the public may be put at risk.
- Research on children or vulnerable adults should be approved only if it is carried out by researchers who have been approved by the Criminal Records Bureau.

Summing it up

- We can estimate the accuracy of our procedures and measures by two means: reliability and validity.

- Psychological tests and procedures should be **reliable**, i.e. consistently measure the same thing.

- Reliability can be assessed by **test-retest**, **split-half** and **inter-rater** methods.

- Tests must also be **valid**, i.e. measure what they set out to.

- We need to be aware of both the **internal** and **external validity** of a study.

- We also need to consider the validity of measures. This can be assessed by **content validity**, **concurrent validity** and **predictive validity**.

- In order to have good external validity, we must carry out research on a representative sample of participants.

- Unrepresentative sampling methods include **opportunity** and **self-selecting** methods.

- Representative sampling methods include **systematic**, **random** and **quota** methods.

- Psychological research often raises **ethical issues**. There are several sets of ethical principles and guidelines which researchers are expected to follow.

- Some of the classic studies in psychology would not have conformed to these guidelines had they existed when the studies were carried out.

- There is sometimes a trade-off between what is ethically acceptable and what would be the most valid procedures to conduct a study.

- Certain kinds of research, for example televised research, raise particular issues and require additional guidelines.

- Various strategies are used to manage ethical issues in research. **Presumptive consent** and **prior general consent** can be employed.

- Role-play can be used in situations that would not be acceptable to create for real.

- Ethics committees are intended to vet all research before it is carried out.

What have I learned?

1 How could you assess the reliability of a questionnaire designed to measure attitudes to *Buffy the Vampire Slayer*?

2 How could you assess the validity of such a questionnaire?

3 What factors affect the ecological validity of an experiment?

4 Under what circumstances might you use unrepresentative sampling methods?

5 Why did Banyard and Flanagan conclude that 'Milgram was a good guy'?

6 What ethical principles become particularly important when research is televised?

7 When is presumptive consent dodgy?

8 What is an ethics committee?

Reading around

■ Banyard, P. and Flanagan, C. (2005) *Ethical Issues and Guidelines in Psychology.* London: Routledge.

■ British Psychological Society (2006) *Ethical Principles for Conducting Research with Human Participants.* Leicester: British Psychological Society.

■ Coolican, H. R. (2004) *Research Methods and Statistics in Psychology*. London: Hodder Arnold.

Analysing data

What should I know?

- Methods of analysis for qualitative data:
  - coding systems
  - categorisation
  - content analysis.
- Methods of analysis for quantitative data:
  - measures of central tendency
  - measures of dispersion
  - graphical representation.

In addition I should be able to:

- recall examples of coding systems and categorisation from the core studies
- recall the use of different measures of central tendency in the core studies
- decide which measures of dispersion could have been used in the core studies.

As you discovered in Chapter 10, quantitative data is readily derived from studies that produce numerical results, such as experiments. It is important to be aware that structured interviews or questionnaires using closed questions also produce quantitative data. Because such data is already categorised by the process of data collection, it is essentially quantitative. However, unstructured interviews or questionnaires with open questions produce rich, detailed information. This type of data raises a key question in analysis –

whether to preserve depth of meaning or to represent the broader picture. Qualitative methods of analysis aim to achieve the former. Alternatively, an indication of the general patterns, themes or issues raised by qualitative findings can be summarised by condensing the data using quantitative analysis.

In the section that follows, we look at ways to represent the findings of qualitative research in quantitative ways.

Methods for analysing qualitative data

In many research situations, it is necessary to develop systematic strategies for collecting data. In an experiment, decisions must be made about how to measure the dependent variable. In methods such as observations, descriptions of the behaviours to be recorded must be developed and agreed between observers when there is more than one. This process of developing a coding system provides an outline of the variables or themes to be used. It serves a similar function to the operationalisation of variables in an experimental study. It aims to structure the data and ensure that researchers are consistent in their approach.

Coding systems

A coding system is a way of identifying or labelling qualitative data items. Each code is intended to represent a small, meaningful unit. The way a coding system is developed depends largely on the research method being employed, although in every case the aim is for a representative and reliable measure. The system must be sufficiently flexible to allow the researcher to include all examples of the variable being measured, but specific enough to ensure that the definition is valid. In essence, a coding system is a way of separating out different elements of the variable(s) being measured.

Coding in observations

One of the key issues in coding behaviours in observations is to break down the stream of behaviour into individual actions. The coding system used must be based on differences which can be seen rather than assumed. For example, in recording indicators of stress in examination candidates, a coding system could use 'biting finger nails' or 'frowning' but not 'feels tense' or 'is guessing' because these attributes cannot actually be observed. Items may also be coded as facial expressions, gestures, postures and speech.

Coding in questionnaires and interviews

When closed questions have been used, coding in self-report measures is relatively easy; the coding system derives directly from the questions themselves. For example, a questionnaire in which a respondent indicates 'Yes' to any of the items on the left or 'No' to any on the right in Box 12.1 could be coded as 'high stress'.

This illustrates that the way questionnaire items are written dictates how they are scored. It is important to note that when designing a questionnaire using Likert scales

---

Box 12.1
Coding in questionnaires

- Do you work more than 60 hours a week?
- Do you have to look after an ill relative?
- When you wake up in the morning do you dread the day?

- Do you have lots of friends to whom you could turn if you were in need?
- If things go wrong do you tend to just shrug them off, knowing there will be something better around the corner?
- Do you indulge in happy daydreams just for the fun of it?

or semantic differentials, some items indicating each extreme should produce a 'No' answer, others a 'Yes' answer (see Chapter 10).

When open questions are used, a coding system must be developed for classifying the responses so that they can be more easily interpreted and analysed. The way in which this is done will depend in part on the theoretical approach of the researcher. For example, in interpreting a response about a phobia, a researcher with a behaviourist perspective is likely to use a different coding system from one taking a psychodynamic perspective. In any situation, possible responses can be divided into different themes. For example, a behaviourist coding an interview about a phobia might look for examples of responses that indicated:

1   a possible source of reinforcement for phobic behaviour
2   indications that the phobic response has been associated with any other, genuinely dangerous or unpleasant situation
3   evidence of a stimulus which could trigger the appearance of phobic behaviours.

These themes could be identified as: reinforcers (1); unconditioned stimuli (2); and conditioned stimuli (3). Interview responses could then be coded using this system.

In contrast, a researcher approaching the same interview from a psychodynamic perspective might look for indications of the following:

1   reluctance to speak about a topic
2   the disguised appearance of a feared situation in the manifest content of a dream
3   descriptions of fears that could have appeared during childhood.

These themes could be identified as: unconscious repression or denial (1); a latent fear being represented in the dream (2); or key experiences from the individual's early childhood (3).

In both cases, the information derived from the interview can be coded using a system that allows the researcher to interpret their findings within a framework. This is useful as it allows situations or individuals to be compared.

> **Box 12.2**
> ## Should theory dictate the coding system or should the coding system evolve from the data?
>
> In one approach to research, **grounded theory**, the explanations arise during the course of the study. This differs from the typical scientific approach in which a theoretical approach determines hypotheses and, in consequence, the nature of the coding system. In grounded theory, by contrast, hypotheses can emerge during the investigation and the coding system is flexible, with new codes and categories being added (or amalgamated or removed) as the research progresses. This inductive process, in which the theory is led by the researchers' observations, has high validity in the sense that it is driven by 'real-world' findings.

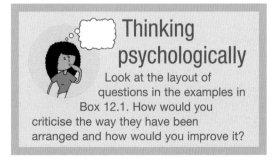

> ## Thinking psychologically
> Look at the layout of questions in the examples in Box 12.1. How would you criticise the way they have been arranged and how would you improve it?

Categorisation

A coding system provides the initial step in organising qualitative data. The next step is to combine these elements into categories. Let's return to the example of phobias. In the first instance, 'reinforcers' could be categorised into positive, negative and vicarious; and in the second, indicators of 'reluctance to speak about a topic' could be categorised into strategies such as silence or evasion.

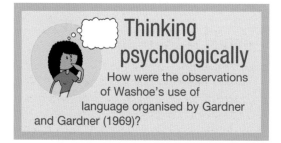

Thinking psychologically

How were the observations of Washoe's use of language organised by Gardner and Gardner (1969)?

It is generally assumed that it is better to begin with many codes that might turn out to be measuring the same phenomenon and eventually combine them than to start with too few. The latter approach risks losing detail and making the analysis less meaningful.

Content analysis

Both coding systems and categorisation are essential to the process of content analysis. This method is an indirect way of investigating sources from the media, such as children's books or television programmes. The technique can be used to investigate real-life issues, such as whether we are exposed to stereotyped models. Media models might illustrate gender-specific behaviours, excessive dieting or violence and these could be investigated using content analysis.

In conducting a content analysis, the first step is for the researcher to decide which material is to be sampled, e.g. the number of TV programmes to be analysed and the channels to be watched. The next decision is about the coding units. For example, in an investigation of gender-role stereotypes in children's TV programmes, coding units could include the gender-role stereotype of each character, activity or scene. In an analysis of a book, the coding units could be words or the themes in each paragraph. Categories can then be constructed, for example 'female in stereotyped female role', 'male in stereotyped female role', 'female in neutral role', etc. Categories could also include whether the portrayal is a positive or a negative one. Examples of actual text with its coding can provide qualitative data. The numerical totals of items in each code or category can provide quantitative data.

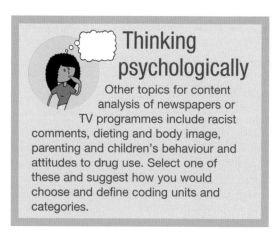

Thinking psychologically

Other topics for content analysis of newspapers or TV programmes include racist comments, dieting and body image, parenting and children's behaviour and attitudes to drug use. Select one of these and suggest how you would choose and define coding units and categories.

Strengths of content analysis

Content analyses are based on real-life sources of information (e.g. current TV programmes, or newspapers) rather than the artificial situations that typify experimentation. This high mundane realism gives content analysis high ecological validity, as it indicates the influences present in media to which we are genuinely exposed. Another advantage of content analyses over other methods is that they can be replicated easily. This is possible because media products (TV programmes, printed material, etc.) are permanent. This means that exactly the same sources can be accessed and used by other researchers for comparison and to replicate the study.

Weaknesses of content analysis

Unlike the conclusions that can be drawn from experiments, causal judgements cannot be made on the basis of a content analysis. Although evidence from sources of media can illustrate patterns, these could be either reflecting or causing differences in the social world. When a researcher selects coding units and categories, their decisions may be biased, which has the potential to lower the objectivity of the method. In addition, the way that they implement the coding units can reduce

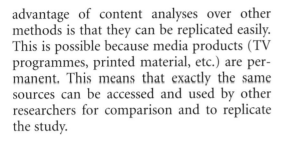

web watch

Use a search engine to find an online newspaper archive. Decide on a topic to investigate (e.g. ageism, raising children bilingually or attitudes to global warming). Search for articles and include one or more key words relating to the topic you want to investigate. For example, you might look for examples of discrimination against homosexuals using the search term 'gay'. Devise a coding system and use this to analyse your articles. It would be interesting to compare your findings with those of another student using the same coding system but who has selected their articles from a different newspaper.

the validity of the findings. One major issue here is the influence of expectations – researchers are likely to find what they expect to find simply because they are more likely to identify examples that confirm their ideas than those which contradict them.

Methods for analysing quantitative data

Collecting numerical data

In general, numerical data is relatively easy to organise. Results from tests or measures used in experiments and other methods designed to generate quantitative data fall into different **levels of measurement**. This refers to the nature of the numerical data and there are four different levels:

1 **Nominal data** – results in named categories. The items do not lie on a linear scale but fall into discrete categories (e.g. Yes/No; or different types of aggressive act: bite, kick or pinch). This generates numerical data because the total number of scores in each category is recorded.

2 **Ordinal data** – points that lie in order on a scale. The points themselves may be numbers or words, but in either case the 'distances' between the values are only representative – the scale does not necessarily have equal divisions. Examples include: a stress scale in which 0 = not stressed and 10 = unbearably stressed; an indicator of the importance of attractiveness in a partner on a rating scale reading very/fairly/somewhat/not at all; or how certain an eyewitness feels about their accuracy, estimated as a

percentage. It is more informative than nominal data as scores have a value, i.e. they are relatively 'bigger' or 'smaller'.

3 **Interval data** – points on a linear scale with equal divisions. The scale has no real zero. Examples include scores on a simple maths test (in which all the sums are equally difficult) or a task using nonsense syllables, each consisting of three consonants. Interval data is useful, as the equal value between each point on the scale means it can be used in more effective mathematical procedures than ordinal data.

4 **Ratio data** – points on a linear scale which has equal divisions between the points and a zero baseline. Examples include the time taken in seconds to complete a Sudoku; the level of cortisol in the blood; or brain volume in cubic centimetres.

You can remember the levels of measurement using the mnemonic NOIR – it tells you the initial letters and which is the least to the most informative type of data.

Measures of central tendency

A measure of central tendency indicates the 'middle' or typical point of a data set. There are three different measures, used with data with different levels of measurement.

The mode

The mode is the most frequent score in the data set. If two (or more) items are equally common there will be two (or more) modes. For example, if two categories of data are most frequent, the data set is described as 'bi-modal'.

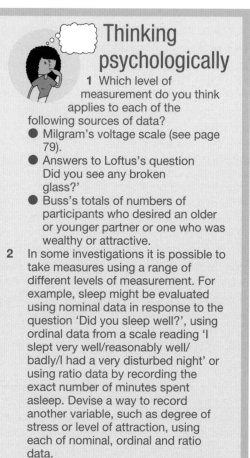

Thinking psychologically

1 Which level of measurement do you think applies to each of the following sources of data?
● Milgram's voltage scale (see page 79).
● Answers to Loftus's question 'Did you see any broken glass?'
● Buss's totals of numbers of participants who desired an older or younger partner or one who was wealthy or attractive.

2 In some investigations it is possible to take measures using a range of different levels of measurement. For example, sleep might be evaluated using nominal data in response to the question 'Did you sleep well?', using ordinal data from a scale reading 'I slept very well/reasonably well/badly/I had a very disturbed night' or using ratio data by recording the exact number of minutes spent asleep. Devise a way to record another variable, such as degree of stress or level of attraction, using each of nominal, ordinal and ratio data.

The mode is easy to calculate and can be used on any level of measurement. It is also useful as it is not affected by extreme scores. However, the mode is not very informative as it does not take into account every score (unlike the mean). Nor is the mode useful for small data sets as it is unlikely to be representative. Because it is not very informative, it tends to be used only with nominal data as other kinds of data can employ other measures of central tendency.

First language of children in two schools	Welsh	English	Bengali	Polish	Other
Number of participants in Ysgol-y-Cwm Dirgel	58	25	8	4	5
Number of participants in Hilltop School	38	38	11	2	4

Table 12.1 Working out the mode for Ysgol-y-Cwm Dirgel
The most frequent first language at Ysgol-y-Cwm Dirgel School had a total of 58, so the mode is Welsh.

The median

The median is the score in the middle when the items in a data set are put in order from smallest to largest (i.e. when they are ranked). If there are two numbers in the middle, these should be added together and divided by two.

The median, unlike the mode, can be used with ordinal, interval or ratio data. It is more representative than the mode and is not affected by very large or small scores. However, the median, unlike the mean, does not represent all of the data because it ignores very large and very small 'outliers'.

The mean

The mean is the arithmetic average. It is worked out by adding up all the scores in the data set and dividing the total by the number of scores. Zero scores should be included in the number of items.

The mean is the most representative measure of central tendency as it takes into account all of the scores. However, precisely because of this, the mean may also be distorted by very large or small 'outlying' scores. Even though it is the most useful measure of central tendency, it can be used only with interval or ratio data.

Boys	2	3	2	2	1	4	5	2	5	5	4	4
Girls	1	2	3	2	2	4	1	1	2	5	2	3

Table 12.2 Rating 1–5 of aggressiveness of children's play
Calculating the median for boys' aggressiveness
Arrange the scores in rank order: 1, 2, 2, 2, 2, 3, 4, 4, 4, 5, 5, 5
Identify the middle score: 1, 2, 2, 2, 2, **3, 4**, 4, 4, 5, 5, 5
Where there are two in the middle, add them together and divide by two: 3 + 4 = 7, 7/2 = 3.5
The median aggressiveness score for boys is 3.5.

Split-brain patients	65	76	58	49	55	76	48	51	53	49
Normal participants	98	76	83	91	88	84	97	95	89	102

Table 12.3 Speed to respond to simultaneous left- and right-brain tasks (in centiseconds)
Calculating the mean for split-brain patients:
Add up all the scores: 65 + 76 + 58 + 49 + 55 + 76 + 48 + 51 + 53 + 49 = 580
Number of scores = 10
Divide the total by the number of scores: 580/10 = 58
The mean for the response speed for split-brain patients is 58 centiseconds.

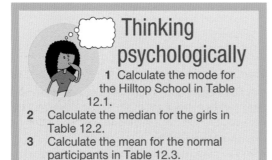

Thinking psychologically

1 Calculate the mode for the Hilltop School in Table 12.1.
2 Calculate the median for the girls in Table 12.2.
3 Calculate the mean for the normal participants in Table 12.3.

Measures of dispersion

The scores within a data set vary. Measures of spread help us to describe the extent of this spread, that is, to provide a simple summary of the variation within the set.

The range

The range is the difference between the largest and smallest scores. This can be represented either by quoting both the biggest and smallest scores or by taking the smallest from the largest to express the range as a single number. For example, the range for the split-brain patients in Table 12.3 can be written as 48 to 76 (the smallest to the largest) or as a single figure (76 to 48 = 28), i.e. 28.

The range is easy to work out and can be used with ordinal, interval or ratio data.

However, the range does not indicate how tightly or widely spread the data points are within the extremes, unlike the standard deviation.

The standard deviation

The standard deviation measures the average variation around the mean. A larger value for the standard deviation of a data set indicates a wider spread than a small value. It is calculated using this formula:

$$\text{standard deviation} = \sqrt{\frac{\Sigma\,(x - \bar{x})^2}{n - 1}}$$
$$(\text{sd or } \sigma)$$

n = the number of scores in the set
x = each score
$\bar{x}$ = the mean
Σ = 'sum of'

The standard deviation is a very sensitive measure of dispersion because it uses all the scores, unlike the range, which is based on just two scores (the largest and smallest). It is, of course, more difficult to work out than the range, which is a disadvantage. Also, it can be used only with interval or ratio data because it relies on the equal intervals between the points on the scale.

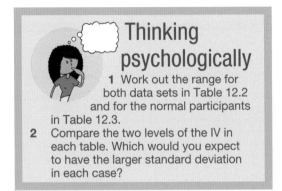

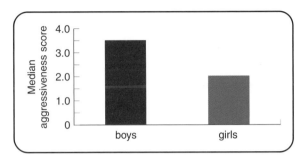

Fig. 12.1 A bar chart has a gap between the bars as the data are in discrete categories

Thinking psychologically

1 Work out the range for both data sets in Table 12.2 and for the normal participants in Table 12.3.
2 Compare the two levels of the IV in each table. Which would you expect to have the larger standard deviation in each case?

Graphical representation

Graphs are used to illustrate aspects of a data set. This may include the central tendency of the data or the spread of a data set. In general, graphs are used to represent the general characteristics of the data, although in some, every single data point is plotted.

Bar charts

The bar chart is used only when the data is in discrete categories. This includes illustrating measures of central tendency (modes, medians or means) and for totals of nominal data. When drawing a bar chart, the bars should be separate. This is because the scale along the x axis is not a continuous scale but represents distinct categories. If plotting the IV and DV, the IV goes on the x axis, the DV on the y axis. Figure 12.1 illustrates this use of the bar chart.

Histograms

The histogram is used when you are representing continuous data. The most common use is to illustrate the frequency of different scores when a measure of the DV is on an ordinal, interval or ratio scale. This is called a frequency histogram. The possible scores on the DV may be grouped into categories (e.g. 0–10, 11–20, 21–30, etc.) and are plotted along the x axis. The frequency of each score or category is represented on the y axis. Unlike the bars on a bar chart, the bars on a histogram are adjacent (along the x axis) because the scale is a continuous measure. This is illustrated in Figure 12.2.

Histograms are used to represent the way that the scores are distributed across the range, so they are also called frequency distributions. A line joining the tops of all the bars would be a frequency distribution curve. When a set of scores is evenly distributed around the mean, the frequency distribution curve makes a symmetrical bell-shape. This is called the normal distribution (Figure 12.2).

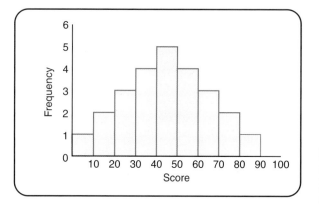

Fig. 12.2 This normal distribution graph is an example of a histogram. On a histogram, the bars are adjacent along the x axis and frequency is plotted on the y axis

Scattergraphs

A scattergraph plots pairs of scores collected in a correlational design. In a correlation each participant has a score on two variables – one variable would be plotted on the *x* axis, the other on the *y* axis. There is no fixed rule for which variable is plotted on which axis as both variables are measured. In a comparison of the scores of pairs of observers, one observer's record would be plotted on one axis, the second observer's records on the other. This is a useful way to compare inter-observer reliability. The shape of the scattergraph should be a diagonal line out from the origin (see Figure 12.3a), this is a positive correlation (e.g. $r=0.9$). In a negative correlation (e.g. $r=-0.8$) the line slopes the other way (see Figure 12.3b). When there is no correlation ($r=0$), the points are randomly scattered (see Figure 12.3c).

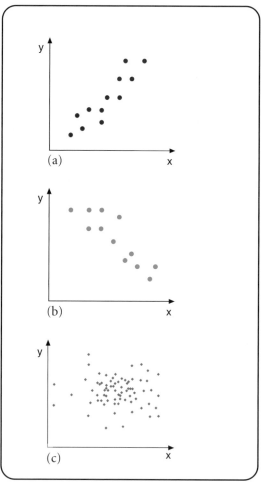

Fig. 12.3 Scattergraphs (a) a positive correlation, (b) a negative correlation, and (c) no correlation

Summing it up

- **Operationalisation** is the use of definitions for variables that ensure researchers are consistent.

- Qualitative data can be analysed by using coding systems and categorisation. This is helpful with data such as the findings of unstructured interviews, open questions in questionnaires and non-focused observations.

- **Content analysis** is a way to obtain qualitative or quantitative data from media sources such as newspapers and TV programmes. Because these are real-world sources the information is likely to be a good indicator of the way that the media affects people.

- Quantitative data is measured on numerical scales. There are four **levels of measurement** (nominal, ordinal, interval and ratio).

- **Measures of central tendency** indicate the middle or average score in a data set. They include the mode, median and mean. The mean is the most informative.

- **Measures of spread** indicate how diverse the points in a data set are. They include the range and standard deviation, the latter being more informative.

- Graphs are used to represent data visually. **Bar charts** are used with nominal data and to illustrate measures of central tendency. **Histograms** are used to illustrate variation within a data set, such as the spread of scores over a range. **Scattergraphs** plot the results of a correlational analysis.

What have I learned?

1   Coding systems are used to analyse qualitative data. In a study looking at the influence of the media on attitudes to health, several themes were identified. These included role models' weight, the exercise they took and their opinions about food. Devise a coding system relating to health, obesity and anorexia. Suggest categories that could be used to analyse the results of interviews on the topic.

2   a Describe how a content analysis is conducted.

    b What are the strengths and weaknesses of this method?

3   a What is meant by the term 'measure of central tendency'?

    b Which measure of central tendency would it be appropriate to use on this data set?

Favourite animal	dog	cat	ferret	goldfish
Number of participants giving that response	42	14	16	28

c If you could, why would it be better to use a mean than a median?

4 a What is the range?

 b Why is the standard deviation a more informative measure than the range?

 c What do both the range and standard deviation measure?

5 a i) What is the difference between a bar chart and a histogram and when is each type of graph used?

 ii) Which one should be used with the data in question 3b and why?

 iii) Plot a graph of the data from question 3b.

 b If you had conducted a study where you had taken a recording of every participant's score on a scale of sleepiness and measured their reaction time, what would you conclude from the results in Figure 12.4?

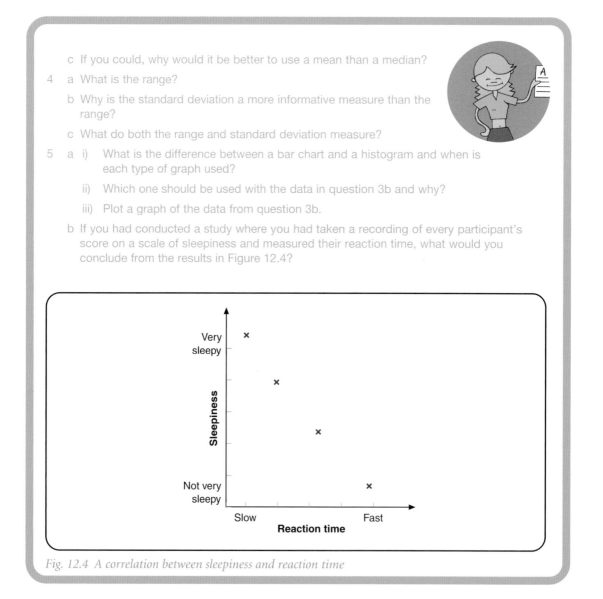

Fig. 12.4 A correlation between sleepiness and reaction time

Reading around

■ Hayes, N. (2000) *Doing Psychological Research: Gathering and analysing data*. Buckingham: Open University Press.

■ Russell, J. and Roberts, C. (2001) *Angles on Psychological Research*. Cheltenham: Nelson Thornes.

Adams, C. E., Rathbone, J., Thornley, B., Clarke, M., Borrill, J., Wahlbeck, K. and Awad, A. G. (2005) 'Chlorpromazine for schizophrenia: a Cochrane systematic review of 50 years of randomised controlled trials.' *BMC Medicine*, 3: 15

Adelman, R., McGhee, P., Power, R. and Hanson, C. (2005) 'Reducing adolescent clients' anger in a residential substance abuse treatment facility.' *Joint Commission Journal of Quality and Patient Safety*, 31: 325–6

Ahn, W. K., Kalish, C. W., Medin, D. L. and Gelman, S. A. (1995) 'The role of covariation versus mechanism information in causal attribution.' *Cognition*, 54: 299–352

Ahn, W. K. and Bailenson, J. (1996) 'Mechanism-based explanations of causal attribution: an explanation of conjunction and discounting effect.' *Cognitive Psychology*, 31: 82–123

Akelaitis, A. J. (1944) 'A study of gnosis, praxis and language following section of the corpus callosum and anterior commissure.' *Journal of Neurosurgery*, 1: 94–102

Anderson, C. A. and Dill, K. E. (2000) 'Video games and aggressive thoughts, feelings, and behaviour in the laboratory and in life.' *Journal of Personality and Social Psychology*, 78(4): 772–90

Andrews, G., Slade, T. and Peters, L. (1999) 'Classification in psychiatry: ICD-10 versus DSM-IV.' *British Journal of Psychiatry*, 174: 3–5

Asch, S. E. (1955) 'Opinions and social pressure.' *Scientific American*, 193: 31–5

Backus, T. B., Fleet, D. J., Parker, A. J. and Heeger, D. J. (2001) 'Human cortical activity correlates with stereoscopic depth perception.' *Journal of Neurophysiology*, 86: 2054–68

Baer, L., Rauch, S. L., Ballantine, H. T. Jr., Martuza, R., Cosgrove, R., Cassem, E., Giriunas, I., Manzo, P. A., Dimino, C. and Jenkie, M. A. (1995) 'Cingulotomy for intractable obsessive-compulsive disorder: prospective long-term follow-up of 18 patients.' *Archives of General Psychiatry*, 52: 384–92

Bandura, A. (1977) *Social Learning Theory*. Englewood Cliffs, New Jersey: Prentice-Hall

Bandura, A., Ross, D. and Ross, S. A. (1961) 'Transmission of aggression through imitation of aggressive models.' *Journal of Abnormal and Social Psychology*, 63(3): 575–82

Bandura, A., Ross, D. and Ross, S. A. (1963) 'Imitation of film-mediated aggressive models.' *Journal of Abnormal and Social Psychology*, 66: 3–11

Banyard, P. and Flanagan, C. (2005) *Ethical Issues and Guidelines in Psychology*. London: Routledge

Baron-Cohen, S. (2006) Empathy – Freudian origins and 21st century neuroscience. *The Psychologist*, 19: 536–7

Bartlett, F. C. (1932) *Remembering: A Study in Experimental and Social Psychology*. Cambridge: Cambridge University Press

Beck, A. (1976) *Cognitive Therapy and the Emotional Disorders*. New York: International Universities Press

Bergstrom, C. T. and Leslie, A. R. (2000) 'Towards a theory of mutual mate choice: lessons from two-sided matching.' *Evolutionary Ecology Research*, 2: 493–508

Blass, T. (1996) 'Attribution of responsibility and trust in the Milgram obedience experiment.' *Journal of Applied Social Psychology*, 26: 1529–35

Blass, T. and Schmitt, C. (2001) 'The nature of perceived authority in the Milgram paradigm: two replications.' *Current Psychology: Developmental, Learning, Personality, Social*, 20: 115–21

Boen, F., Auweele Y. v., Claes, E., Feys, J. and Cuyper, B. D. (2006) 'The impact of open feedback on conformity among judges in rope skipping.' *Psychology of Sport and Exercise*, 7: 577–90

Bond, R. and Smith, P. B. (1996) Culture and conformity: a meta-analysis of studies using Asch's 1952/1966 line-judging task. *Psychological Bulletin*, 119: 111–37

Borison, R. L. (1995) 'Clinical efficacy of serotonin-dopamine antagonists relative to classic neuroleptics.' *Journal of Clinical Psychopharmacology*, 15 (1, supplement 1): 24S–29S

Bowlby, J. (1944) 'Forty-four juvenile thieves.' *International Journal of Psychoanalysis*, 25: 19–52

British Psychological Society (2006) *Ethical Principles for Conducting Research with Human Participants*. Leicester: British Psychological Society

Buss, D. (1989) 'Sex differences in human mate preferences.' *Behavioural and Brain Sciences*, 12: 1–49

Cahill, J., Barkham, M., Hardy, G., Rees, A., Shapiro, D. A., Stiles, W. B. and Macaskill, N. (2003) 'Outcomes of patients completing and not completing cognitive therapy for depression.' *British Journal of Clinical Psychology*, 42: 133–43

Carmichael, L. C., Hogan, H. P. and Walter, A. A. (1932) 'An experimental study of the effect of language on the reproduction of visually perceived forms.' *Journal of Experimental Psychology*, 15: 73–86

Charlton, T., Gunter, B. and Hannan, A. (eds) (2000) 'Broadcast television effects in a remote community.' Mahway, N. J.: Lawrence Erlbaum Associates

Cohen, R. A., Kaplan, R. F., Zuffante, P., Moser, D. J., Jenkins, M. A., Salloway, S. and Wilkinson, H. (1999) 'Alteration of intention and self-initiated action associated with bilateral anterior cingulotomy.' *Journal of Neuropsychiatry and Clinical Neuroscience*, 11: 444–53

Conway, L. G. and Schaller, M. (2005) 'When authorities' commands backfire: attributions about consensus and effects on deviant decision making.' *Journal of Personality and Social Psychology*, 89: 311–26

de Groot, J., Boersma, W. J. A., Scholten, J. W. and Koolhaas, J. M. (2002) 'Social stress in male mice impairs long-term antiviral immunity selectivity in wounded subjects.' *Physiology and Behavior*, 75: 277–85

Dickemann, M. (1981) 'Paternal confidence and dowry competition.' In Alexander, R. D. and Tinkle, D. W. (eds) *Natural Selection and Social Behaviour*. Chiron Press, New York

Duker, P. C. and Seys, D. M. (2000) 'A quasi-experimental study on the effect of electrical aversion treatment on imposed mechanical restraint for severe self-injurious behaviour.' *Research in Developmental Disabilities*, 21: 235–42

Ehrensaft, M. K., Cohn, P., Brown, J., Smailes, E., Chen, H. and Johnson, J. G. (2003) 'Intergenerational transmission of partner violence: a 20-year prospective study.' *Journal of Consulting and Clinical Psychology*, 71: 741–53

Eley, T. C. and Stevenson, J. (2000) 'Specific life-events and chronic experiences differentially associated with depression and anxiety in young twins.' *Journal of Abnormal Child Psychology,* 28: 383–94

Ellis, A. (1977) 'The basic clinical theory of rational emotive therapy.' In Ellis, A. and Grieger, R. (eds) *Handbook of Rational Emotive Therapy.* Monterey: Brooks/Cole

Engels, G. I., Garnekski, N. and Diekstra, R. R. W. (1993) 'Efficacy of rational-emotive therapy: a quantitative analysis.' *Journal of Consulting and Clinical Psychology,* 61: 1083–90

Epping-Jordan, J. E., Compas, B. E. and Howell, D. C. (1994) 'Predictors of cancer progression in young adult men and women: avoidance, intrusive thoughts, and psychological symptoms.' *Health Psychology,* 13: 539–47

Eron, L. (1995) 'Media violence: how it affects kids and what can be done about it.' Invited address presented at the annual meeting of the American Psychological Association, New York

Eron, L. D. and Huesmann, L. R. (1986) 'The role of television in the development of antisocial and prosocial behaviour.' In Olweus, D., Block, J. and Radke-Yarrow, M. (eds) *Development of Antisocial and Prosocial Behaviour, Theories and Issues.* New York: Academic Press

Eron, L. D., Huesmann, L. R., Leftowitz, M. M. and Walder, L. O. (1972) 'Does television violence cause aggression?' *American Psychologist,* 27: 253–63

Fava, G. A., Rafanelli, C., Grandi, S., Conti, S. and Belluardo, P. (1998) 'Prevention of recurrent depression with cognitive behavioural therapy: preliminary findings.' *Archives of General Psychiatry,* 55: 816–20

Fink, G. R., Halligan, P. W., Marshall, J. C., Frith, C. D., Frackowiak, R. S. J. and Dolan, R. J. (1996) 'Where in the brain does visual attention select the forest and the trees?' *Nature,* 382: 626–8

Freud, S. (1900) *The Interpretation of Dreams.* London: Hogarth

Freud, S. (1905) *Three Essays on Sexuality.* London: Hogarth

Freud, S. (1915) *Introductory Lectures on Psychoanalysis.* London: Hogarth

Freud, S. (1917) 'Mourning and melancholia.' *Collected Works Volume 14.* London: Hogarth

Freud, S. (1923) *The Ego and the Id.* London: Hogarth

Freud, S. (1933) *New Introductory Lectures on Psychoanalysis.* London: Hogarth

Friedman, M. and Rosenman, R. H. (1974) *Type A Behavior and Your Heart.* New York: Knopf

Frydenberg, E., Lewis, R., Kennedy, G., Ardila, R., Fridte, W. and Hannoun, R. (2003) 'Coping with concerns: an exploratory comparison of Australian, Columbian, German and Palestinian adolescents.' *Journal of Youth and Adolescence,* 32: 59–66

Gardner, B. T. and Gardner, R. A. (1969) 'Teaching sign language to a chimpanzee.' *Science,* 165: 664–72

Gibson, E. J. and Walk, R. (1960) 'The visual cliff.' *Scientific American,* 202: 67–71

Golombok, S. (2000) *Parenting: What Really Counts?* London: Routledge

Grazioli, R. and Terry, D. J. (2000) 'The role of cognitive vulnerability and stress in the prediction of postpartum depressive symptomatology.' *British Journal of Clinical Psychology,* 39: 329–47

Greene, W. A. (1954) 'Psychological factors and reticuloendothelial disease – I. Preliminary observations on a group of males with lymphomas and leukemias.' *Psychosomatic Medicine,* 16: 3

Greene, W. A., Young, L. E. and Swisher, S. N. (1956) 'Psychological factors and reticuloendothelial disease – II. Observations on a group of women with lymphomas and leukemias.' *Psychosomatic Medicine,* 18: 4

Gupta, M. A. and Gupta, A. K. (2004) 'Stressful major life events are associated with a higher frequency of cutaneous sensory symptoms: an empirical study of non-clinical subjects.' *Journal of European Academy Dermatology and Venerology,* 8(5): 560–5

Hagell, A. and Newbury, T. (1994) *Young Offenders and the Media.* London: Policy Studies Institute

Harrington, R., Campbell, F., Shoebridge, P. and Whittaker, J. (1998) 'Meta-analysis of CBT for depression in adolescents.' *Journal of the Academy of Child and Adolescent Psychiatry,* 37: 1005–6

Haslam, A. and Reicher, S. (2003) 'A tale of two prison experiments: beyond a role-based explanation of tyranny.' *Psychology Review,* 9: 2–6

Hauff, E., Varvin, S., Laake, P., Melle, I., Vagium, P. and Friis, S. (2002) 'Inpatient psychotherapy compared to usual care for patients who have schizophrenic psychoses.' *Psychiatric Services,* 53: 471–3

Hawkins, N. G., Davies, R. and Holmes, T. H. (1957) 'Evidence of psychological factors in the development of pulmonary tuberculosis.' *American Review of Tuberculosis,* 75(5): 768–80

Hayes, K. H. and Hayes, C. (1951) 'Imitation in a home-raised chimpanzee.' *Journal of Comparative Physiology and Psychology,* 45: 450–9

Heider, F. (1958) *The Psychology of Personal Interpersonal Relationships.* New York: Wiley

Herbert, T. B. and Cohen, S. (1993) 'Stress and immunity in humans: a meta-analytic review.' *Psychonomic Medicine,* 55: 364–79

Hobson, J. A. and McCarley, R. W. (1977) 'The brain as a dream state generator: an activation-synthesis hypothesis of the dream process.' *American Journal of Psychiatry,* 134: 1335–48

Holmes, T. H. and Rahe, R. H. (1967) 'The social readjustment rating scale.' *Journal of Psychosomatic Research,* 11: 213–8

Home Office Select Committee Report on Home Affairs (2001–2) accessed electronically at http://www.publications. parliament.uk/pa/cm200102/cmselect/cm haff/836/83604.htm#a7 [15/01/07]

Insel, T. R. (2006) 'Beyond efficacy: the STAR*D trial.' *American Journal of Psychiatry,* 163: 1

Ito, M. (1998) 'Consciousness from the viewpoint of the structural-functional relationships of the brain.' *International Journal of Psychology,* 33: 191–7

Jacobs, M. A., Anderson, L. S., Champagne, E., Karush, N., Richman, S. J. and Knapp, P. H. (1966) 'Orality, impulsivity and cigarette smoking in men: further findings in support of a theory.' *Journal of Nervous and Mental Disease,* 143: 207–19

Jarvis, M. (2004) *Psychodynamic Psychology: Classical Theory and Contemporary Research.* London: Thomson

Jones, E. E. and Davis, K. E. (1965) 'From acts to dispositions: the attribution process in person perception.' In Berkowitz, L. (ed.) *Advances in Experimental Social Psychology,* vol 2. New York: Academic Press

Joy, L. A., Kimball, M. M. and Zabrack, M. L. (1986) 'Television and children's aggressive behavior.' In Williams, T. M. (ed.) *The Impact of Television: A Natural Experiment in Three Communities.* Orlando, F. L.: Academic Press, 303–60

Kelley, H. H. (1967) 'Attribution theory in social psychology.' In Levine, D. (ed.) *Nebraska Symposium on Motivation,* vol 15. Lincoln N. E.: Nebraska University Press

Kellogg, W. N. and Kellogg, L. A. (1933) *The Ape and the Child.* New York: McGraw-Hill

Kostinsky, S., Bixler, E. O. and Kettl, P. A. (2001) 'Threats of school violence after media coverage of the Columbine High School massacre: examining the role of imitation.' *Archives of Pediatric and Adolescent Medicine,* 155(9): 994–1001

Lang, P. J. and Lazovik, A. D. (1963) 'Experimental desensitization of a phobia.' *Journal of Abnormal and Social Psychology,* 66: 519–25

Lashley, K. S. and Russell, J. T. (1934) 'The mechanism of vision: a preliminary test of innate organisation.' *Journal of Genetic Psychology,* 45: 136–44

le Doux, J. E., Wilson, D. H. and Gazzaniga, M. S. (1977) 'A divided mind: observations on the conscious properties of the separated hemispheres.' *Annals of Neurology,* 2: 417–21

Leichsenring, F. (2001) 'Comparative effects of short-term psychodynamic psychotherapy and cognitive-behavioural therapy in depression: a meta-analytic approach.' *Clinical Psychology Review,* 21: 401–19

Liberzon, I., Abelson, J. L., Flagel, S. B., Raz, J. and Young, E. A. (1999) 'Neuroendocrine and psychophysiologic responses in PTSD: symptom provocation studies.' *Neuropsychopharmacology,* 21: 40–50

Loftus, E. F. (1975) 'Leading questions and the eyewitness report.' *Cognitive Psychology,* 1: 560–72

Loftus, E. F. and Palmer, J. C. (1974) 'Reconstruction of automobile destruction: an example of the interaction between learning and memory.' *Journal of Verbal Learning and Behavior,* 13: 585–9

Loftus, E. F. and Zanni, G. (1975) 'Eyewitness testimony: the influence of wording of a question.' *Bulletin of the Psychonomic Society,* 5: 86–8

Luttke, H. B. (2004) 'Experiments within the Milgram paradigm.' *Gruppendynamik und Organisationsberatung,* 35: 431–64

Maki, P., Hakko, H., Joukamaa, M., Laara, E., Isohanni, M. and Veijola, J. (2004) 'Parental separation at birth and criminal behaviour in adulthood: a long-term follow-up of the Finnish Christmas Seal Home Children.' *Journal of Social Psychiatry and Psychiatric Epidemiology,* 38: 354–9

Malan, D. (1995) *Individual Psychotherapy and the Science of Psychodynamics.* London: Butterworth-Heinemann

Marshall, W. L. (2006) 'Ammonia aversion with an exhibitionist: a case study.' *Clinical Case Studies,* 1: 15–24

Marshall, J. C. and Halligan, P. W. (1995) 'Seeing the forest but only half the trees.' *Nature,* 373: 521–3

Mashour, G. A., Walker, E. E. and Martuza, R. L. (2005) 'Psychosurgery: past, present and future.' *Brain Research Reviews,* 48: 409–19

Massie, H. and Szeinberg, N. (2002) 'The relationship between mothering in infancy, childhood experience and adult mental health.' *International Journal of Psychoanalysis,* 83: 35–55

Masui, T., Kusumi, I., Takahashi, Y. and Koyama, T. (2005) 'Efficacy of carbamazepine against neuroleptic-induced akathisia in treatment with perospine: case series.' *Progress in Neuro-psychopharmacology and Biological Psychiatry,* 29: 343–6

McKnight, J. and Sutton, N. (1994) *Social Psychology.* Sydney: Prentice Hall

McVey, C., McKechnie, K., Thomson, K. and Watt, S. (2003) 'Group dynamics: the effects of a bipartite selection on social interaction of castaways on a Scottish island.' *Proceedings of the British Psychological Society,* 11: 4

Mendels, J. and Weinstein, N. (1972) 'The schedule of recent experiences: a reliability study.' *Psychosomatic Medicine.* 34(6): 527–32

Milgram, S. (1963) 'Behavioural study of obedience.' *Journal of Abnormal and Social Psychology,* 67: 371–8

Musher-Eizenman, D. R., Holub, S. C., Miller, A. B., Goldstein, S. E. and Edwards-Leeper, L. (2004) 'Body size stigmatisation in pre-school children: the role of control attributions.' *Journal of Paediatric Psychology*, 29: 613–20

Myers, R. E. (1961) 'Corpus callosum and visual gnosis.' In Delafresnaye, J. F. (ed.) *Brain Mechanisms and Learning*. Oxford: Blackwell

Neenan, M. (2004) 'REBT 45 years on: still on the sidelines.' *Journal of Rational Emotive and Cognitive Therapy*, 19: 31–41

O'Neill, R. M., Greenberg, R. P. and Fisher, S. (1992) 'Humour and anality.' *Humour: International Journal of Humour Research*, 5: 283–91

Palmer, S. and Dryden, W. (1995) *Counselling for Stress Problems*. London: Sage

Parker, G., Mitchell, P. and Wilhelm, K. (2000) 'Twelve month episodes of non-melancholic depressive subjects: refinements of subgroups by examination of trajectories.' *Annals of Clinical Psychiatry*, 12: 219–25

Pavlov, I. P. (1927) *Conditioned Reflexes*. Oxford: Oxford University Press

Pei, F., Pettet, M. W. and Norcia, A. M (2007) 'Sensitivity and configuration-specificity of orientation-defined texture processing in infants and adults.' *Vision Research*, 47: 338–48

Perez, M. G., Rivera, R. M., Banos, F. and Amparo, B. (1999) 'Attentional bias and vulnerability to depression.' *Spanish Journal of Psychology*, 2: 11–19

Perrin, S. and Spencer, C. (1980) The Asch effect – a child of its time. *Bulletin of the BPS*, 33: 405–6

Perry, A. R. and Baldwin, D. A. (2000) 'Further evidence of associations of type A personality scores and driving-related attitudes and behaviors.' *Perceptual Motor Skills*, 91(1): 147–54

Pert, C. B. and Snyder, S. H. (1973) 'The opiate receptor: demonstration in nervous tissue.' *Science*, 179: 1011–14

Pillsworth, E. G., Hasleton, M. G. and Buss, D. M. (2004) 'Ovulatory shifts in female sexual desire.' *Journal of Sex Research*, 41: 55–65

Pines, A. M. (2002) 'Teacher burnout: a psychodynamic perspective'. *Teachers and Teaching: Theory and Practice*, 8: 121–40

Pippard, J. (1955a) 'Rostral leucotomy: a report on 240 cases personally followed up.' *Journal of Mental Science*, 101: 756–73

Pippard, J. (1955b) 'Personality changes after rostral leucotomy.' *Journal of Mental Science*, 101: 774–87

Plotsky, P. M. and Meaney, M. J. (1993) 'Early, postnatal experiences alters hypothalamic corticotropin-releasing factor (CRF) mRNA, median eminence CRF content and stress-induced release in adult rats.' *Brain Research and Molecular Brain Research*, 18: 195–200

Pole, N. and Jones, E. E. (1998) 'The talking cure revisited: content analysis of a two year psychodynamic therapy.' *Psychotherapy Research*, 8: 171–89

Rahe, R. H., Meyer, M., Smith, M., Kjaer, G. and Holmes, T. H. (1964) 'Social stress and illness onset.' *Journal of Psychosomatic Research*, 8: 35–44

Rahe, R. H., Mahan, J. L. and Arthur, R. (1970) 'Prediction of near-future health change from subjects' preceding life changes.' *Journal of Psychosomatic Research*, 14: 401–6

Raphael, K. G., Cloitre, M. and Dohrenwend, B. P. (1991) 'Problems of recall and mis-classifications with checklist methods of measuring stressful life events.' *Health Psychology*, 10: 62–74

Risbrough, V. B., Hauger, R. L., Roberts, A. L., Vale, W. W. and Geyer, M. A. (2004) 'Corticotropin-releasing factor receptors

CRF1 and CRF2 exert both additive and opposing influences on defensive startle behaviour.' *Journal of Neuroscience*, 24(29): 6545–52

Roberts, S. C., Havlicek, J., Flegr, J., Hruskova, M., Little, C., Jones, B. C., Perrett, D. I. and Petrie, M. (2004) 'Female facial attractiveness increases during the fertile phase of the menstrual cycle.' *Proceedings of the Royal Society*, 10: 1098np

Rose, H. and Rose, S. (2000) *Alas Poor Darwin*. London: Vintage

Rosenhan, D. L. (1973) 'On being sane in insane places.' *Science*, 179: 250–8

Rosenman, R. H. and Friedman, M. (1958) 'The possible relationship of occupational stress to clinical coronary heart disease.' *California Medicine*, 89(3): 169–74

Rothbaum, B. O., Hodges, L., Smith, S., Lee, J. H. and Price, L. (2000) 'A controlled study of virtual reality exposure therapy for the fear of flying.' *Journal of Consulting and Clinical Psychology*, 68: 1020–26

Roussy, F., Camirand, C., Foulkes, D., Dekoninck, J., Loftis, M. and Kerr, N. (1996) 'Does early night REM dream content reflect presleep state of mind?' *Dreaming*, 6: 121–30

Rutter, M. (1981) *Maternal Deprivation Reassessed*. Harmondsworth: Penguin

Sandahl, C., Herlitz, K. and Ahlin, G. (1998) 'Time-limited group psychotherapy for moderately alcohol dependent patients: a randomised controlled clinical trial.' *Psychotherapy Research*, 8: 361–78

Sandell, R. (1999) 'Long-term findings of the Stockholm Outcome of Psychotherapy and Psychoanalysis Project (STOPP).' Paper presented at the 'Psychoanalytic long-term treatment: a challenge for clinical and empirical research in psychoanalysis' meeting, Hamburg

Sautter, F. J., Bissette, G., Wiley, J., Manguno-Mire G., Schoenbachler, B., Myers, L., Johnson, J. E., Cerbone, A. and Malaspina, D. (2003) 'Corticotropin-releasing factor in posttraumatic stress disorder (PTSD) with secondary psychotic symptoms, nonpsychotic PTSD, and healthy control subjects.' *Biological Psychiatry*, 54: 1382–8

Schmitt, D. P. (2003) 'Universal sex differences in the desire for sexual variety: tests from 52 nations, 6 continents and 13 islands.' *Journal of Personality and Social Psychology*, 85: 85–104

Seifert, K. (2003) 'Attachment, family violence and disorders of childhood and adolescence.' *Paradigm*, Summer: 14–18

Selye, H. (1947) *Textbook of Endocrinology*. Montreal: University of Montreal

Sinai, M. J., Ooi, T. L. and He, Z. H. (1998) 'Terrain influences the accurate judgement of distance.' *Nature*, 395: 497–500

Smallbone, S. W. and Dadds, M. R. (2004) 'Attachment and coercive sexual behaviour.' *Sexual Abuse: A Journal of Research Treatment*, 12: 3–15

Solms, M. (2000) 'Freudian dream theory today.' *The Psychologist*, 13: 618–19

Sperry, R. W. (1967a) 'Mental unity following surgical disconnection of the hemispheres.' *The Harvey Lectures*, series 62. New York: Academic Press

Sperry, R. W. (1967b) 'Split-brain approach to learning problems.' In Quarton, G. C. Melnechuk, T. and Schmidtt, F. O. (eds) (1967) *The Neurosciences: A Study Program*. New York: Rockerfeller University Press

Sperry, R. W. (1968) 'Hemisphere deconnection and unity in conscious awareness.' *American Psychologist*, 23: 723–33

Stander, V. A., Hsiung, P. and MacDermid, S. (2001) 'The relationship of attributions to marital distress: a comparison of mainland Chinese and US couples.' *Journal of Family Psychology*, 15: 124–34

Stewart, A. E. (2005) 'Attributions of responsibility for motor vehicle crashes.' *Accident Analysis and Prevention,* 37: 681–8

Tarnow, E. (2000) 'Self-destructive obedience in the airplane cockpit and the concept of obedience optimisation.' In Blass, T. (ed.) *Obedience to Authority.* Mahwah: Lawrence Erlbaum

Theorell, T., Lind, E. and Floderus, B. (1975) 'The relationship of disturbing life changes and emotion to the early development of myocardial infarction and other serious illnesses.' *International Journal of Epidemiology,* 4: 281–93

Thornhill, R. and Palmer, C. (2000) *A Natural History of Rape.* Cambridge, USA: MIT Press

Tondel, G. M. and Candy, T. R. (2007) 'Human infants' accommodation responses to dynamic stimuli.' *Investigative Ophthalmology and Visual Science,* 48: 949–56

Toneatto, T. and Kosky, B. (2006) 'Problem gambling treatment research: an annotated bibliography.' *Journal of Gambling Issues,* 17. Accessed electronically at http://www.camh.net/egambling/issue17/pdfs/complete.pdf [30/1/07]

Tooth, J. C. and Newton, M. P. (1961) 'Leucotomy in England and Wales 1942–1954. Reports on public health and medical subjects No. 104.' London: Her Majesty's Stationary Office

Trivedi, M. H., Rush, A. J., Wisniewski, S. R., Nierenberg, A. A., Warden, D., Ritz, L., Norquist, G., Howland, R. H., Lebowitz, B., McGrath, P. J., Shores-Wilson, K., Biggs, M. M., Balasubramani, G. K. and Fava, M. (2006) 'Evaluation of outcomes with Citalopram for depression using measurement-based care in STAR*D: implications for clinical practice.' *American Journal of Psychiatry,* 163: 28–40

Trivers, R. L. (1972) 'Parental investment and sexual selection.' In Campbell, B. (ed.) *Sexual Selection and the Descent of Man.* Chicago: Aldine Publishing

Troseth, G. L. (2003) 'Two-year-old children learn to use video as a source of information.' *Developmental Psychology,* 39(1): 140–50

Trower, P. and Jones, J. (2001) 'How REBT can be less disturbing and remarkably more influential in Britain: a review of views of practitioners and researchers.' *Journal of Rational Emotive and Cognitive Therapy,* 19: 21–30

Ulmann, E. and Swanson, J. (2004) 'Exposure to violent video games increases automatic aggressiveness.' *Journal of Adolescence,* 27: 42–51

Vidal, A., Gomez-Gil, E., Sans, M., Portella, M. J., Salamero, M., Pique, J. M. and Panes, J. (2006) 'Life events and inflammatory bowel disease relapse: a prospective study of patients enrolled in remission.' *American Journal of Gastroenterology,* 101(4): 775–81

Vidal-Vazquez, M. A. and Clemente-Diaz, M. (2000) 'The attraction of media violence.' *PSCIO,* 31(2): 49–80

Vonk, R. and Konst, D. (1998) 'Intergroup bias and correspondent inference bias: people engage in situational correction when it suits them.' *British Journal of Social Psychology,* 37: 379–85

Wall, T. N. and Hayes, J. A. (2000) 'Depressed patients' attributions of responsibility for the causes of and solutions to their problems.' *Journal of Counselling and Development,* 78: 81–6

Watson, J. B. and Rayner, R. (1920) 'Conditioned emotional responses.' *Journal of Experimental Psychology,* 3(1): 1–14

Weinrott, M. R., Riggan, M. and Frothingham, S. (1997) 'Reducing deviant arousal in juvenile sex offenders using vicarious sensitisation.' *Journal of Interpersonal Violence,* 12b: 704–728

Wolpe, J. (1958) *Psychotherapy by Reciprocal Inhibition.* Stanford, C.A.: Stanford University Press

Wolpe, J. (1969) 'Basic principles and practices of behavior therapy of neuroses.' *American Journal of Psychiatry,* 125: 1242–7

Workman, J. E. and Freeburg, E. W. (1999) 'An examination of date rape, victim distress and perceiver variables within the context of attribution theory.' *Sex Roles,* 41: 261–77

Wright, D. B., Loftus, E. F. and Hall, M. (2001) 'Now you see it, now you don't: inhibiting recall and recognition of scenes.' *Applied Cognitive Psychology,* 15: 471–82

Yost, J. H. and Weary, G. (1996) 'Depression and correspondent inference bias: evidence for more effortful processing.' *Personality and Social Psychology,* 22: 192–200

Zanni, G. (1975) 'Eyewitness testimony: the influence of wording of a question.' *Bulletin of the Psychonomic Society,* 5: 86–8

Zorrilla, E. P. and Koob, G. F. (2004) 'The therapeutic potential of CRF1 antagonists for anxiety.' *Expert Opinion on Investigational Drugs,* 13: 799–828

Index

The index is in word-by-word order. Tables, figures and diagrams are indicated by non-bold *italics*; information in boxes by **bold**; and glossary entries by ***bold italics***. Research studies are indexed under first author's name and also descriptively under the main heading 'studies'.